Light & Easy
CHOICES® AND DESSERTS

Recipes for Healthy Eating

Kay Spicer

MIGHTON
HOUSE

Canadian Cataloguing in Publication Data

Spicer, Kay
Light & easy choices® and desserts

Rev. ed.
Published in co-operation with the Canadian Diabetes Association.
Compilation of Kay Spicer's light & easy choices and Light & easy choice desserts

Includes index.
ISBN 0-9695688-0-0

1. Cookery. 2.   Desserts. 3.   Low-calorie, low-fat diet -
Recipes 4.   Diabetes - Diet therapy - Recipes.
I. Canadian Diabetes Association. II. Title.

TX714.S65 1992   641. 5'63   C91-905704-5

Published by:
Mighton House
Box 399,
Campbellville, Ontario
L0P 1B0

Printed and bound in Canada
Cover Design: Mary O'Neil
Illustrations: Linda Hendry
Photography: Fred Bird
Printing and Binding: Friesen Printers
Typography: Greg Golding

Front cover: Pork Veronique, Ginger Orange Carrots
Back cover: Citrus Banana Cheesecake

Table of Contents

Author's Acknowledgements

The time I spent on developing *Light & Easy Choices and* then *Light & Easy Choice Desserts* was special. I learned more about people with diabetes and it was a joy to create recipes for them for foods to fit into their healthy eating plans. Now I have created this compilation of the best from the two cookbooks for everyone interested in healthy food as it relates to wellness, as well as for those committed to a specific diet plan because of diabetes.

My thanks go out to everyone who assisted me throughout writing the first two cookbooks and creating this one.

To my daughter and fellow home economist, Susan Spicer, goes my appreciation for the hours and hours of testing, tasting and typing, and for enduring, with enthusiasm, the heavy work load.

I am grateful for the help and expertise of dietitians, the late Cathy Patterson, R.P.Dt. (to whom I dedicated Light & Easy Choice Desserts), and Susan Gatchell, R.P.Dt., for calculating all the food values; for the technical and professional guidance of Jan Eno, M.Sc., R.P.Dt., Director of Education, Research and Service, Canadian Diabetes Association (CDA); Marjorie Hollands, M.S.c., R.P.Dt., C.D.E., Former chairman, National Nutrition Committee, CDA; Lynda Cole, R.P.Dt., past chairman, Youth Committee; and Janie Sanderson, M.Sc., R.P.Dt., Manager of Nutrition Education & Services, CDA.

I appreciate the opportunities Judy Brandow, Carol Ferguson, Marg Fraser and Elizabeth Baird have given me to share my creative cookery with the readers of *Canadian Living*. A few of the recipes in this book have been adapted from features printed in the magazine. And, thanks to Mary O'Neil for designing the cover; to Greg Golding for the printed pages; and to Fred Bird for taking appealing food photographs.

Finally, special thanks to my children, Susan, Patti and Bob Spicer, and to my husband, Jim Mighton, for their encouragement, enthusiasm and support.

Kay Spicer

Foreword

You don't have to have diabetes to enjoy this cookbook. It's for all those interested in their good health and in eating food that tastes great.

Light & Easy Choices and Desserts was developed especially for the young person learning to cook and plan meals, perhaps for the first time. For the more experienced cook, the recipes are fantastically easy and convenient. Kay Spicer has shared many of her good ideas for cooking and preparing enjoyable meals that look as good as they taste. Family and friends can't help but want to join you in trying them. Best of all, Kay's recipes make you feel like a superb cook because they always work and the results are a big hit with everyone.

I wish that Kay Spicer's *Light & Easy Choices and Desserts* had been available to me at age fourteen when I developed diabetes. It would have made diabetes a little easier to live with, for me and for my family too. Although my family usually ate the meals that were planned around my needs, it was at dessert time that I felt singled out. Everyone else in the family would have apple pie and I would have applesauce. Without anyone saying so, I felt my food was second class. If it was so good, why weren't they eating it too? With Kay's recipes in *Light & Easy Choices and Desserts* I could have made a dessert the whole family would have enjoyed. That would have given me a lot of important comfort and support at a crucial time in my life.

When I read the meal planning section of this book, I instantly liked the idea of making menu cards for each meal. It reminded me of the way I visualized my diet at age fourteen. At home we had an old pigeon hole desk, the kind with slots to hold envelopes and such. I imagined that my meal plan was like that desk and that each meal or snack had a set of pigeon holes — three for protein, two for starch and so on. Meal planning was simply making food choices to fill all the slots; an empty slot meant I must eat more and when the slots were filled in each food group, the meal was complete. The menu cards in this book show how you can put together many different recipes and food combinations using your own eating plan as a guide. The food lists of the Canadian Diabetes Association's Good Health Eating Guide allow you to have variety in your food choices while using the same eating plan each day. If you have diabetes, your eating plan is important because it is designed to give you the right kinds of food in the right amounts at the right times to meet your needs.

This book is designed for you. I hope you enjoy it.

Jan Eno, M.Sc., R.P.Dt.
Director of Education, Research and Service
Canadian Diabetes Association

As a physician who has cared for children with diabetes mellitus for many years, I am well aware that one of the most difficult parts of their treatment program is the need to follow a careful diet. Eating the same amount and type of food at the same time every day can be difficult to do over many years. Breaks in diet routines occur commonly and are probably unavoidable with the type of lifestyle most children follow. Thus anything which will make a diabetic diet more attractive and interesting should be welcomed by diabetics. Kay Spicer's new cookbook *Light & Easy Choices* offers a variety of recipes sure to excite the most discerning gourmet. She incorporates the latest information on food groups so that servings of each recipe can easily be incorporated into individual meal plans. I am sure that those who can use this book will be delighted with the results.

Robert M. Ehrlich, M.D., F.R.C.P. (C)
Chief, Division of Endocrinology
The Hospital for Sick Children,
Toronto

Desserts with Sugar?

People with diabetes may be concerned that some of the recipes in *Light & Easy Choices and Desserts* contain small amounts of sugar. By using the assigned Food Choice Values, a *carefully measured* serving of the desserts in this book can be *substituted* into your meal plan. All natural and added sugars have been included in the carbohydrate and Food Choice Values given for each recipe.

Sugar comes in many forms. The most commonly added sugars are white and brown sugar, honey, syrups and molasses. Natural sugars are found in fruits, juices, vegetables and milk. These foods are listed in the ◢ Fruits & Vegetables group and ◆ Milk group of the Good Health Eating Guide by the Canadian Diabetes Association.

Many factors affect how the body digests sugar. A key factor is the amount you eat. Natural sugars can raise your blood sugar as quickly as those that you add. For this reason, it is important for people with diabetes to eat any natural or added sugars in *controlled* amounts.

Almost everyone loves desserts. Having diabetes doesn't mean you lose your desire for sweet treats. *Light & Easy Choices and Desserts* lets you follow your meal plan and still satisfy your sweet tooth.

Susan Gatchell, B.A. Sc., R.P.Dt.
Former Nutrition Program Assistant
Canadian Diabetes Association

Introduction

The choices in this cookbook are light and easy. It is the way I have been cooking and eating ever since working on *Choice Cooking* for the Canadian Diabetes Association (CDA) in 1982 and writing *Light & Easy Choices* (1985) and *Light & Easy Choice Desserts* (1987) Now this cookbook has also been developed in co-operation with CDA.

There is a lighter touch to all the dishes — less fat, sugar and salt. As well, they are prepared in the easiest way possible. I like the nutritious, delicious results and so do my family and friends. They have become fans of this healthier style of cooking.

As I began to develop recipes for the *Light & Easy* cookbooks, it came to me loud and clear that the Choice system of diet developed by the Canadian Diabetes Association is a perfectly good balanced diet for everyone. It is based on Canada's Food Guide and is recommended by both the CDA and the Juvenile Diabetes Foundation for young people and others with diabetes. The more I read the experts and study research findings on nutrition, the more sure I am that the regime is definitely a healthy one.

Mealtime is very special to someone with diabetes because eating must be planned according to the amount of insulin available to the body. Individuals with diabetes must have their nutrition in measured amounts at regular evenly spaced meal and snack times, in balance with physical activities. For a person with diabetes, food is a tool for controlling the disease.

Throughout the development of *Light & Easy Choices* I have purposely kept the use of fat and salt, as well as sugar, to the bare minimum. With all the reports of the effect of these foods on our general well-being, I'm convinced it is the most healthy way for all of us to cook and eat. Also, where applicable, I have used ingredients that contribute significant amounts of dietary fibre to the finished product.

The recipes are helpful because they have the Canadian Diabetes Association Food Choice Value for a single-serving portion. As well, the carbohydrate, protein, fat and energy (kilojoule/Calorie) values are indicated at the end of each recipe. This information makes it easy for people with diabetes to plan their meals. It is important that they measure and count servings carefully, since changing the serving size will increase or decrease the food values listed for each dish. The calculations are also helpful for individuals who are keeping track of grams fat and energy value (kilojoules/Calories) in the food they eat.

People with diabetes are usually advised to avoid added sugar. It's impossible, however, to bake any semblance of a cake without using some sugar. Some other doughs and batters also require a little sugar in combination with the other ingredients – flour, fat, eggs – to achieve the best results with a recipe. When sugar is called for in any of the recipes its carbohydrate and energy values are included in the calculations and Food Choice Values following the recipe.

A volume (mL/cup) measure is given following many of the recipes to describe the amount of one serving. However, this measure is approximate since the total yield of the recipe often depends on several variables, such as, the volume of beaten egg white, the evaporation of liquid during cooking and how finely ingredients are cut up. Therefore, it is important to divide each completed dish into the number of servings indicated in the recipe.

A few of the recipes call for small amounts of alcoholic beverages. Unless the alcohol has evaporated out of the dessert by heating or flaming, the amount and energy value of the alcohol is included in my calculations.

When a recipe calls for a sugar substitute, choose the one you like best and always read the label to know how much to use for the sweetness desired. Sodium cyclamate maintains its sweetness when heated; saccharin-based sweeteners seem to develop a bitter taste when heated; aspartame-based sweeteners lose their sweetening power at the high temperatures required for baking and cooking.

Sugar substitutes and artificial sweeteners are available in grocery stores, supermarkets and drug stores in the following forms:

> 1) Liquid, available in a bottle, is concentrated: 1 mL (1/4 tsp) equals the sweetness of 5 mL (1 tsp) sugar and has no energy value.
>
> 2) Bulk granulated sweeteners look, pour and measure like sugar. They yield 4 kilojoules (1 Calorie) per 5 mL (1 tsp), and sweeten like 5 mL (1 tsp) sugar
>
> 3) Packets, are handy to carry for sweetening beverages. The contents of 1 paper packet sweetens as much as 10 mL (2 tsp) sugar and may yield 8 kilojoules (2 Calories).
>
> 4) Tablets which are bottled, are usually sold 100 to a bottle. One tablet sweetens as much as 5 mL (l tsp) sugar and yields less than 4 kilojoules (1 Calorie).

All of my recipes have easy-to-follow, step-by-step directions. All of the dishes are kitchen-tested and made from scratch with ordinary ingredients that are readily available in grocery stores and supermarkets across the country.

The foods prepared from the recipes in this book are not only good for you, they are good-looking and good-tasting. And, as an added bonus, they are light and easy to make.

Kay Spicer
1992

Kitchen Talk

Cooking is a science involving weights and measures, temperatures, formulas and methods.

While developing the recipes, I did the experimenting and testing. Now, all you have to do when you choose the dishes you want to make is measure the ingredients carefully, combine them as directed, and cook them at the temperatures indicated for good results, every time.

Measures for ingredients used in the recipes in this book are both metric and imperial. Choose one of the systems and follow through using the measures, weights and temperatures for that system. You may have problems if you mix the two, because slight variations sometimes occur in the adaptation of one system to the other.

Teaspoons, tablespoons, cups and quarts are the measures, and ounces and pounds are the weights for the imperial system. Temperatures are given in Fahrenheit readings.

In metric recipes, small measures, dry measures and liquid measures are in milliliters; weights are in grams and kilograms. Temperatures are in Celsius readings.

Ingredients are measured for both systems in exactly the same way. When the recipe calls for 15 mL (or 1 tbsp) of liquid or 250 mL (or 1 cup) of a dry ingredient, the measure is always level. I never use a heaping or a scant measure of any ingredient in any of the recipes.

> *"Always use a measure, never guess*
> *Then cooking will be a pleasure, never a mess."*

How to Measure Exactly

A good cook starts off with a correct set of measures. They are available in hardware and department stores and kitchenware shops.

Graduated measures or cups for dry ingredients:
   Imperial 1/4 cup; 1/3 cup; 1/2 cup; 1 cup
   Metric 50 mL; 75 mL; 125 mL; 250 mL

Measures or cups with lips for liquids:
   Imperial 1 cup; 2 cups; 4 cups
   Metric 250 mL; 500 mL; 1 L

Small measure or spoons for both dry and liquid ingredients:
   Imperial 1/4 tsp; 1/2 tsp; 1 tsp; 1 tbsp
   Metric 1 mL; 2 mL; 5 mL; 15 mL; 25 mL

Abbreviations: g - gram; kg - kilogram; mL - milliliter; L -litre;
   lb - pound; oz - ounce; in -inch;
   tsp - teaspoon; tbsp - tablespoon

Measuring Dry and Liquid Ingredients:

To measure dry ingredients use graduated-type measures with no lip. Lightly spoon flour, bulk granulated sweetener and granulated sugar into desired cup or measure until it is heaping full then level it off with a straight-edged spatula or kitchen knife. Never push it down or shake or tap the container.

Use small measures or spoons for salt, baking powder or soda, cornstarch, herbs and spices. Stir to loosen in container. Fill measure or spoon heaping full. Level off. Lightly pack raisins, nuts, seeds and cut-up or chopped foods, such as celery, onions, meats and bread crumbs into cup or measure until level with the top.

To measure liquid ingredients, use pitcher-style measures: Place cup or measure on level surface, such as counter or table. Pour in liquid to mark off amount required. Bend down and look at mark at eye level to be sure it is correct.

Measure margarine, butter or shortening by packing it into cup or measure with a spoon or spatula and then leveling it off with a straight edge. Make sure all of it is scraped out for its use in a recipe.

For liquids such as vinegar, vanilla, oil, juice and milk, slowly pour from the bottle into the measure or spoon right to its rim, taking care that the liquid does not spill over the edge. Do this over a small bowl or saucer rather than directly over the food to which the liquid is being added to avoid spilling in too much.

Cooking Language

These cooking terms are used in the recipe instructions. They explain how to handle the ingredients.

Bake: Cook in dry heat in an oven or oven-type appliance.

Barbecue: Broil or roast food on a rack or spit over hot coals.

Baste: Moisten food as it cooks by brushing liquid, juice, vegetable oil, sauce or pan drippings over food to add flavor and prevent it from drying out.

Beat: Make a mixture smooth and lighter by stirring vigorously in an over-and over action with a spoon, fork, or whisk, or an around-and-around action with a beater.

Blanch: Place food in boiling water for a short time and then plunge into cold water to stop further cooking.

Blend: Mix or stir two or more ingredients together until mixture is smooth, or mix food in a blender.

Boil: Cook food in liquid over enough heat to make bubbles constantly rise to the surface and break.

Braise: Cook food in a small amount of liquid in a covered pan.

Broil: Cook under "broiler" unit in range or on a rack over hot coals or burner.

Chop: Cut into pieces with a knife or chopper.

Coat: Cover all sides of food with another ingredient such as egg, flour or crumbs.

Combine: Mix foods together.

Crisp: Make food firm and crunchy by letting vegetables stand in ice water or bread dry in an oven.

Cube: Cut into small squares, 1 to 2 cm (1/2 to 3/4 inch).

Cut in: Work fat into flour mixture evenly with a pastry blender, a fork, or by cutting action of two knives.

Dice: Cut into very small squares, 5 mm (1/4 inch).

Disjoint: Cut poultry apart at its joints, such as cutting drumstick from body of chicken.
Drain: Pour off liquid or place food in strainer to allow liquid to run off food.
Dredge: Coat food with flour.
Fold: Mix with spoon or rubber scraper with a down-and-across bottom of bowl and an up-and-over action until mixture is blended.
Fry: Cook in hot fat in skillet or fryer.
Garnish: Decorate cooked or prepared dishes with attractive pieces of food in a contrasting color, such as parsley, green onion, fresh lemon slices, whipped topping.
Grate: Rub food against rough part of grater to make very fine bits of food.
Grease: Spread baking sheets and pans with a thin coat of oil or margarine, butter or shortening to keep food from sticking. A small brush does it best.
Grind: Cut food, such as meat, into tiny particles by putting it through a grinder.
Julienne: Cut vegetables into thin, matchstick-size strips.
Knead: Work food, usually doughs, by hand by folding over toward you, then pushing away by pressing with heel of hand.
Marinate: Let food stand or soak in a flavored liquid to tenderize and flavor it.
Melt: Heat food to change it from a solid to a liquid.
Microwave: Cook food in a microwave oven.
Mix: Combine or stir ingredients together until evenly blended.
Poach: Cook gently in simmering water over enough heat so that the surface of the water juggles slightly, but does not boil.
Purée: Process food in a blender or food processor until blended and smooth.
Reduce: Boil or simmer liquid, such as broth, to evaporate moisture and decrease the amount of liquid.
Roast: Cook, uncovered, by dry heat, as in an oven.
Roll: Move rolling pin over food, such as dough or crackers, to flatten or crush it.
Sauté: Cook in a small amount of fat over medium to high heat.
Season: Flavor food by sprinkling with flavorings such as vanilla, herbs such as oregano, and spices such as pepper.
Shred: Cut food into very fine slivers or thin strips with a knife or shredder.
Simmer: Cook slowly in water over enough heat so that water barely ripples.
Skewer: Fasten or close with metal or wooden pins.
Skim: Remove top layer of food from bottom layer such as fat from top of soup.
Slice: Place food on a cutting board and cut across or down and away from you into thin pieces.
Steam: Cook in a container with holes over boiling water.
Stew: Simmer in liquid on top of range or in the oven.
Stir: Mix food with a spoon in a circular motion until ingredients are evenly distributed.
Stir-braise: Mix food as it cooks with a liquid in a hot saucepan or skillet.
Stir-cook: Mix food as it cooks.
Stir-fry: Mix food as it cooks with fat or oil in a hot skillet or wok.
Toast: Brown food by dry heat in toaster or oven.
Toss: Mix foods by lifting them lightly with two forks or spoons.
Unmold: Remove food such as a jelly that has set from mold.
Whip: Beat rapidly with a whisk or beater until mixture expands and is light.
Whisk: Whip food with a wire whisk made for this purpose.

Safety First Tips

- Cut, slice or chop down and away from you on a cutting board. When using a vegetable peeler, work away from you, as well.
- Always wear oven mitts or use a thick, dry cloth to remove pans and dishes from a hot oven.
- Turn handles to back or side of burners so they don't stick out over the front of the range where they might be knocked and the pan upset.
- Remember to turn off stove or oven when finished cooking or baking.

Cooking Equipment

The following is the list of essentials I feel I must have in my kitchen for preparing the recipes in this book. If you have the same equipment, you will be able to cook up a storm whenever you choose.

For Preparation:

Hard wooden board or plastic slab for cutting and chopping.
Paring, utility, chopping and carving knives - and they must be sharp. It is also nice to have a bread knife with a serrated edge.

Vegetable peeler	Kitchen scissors
Grater	Strainer or sieve
Juicer	Can opener

For Measuring:

Measures and measuring cups for liquid ingredients, graduated set for dry ingredients, and small ones for both.
Rubber scraper
Gram scale for weighing ingredients and portions
Roast meat thermometer for checking the doneness of roasted meats and poultry

For Mixing:

Wooden spoon for stirring and mixing
Pastry blender for cutting margarine or butter into flour
Whisk. This looks like a group of wires in a balloon shape with their ends stuck into a handle. It is used for beating or blending.
Rotary egg beater and/or electric mixer
Table knives and forks for cutting and beating
Rubber spatula
Mixing Bowls. It is nice to have at least two large and two small.
For cooking on top of the range or baking
In the oven I prefer using nonstick skillets and baking sheets. As well I find it important to use heavy-bottomed saucepans, especially for many of the dishes in this book which do not call for fat but instead use water or broth for braising.

For Cooking on Top of the Range:

Heavy skillets. I would not be without a small one for omelets
and crêpes, about 15 cm (6 in) in diameter, and a large one 25 to 30 cm (10 to 12 in) in diameter.
Saucepans. These should also be heavy and it is great to have two or three, one of them at least 3 L (12 cups) for cooking pasta and making soup.

Steamer for cooking vegetables
Metal lifter or spatula

For Baking in the Oven:

Cake pans. 20 to 23 cm (8 to 9 in)
Jelly Roll pan. Can also be used as a baking sheet for cookies.
Baking sheets for cookies (preferably non-stick)
Pie pans or plates (23 cm/9 in)
Muffin pan for medium-size muffins
Brushes for lightly greasing pans and basting. I use small paint brushes with good hair bristles.

Rolling pin	Biscuit cutters
Molds or souffle dish	Springform pan
Wide spatula for lifting cookies	Pot holders or oven mitts
Foil	

For Storing:

Glass jars with lids	Plastic containers with lids
Plastic bags	Plastic wrap

Other Larger Equipment - Nice to have but not necessary:

Toaster	Microwave Oven
Blender	Electric skillet
Food Processor	Toaster Oven

Cooking Ingredients

The choice of foods in our supermarkets today is mind boggling. Even a shopping trip to the corner grocer can buy almost anything we need to cook and eat. I kept a supply of staples and non-perishable ingredients on hand while developing the recipes for this collection. Then all I had to buy every couple of days were the fresh meats, poultry, fish, vegetables and fruits I needed. You might like to do the same. Here is the list of ingredients to keep on hand:

In the Kitchen Cupboard

Baking Needs:
All-purpose flour
Whole wheat flour
Quick-cooking rolled oats
Cornmeal
Sugar substitute
Granulated sugar
Corn syrup
Molasses
Baking powder
Baking soda
Dry unsweetened cocoa
Vanilla
Almond extract
Semi-sweet chocolate chips

Canned and Bottled Goods

Tomatoes
Kidney Beans
Romano Beans
Lentils
Chick peas
Soy sauce
Worcestershire sauce
Hot pepper sauce
Peanut butter
Unsweetened pineapple
Unsweetened apple, pineapple and grape juice
Catsup
Chili sauce

Dried Goods

Pasta (macaroni, spaghetti, lasagna noodles)
White long grain rice and short grain rice
Brown rice
Raisins
Dried apricots
Instant bouillon mix or cubes for chicken and beef broth
Seeds and nuts - sesame and sunflower seeds, walnuts, almonds, pecans
Corn oil
Vinegar

Herbs and Spices:

This list seems long. Buy one or two at a time. These are the ingredients that help flavor cooked foods: Chili powder, cayenne, pepper, curry powder, dried basil, bay leaves, celery seed, thyme, oregano, marjoram, tarragon, paprika, cinnamon, cloves, ground ginger, nutmeg, cardamom, coriander, allspice, cream of tartar.

In the Refrigerator

Cheddar, mozzarella	Unsalted butter
Parmesan cheese	2% cottage cheese
Dijon mustard	2% yogurt
Lemons	2% milk
Oranges	Skim milk
Carrots	Eggs
Green onions	Celery
Parsley	

In a Vegetable Bin

Cooking onions
Garlic
Potatoes

Make It a Game

Everyone Wins

When a person has diabetes it is important to balance the protein, carbohydrate and fat in a meal to control how much sugar will enter the bloodstream after the meal. The Food Group System with its Choices, used with a meal plan, makes this balance possible.

A suitable meal plan can be worked out with a dietitian who understands how to plan meals to meet your energy needs, taking into consideration your insulin and exercise pattern. The dietitian will help you decide how many Choices from each food group you wish to have at each meal. Then your dietitian's guide is your meal plan... and how you play the game is up to you. The choice is yours and this cookbook will help you add variety to your meals. The Food Choice value for a serving of a certain size has been worked out for you for each recipe so that you can fit your favorites into your own meal plan.

The following sample menus were planned using different meal plans for Sammy and Ted, Jane, Pat and Bob - all different young people - different ages, different food preferences, different energy needs. Their plan for a particular meal may or may not be the same as yours.

Take your own meal plan (or diet) and write up menu cards in the same way, only using the number of Food Choices from each food group on your own Good Health Eating Guide. Decide what and how much you are going to eat at a meal, and then you will have a meal that is nutritious, delicious - and balanced with your insulin supply and your energy needs.

Recipes in *Light & Easy Choices and Desserts* are indicated by an asterisk (*).

For example, your game plan for breakfast might consist of:

2 ▢ Starchy Choices
1 ◪ Fruits & Vegetables Choice
2 ◈ Milk Choices (2%)
1 ◩ Protein Choice
2 ▲ Fats & Oils Choices

Sample Breakfast	Food Choice Groups							Energy	
For: Sammy **Meal:** Breakfast 8:00 am	Starchy ▢	Fruits & Vegetables ⬦	Extra Vegetables ⊞	Milk ◇	Protein ⬙	Fats & Oils △	Extra ⊞	kilojoules	Calories
Orange Juice (125 mL/1/2 cup)		1						245	58
Poached Egg on					1			330	79
1 slice whole wheat toast	1							300	72
with margarine (5 mL/1 tsp)						1		150	36
1 Orange Cornmeal Muffin*	1							290	69
with margarine (5 mL/1 tsp)						1		150	36
Milk (250 mL/1 cup 2%)			2(2%)					540	129
Total Choices on Meal Plan	2	1		2(2%)	1	2			
Total Energy Value								2005	479

Meal planning is as simple as that!

To plan a meal, first list the total number of the Choices allowed from each Food Group for that meal on your own personal meal plan. Go through the recipes and as you select one, see what Choices will be used up in a serving. Subtract that from the total; then you can see what you have as you go along and what Choices need to be added to the meal. Be sure to count only the measured amount for a serving. If you want to eat 1½ or 2 servings of a certain dish, remember to count 1½ or 2 times the number of Choices in your meal. Everything you plan to eat at a meal must be included in your game plan unless they are ⊞ Extras.

This mixing and matching makes meal planning a game. It is a good idea to keep a copy of your menus on cards or in a book to help you remember combinations that you like and that work for you. It will be a handy and time-saving record to have at your fingertips.

When you use the recipes in this book with your own eating plan, you will be able to enjoy light, lively and luscious meals planned just for you.

16

Special Family Dinner / Food Choice Groups / Energy

For: Bob
Meal Evening 7:00 pm

Special Family Dinner	Starchy	Fruits & Vegetables	Extra Vegetables	Milk	Protein	Fats & Oils	Extra	kilojoules	Calories
*Potted Cheese in					1			230	55
Celery Sticks			++						
*Roast Chicken					3			690	165
*Grandma's Bread Stuffing (2 servings)	2					1		780	118
*Schnippled Green Beans			++					80	20
*Ginger Orange Carrots		1						240	57
*Cheesy Chive Potatoes	1							270	64
*Chocolate Mousse				1(skim)		1		300	72
Milk (125 mL/1/2 cup 2%)				1(2%)				270	65
Total Choices on Meal Plan	3	1	++	2(2%)	4	2			
Total Energy Value								2860	616

Snack Supper / Food Choice Groups / Energy

For: Pat
Meal: Evening 5:30 pm

Snack Supper	Starchy	Fruits & Vegetables	Extra Vegetables	Milk	Protein	Fats & Oils	Extra	kilojoules	Calories
*Bunch of Crunch with			++						
*Basil Cheese Dip					1			190	45
*Mini Pizza (2 Servings)	2				2	2		1480	350
*Apricot Sherbet (2 servings)		2						200	48
Milk (250 mL/1 cup 2%)				2(2%)				540	129
Total Choices on Meal Plan	2	2	++	2(2%)	3	2			
Total Energy Value								2410	572

School Lunch For: Ted Meal: Noon-time 12:00 pm	Starchy □	Fruits & Vegetables �	Extra Vegetables ++	Milk ◆	Protein ∅	Fats & Oils △	Extra ++	kilojoules	Calories
Tuna Sandwich	2				2			920	220
Celery Sticks			++						
*Butterscotch Peanut Cookies (4)	1					2		760	180
Milk (250 mL/1 cup 2%)				2(2%)				540	129
Total Choices on Meal Plan	**3**		**++**	**2(2%)**	**2**	**2**			
Total Energy Value								**2220**	**529**

Week-day Breakfast For: Jane Meal: Breakfast 8:00 am	Starchy □	Fruits & Vegetables �	Extra Vegetables ++	Milk ◆	Protein ∅	Fats & Oils △	Extra ++	kilojoules	Calories
Half Grapefruit		1						190	45
Scrambled Egg					1			330	79
English Muffin	2							640	153
Margarine (5 mL/1 tsp)						1		150	36
Lo-Cal Spread							++	21	5
*Frothy Rich Hot Chocolate				2(skim)				350	84
Total Choices on Meal Plan	**2**	**1**		**2(skim)**	**1**	**1**	**++**		
Total Energy Value								**1681**	**402**

The Canadian Diabetes Association's Food Group System

Tasty, wholesome food provides great enjoyment. It also supplies energy and the essential nutrients for building and maintaining a healthy body. While people with diabetes have the same nutritional needs as anyone else, they must also balance the kind and amount of food they eat with their limited insulin supply. A qualified dietitian or nutritionist can help them achieve this balance by designing an individually tailored *Eating Plan*. Factors such as activity level, weight, age, medication and food preferences are considered by the dietitian as the plan is prepared and discussed with the person with diabetes. An *Eating Plan* based on either the Food Group System or Exchange System can include meals prepared using this specially developed collection of recipes.

A comparison of the two systems is summarized below.

Canadian Diabetes Association	**American Diabetes Association**
Choice System	*Exchange System*
1 Starchy Foods *Choice*	1 Starch *Exchange*
1 Fruits & Vegetables *Choice*	2 Fruit *Exchange*
1 Fruits & Vegetables *Choice*	2/3 Vegetable *Exchange*
Extra Vegetables	(no equivalent)
1 Milk (Skim) *Choice*	1/2 Milk *Exchange*
1 Protein Foods *Choice**	1 Lean Meat *Exchange*
1 Fats & Oils *Choice*	1 Fat *Exchange*
Extras (unmeasured)	Calorie-Free Foods, List A
Extras (small measures)	Calorie Poor Foods, List B

The *Food Group System* is a revised form of the Exchange System of meal planning. It is based on *Canada's Food Guide*, with modifications to make it suitable for people with diabetes. In the *Food Group System*, foods are classified into six groups according to their carbohydrate, protein and fat content. These groups are identified by different symbols.

The word *CHOICE* refers to a measured (or weighed) amount of food which can be replaced by another in that Food Choice Group. This system can be used to plan menus

---

*Dietary calculations are based on protein foods low in fat. If protein foods high in fat are chosen frequently, the dietary calculations would be adjusted to account for the extra "hidden" fat.

for the whole family, but the serving sizes will vary according to individual needs.

These recipes have been developed in both metric and imperial measures. Choose the system of measures that you prefer and use the tools designed for that system. Slight variations sometimes occur between the two systems, therefore it is most important to follow through the recipe using one system— metric or imperial—only.

Nutrient Values have been calculated for single servings of each recipe using current Food Composition tables. These figures should be regarded as approximate due to the variations between tables and the many factors which can alter the yield of a recipe.

The Food Groups

Starchy Foods 🔲

This group includes breads, cereals, grains, pasta, dried beans and peas, starchy vegetables and some prepared foods. Starch is a complex carbohydrate which gradually breaks down to sugar during digestion.

Some starchy foods are valuable sources of dietary fibers. These fibers are the portions of edible plants that are not digested by humans. Some of these fibers, such as those from dried peas and beans, delay carbohydrate absorption and thus slow the entry of sugar into the blood stream. Other fibers, such as cereal fibers, aid in elimination. A high-fiber diet also may help to promote weight loss by creating a feeling of fullness and satisfaction. To increase the fiber in your diet, try to choose more high-fiber foods such as dried beans, peas, lentils, whole grain breads and cereals.

One Choice from the Starchy Foods Group 🔲 contains approximately 15 g starch (carbohydrate) and 2 g of protein and yields an energy value of about 290 kilojoules (68 Calories).

	Breads	
25 g	Bagel, Kaiser Roll	1/2
20 g	Bread Sticks, 11 cm x 1 cm (4¹/₂" x ¹/₂")	2
45 g	Brewis, cooked	50 mL (1/4 cup)
25 g	English Muffin, Crumpet	1/2
30 g	Hamburger Bun, Hot Dog Bun	1/2
20 g	Matzoh, 15 cm (6" square)	1
15 g	Melba Toast, rectangular	4
25 g	Plain Roll	1 small
20 g	Rusks	2
25 g	Rye, coarse or Pumpernickel, 10 cm x 10 cm x 8 mm (4" x 4" x ³/₈")	1/2 slice
20 g	Soda Crackers	8 small, 6 medium
25 g	Whole Wheat, Cracked Wheat, Rye, White Enriched	1 slice
	Pastas	
70 g	Macaroni — cooked	125 mL (1/2 cup)
80 g	Noodles — cooked	125 mL (1/2 cup)

70 g	Spaghetti — cooked	125 mL (1/2 cup)

Cereals

125 g	Cooked Cereals — cooked	125 mL (1/2 cup)
20 g	— dry	30 mL (2 tbsp)
125 g	Cornmeal — cooked	125 mL (1/2 cup)
20 g	— dry	30 mL (2 tbsp)
20 g	*Ready-to-Eat Unsweetened Cereal	125 mL (1/2 cup)
20 g	Shredded Wheat Biscuit, rectangular or round	1
30 g	Wheat Germ	75 mL (1/3 cup)

Grains

120 g	Barley — cooked	125 mL (1/2 cup)
20 g	— dry	30 mL (2 tbsp)
70 g	Bulgar, Kasha — cooked, moist	125 mL (1/2 cup)
40 g	— cooked, crumbly	75 mL (1/3 cup)
20 g	— dry	30 mL (2 tbsp)
70 g	Rice — cooked, loosely packed	125 mL (1/2 cup)
70 g	— cooked, tightly packed	75 mL (1/3 cup)

Starchy Vegetables

80 g	Beans & Peas (dried) — cooked	125 mL (1/2 cup)
85 g	Corn — canned, whole kernel	125 mL (1/2 cup)
60 g	— canned, creamed	75 mL (1/3 cup)
140 g	Corn, on the cob, 13 cm, 4 cm diameter (5", 1¹/₂" diameter)	1 small cob
20 g	Popcorn, unbuttered, large kernel	750 mL (3 cups)
105 g	Potatoes, whipped	125 mL (1/2 cup)
95 g	Potatoes, whole 13 cm, 5 cm diameter (5", 2" diameter)	1/2
75 g	Yam, Sweet Potatoes 13 cm, 5 cm diameter (5", 2" diameter)	1/2

Cookies and Biscuits
See "Prepared Foods," following. For more detail refer to Convenience Foods, Canadian Diabetes Association.

*For more exact measures of various types of ready-to-eat cereals, see the cereals section of Convenience Foods which is available from the Canadian Diabetes Association.

Food items found in this category contain an additional 5 g fat and consequently an extra 190 kilojoules (45 Calories) = 1 ▲ Fats & Oils Choice.

Prepared Foods

30 g	Baking Powder Biscuit, 5 cm diameter (2" diameter)	1
20 g	*Cookies, plain, (e.g. Digestive, Oatmeal)	2

35 g	Cup Cake, un-iced, 5 cm diameter (2" diameter)	1 small
30 g	Doughnut, cake type, plain, 7 cm diameter (2³/₄" diameter)	1
40 g	Muffin, plain, 6 cm diameter (2¹/₂" diameter)	1 small
50 g	Pancake, homemade using 50 mL (1/4 cup) batter	1 small
65 g	Potatoes, French Fried, 5 cm x 1 cm x 1 cm (2" x ¹/₂" x ¹/₂")	10
260 g	*Soup, canned (Prepared with equal volume of water)	250 mL (1 cup)
35 g	Waffle, homemade using 50 mL (1/4 cup) batter	1 small

*For more exact measures of various types of cookies and canned soups, see the appropriate section of Convenience Foods which is available from the Canadian Diabetes Association.

Fruits & Vegetables ◢

This group includes fruits and many vegetables. Since certain vegetables such as corn and potatoes are high in starch, they are included in the Starchy Foods Group.

Fruits and vegetables are excellent sources of many vitamins and minerals as well as dietary fibers. Select a wide variety from this group for good health. Many fruits and vegetables (such as oranges, strawberries and turnips) are a valuable source of Vitamin C. Deep yellow fruits and dark green vegetables (such as peaches and winter squash) are usually high in Vitamin A.

Plan to have solid fruits and vegetables instead of juices. The natural sugar present in juice enters the blood rapidly, whereas the fiber content of solid fruits and vegetables slows the entry of sugar into the blood.

One Choice from the Fruits & Vegetables Group ◢ contains approximately 10 g of simple sugar (carbohydrate) and 1 g of protein, and yields an energy value of about 190 kilojoules (44 Calories).

	Fruits	
	Fresh, frozen without sugar, canned in water	
75 g	Apple — raw	1/2 medium
120 g	— sauce	125 mL (1/2 cup)
115 g	Apricot — raw	2 medium
110 g	— canned, in water	4 halves, plus 30 mL (2 tbsp) liquid
75 g	Banana, 15 cm (6"), with peel	1/2 small
70 g	Blackberries — raw	125 mL (1/2 cup)
100 g	— canned, in water	125 mL (1/2 cup), includes 30 mL (2 tbsp) liquid
70 g	Blueberries, raw	125 mL (1/2 cup)
240 g	Cantaloupe, wedge with rind, 13 cm diameter (5" diameter)	1/4

160 g	cubed or diced	250 mL (1 cup)
75 g	Cherries — raw, with pits	10
90 g	— canned, in water, with pits	75 mL (1/3 cup), includes 30 mL (2 tbsp) liquid
120 g	Fruit Cocktail, canned, in water	125 mL (1/2 cup), includes 30 mL (2 tbsp) liquid
120 g	Fruit, mixed, cut-up	125 mL (1/2 cup)
185 g	Grapefruit — raw, with rind	1/2 small
100 g	— raw, sectioned	125 mL (1/2 cup)
120 g	— canned, in water	125 mL (1/2 cup), includes 30 mL (2 tbsp) liquid
75 g	Grapes — raw	125 mL (1/2 cup)
115 g	— canned, in water	75 mL (1/3 cup), includes 30 mL (2 tbsp) liquid
225 g	Honeydew Melon — raw, with rind	1/10
170 g	— cubed or diced	250 mL (1 cup)
155 g	Kiwifruit, raw, with skin	2 small
100 g	Mandarin Oranges, canned, in water	125 mL (1/2 cup) includes 30 mL (2 tbsp) liquid
75 g	Nectarine	1/2 medium
130 g	Orange — raw, with rind	1 small
95 g	— raw, sectioned	125 mL (1/2 cup)
130 g	Peaches — raw, with seed and skin, 6 cm (2-1/2") diameter	1 large
100 g	— raw, sliced, diced	125 mL (1/2 cup)
120 g	— canned, in water, halves or slices	125 mL (1/2 cup), includes 30 mL (2 tbsp) liquid
90 g	Pear — raw, with skin and core	1/2
90 g	— canned, in water, halves	2 halves, plus 30 mL (2 tbsp) liquid
75 g	Pineapple — raw	1 slice, 8 cm diameter, 2 cm thick (3 1/4"diameter, 3/4" thick)
75 g	— raw, diced	125 mL (1/2 cup)
55 g	— canned, in juice, sliced	1 slice, plus 15 mL (1 tbsp) liquid
55 g	— canned in juice, diced	75 mL (1/3 cup), includes 15 mL (1 tbsp) liquid
60 g	Plums — raw, prune type	2

100 g	— canned, in water	3, plus 30 mL (2 tbsp) liquid
70 g	— canned, in apple juice	2, plus 30 mL (2 tbsp) liquid
65 g	Raspberries, raw, black or red	125 mL (1/2 cup)
150 g	Strawberries, raw	250 mL (1 cup)
115 g	Tangerine — raw	1
100 g	— raw, sectioned	125 mL (1/2 cup)
310 g	Watermelon — raw with rind	1 wedge, 125 mm triangle, 22 mm thick (5" triangle, 1" thick)
160 g	— cubed or diced	250 mL (1 cup)

Fresh Fruits

Fruits can vary a great deal in size. Many of the recipes in Light & Easy Choices and Desserts call for a certain size piece of fruit. If you substitute a smaller or larger piece, you may change the amount of carbohydrate and Food Choice Values of each serving of the prepared dessert. The following chart will help you choose the right size fruit piece. The weights are for fruits as they are purchased and include peel, pits or seeds.

Apple, small	115g	Grapefruit, medium	480g	Pear, medium	185g
Apple, medium	150g	Cantaloupe	1060g	Kiwifruit	90g
Apricot	40g	Orange, small	130g	Nectarine	150g
Banana, small	140g	Orange, medium	210g	Prune plum	130g
Dates, 2	15g	Peach, medium	115g	Mango	300g
Grapefruit, small	400g	Peach, large	175g	(Notes from Susan Gatchell, R.P.Dt.)	

	Dried Fruit	
15 g	Dates, without pits	2
15 g	Prunes, raw, with pits	2
15 g	Raisins, Currants	30 mL (2 tbsp)

	Juices No sugar added or unsweetened	
55 g	Apricot, Grape, Guava, Mango, Prune	50 mL (1/4 cup)
80 g	Apple, Carrot, Pineapple	75 mL (1/3 cup)
130 g	Grapefruit, Orange	125 mL (1/2 cup)
255 g	Tomato, Tomato based mixed vegetables	250 mL (1 cup)

	Vegetables Fresh, frozen or canned	
85 g	Beets, diced or sliced	125 mL (1/2 cup)
75 g	Carrots, diced	125 mL (1/2 cup)
80 g	Parsnips, mashed	125 mL (1/2 cup)
80 g	Peas — fresh or frozen	125 mL (1/2 cup)
55 g	— canned	75 mL (1/3 cup)
235 g	Sauerkraut	250 mL (1 cup)
100 g	Snowpeas	10 pods
115 g	Squash, yellow or winter, mashed	125 mL (1/2 cup)

240 g	Tomatoes, canned	250 mL (1 cup)
115 g	Turnip, mashed	125 mL (1/2 cup)
90 g	Vegetables, mixed	125 mL (1/2 cup)
50 g	Water Chestnuts	8 medium

Extra Vegetables ⬛

The vegetables in this group are low in natural sugar and energy value. However, they are high in dietary fibers, vitamins and minerals. Use them when you feel like nibbling. Moderate amounts of these vegetables do not have to be measured or calculated in your meal plan. Usually 125 mL (1/2 cup) cooked vegetables from this group contains less than 3.5 g of carbohydrate and yields an energy value of 60 kilojoules (14 Calories) or less. For some vegetables, 250 mL (1 cup) would be counted as one Fruits & Vegetables Choice ◨ . These are indicated with an asterisk (*) in the following list.

Artichokes,	*Brussels Sprouts	*Kohlrabi	Radish
Globe or French	Cabbage	*Leeks	*Rhubarb
Asparagus	Cauliflower	Lettuce	Spinach
Bamboo shoots	Celery	Mushrooms	Sprouts:
Beans, String,	Chard	*Okra	Alfalfa, Radish, etc.
green or yellow	Cucumber	Onions, green	*Tomato, raw
Bean Sprouts,	*Eggplant	*Onions, mature	Vegetable Marrow
Mung or Soy	Endive	Parsley	Watercress
Broccoli	Kale	Pepper, green or red	Zucchini

Some vegetables are high in dietary fiber and low in available carbohydrate. They may be counted as ⬛ Extra Vegetables if they are eaten in the portion size indicated with recipe, because only part of the carbohydrate is actually available to the blood sugar.

Milk ◆

This group includes milk and yogurt. Your dietitian will indicate the type of milk you should use in your *Eating Plan*.

Plain yogurt may be substituted for milk, but avoid sweetened yogurts which have a "fruit bottom" or added syrup. They contain extra sugar. Try making your own fruit-flavored yogurt by combining one Milk Choice as plain yogurt with one Fruits & Vegetables Choice. For a completely new taste, add bits of cut-up cucumber, green pepper and tomato to plain yogurt. Plain yogurt plus dill and other herbs such as thyme and parsley may be used as a tasty dressing for salads. You may use 25 mL (2 tbsp) of this mixture as an Extra ⬛ in your meal plan.

The Milk Food Choices are a valuable source of many nutrients — protein, calcium and phosphorous (needed for strong bones and teeth), thiamine and riboflavin. Since milk and plain yogurt are a source of carbohydrate (lactose or milk sugar) they are included in measured amounts in meal planning.

One Choice from the Milk Group ◆ contains approximately:

	Skim Milk	
6 g	Carbohydrate	170 kilojoules
4 g	Protein	(40 calories)
0	Fat	

2% Milk

6 g	Carbohydrate	240 kilojoules
4 g	Protein	(58 calories)
2 g	Fat	

Whole Milk

6 g	Carbohydrate	320 kilojoules
4 g	Protein	(76 calories)
4 g	Fat	

125 g	Milk, Buttermilk	125 mL (1/2 cup)
50 g	Evaporated Milk	50 mL (1/4 cup)
15 g	Powdered Milk, regular	30 mL (2 tbsp)
15 g	instant	50 mL (1/4 cup)
125 g	Unflavored yogurt	125 mL (1/2 cup)

Protein Foods ⬛

This group includes meat, fish, poultry, cheese and eggs. These are excellent sources of protein, which is essential for life. It is used for building, maintaining and repairing body tissues and also forms an important part of hormones and antibodies.

When shopping for meat, select cuts which look lean and have little visible fat distributed (marbled) throughout. Buy enough meat to allow for shrinkage during cooking—100 g (4 oz) raw, boneless meat will yield about 75 g (3 oz) cooked. When selecting chops or poultry, purchase double the weight required—500 g (1 lb) raw poultry or chops will yield about 250 g (1/2 lb) cooked.

Protein foods low in fat are listed first in the following chart. Choose them often, especially if you need to lose weight.

One choice from the Protein Foods Group ⬛ contains approximately 7 g protein and 3 g fat and yields an energy value of about 230 kilojoules (55 Calories). All weights and measures are for cooked meats, fish and poultry unless otherwise stated.

Cheese

25 g	All types, made from partly skim milk, e.g. Mozzarella, part-skim	1 piece 5 cm x 2 cm x 2 cm (2" x ³/₄"x ³/₄")
55 g	Cottage Cheese, all types	50 mL (1/4 cup)

Fish

30 g	Canned, drained, e.g. Chicken Haddie, Mackerel, Salmon, Tuna	50 mL (1/4 cup)
50 g	Cod Tongues/Cheeks	75 mL (1/3 cup)
30 g	Fillet or Steak, e.g. Boston blue, Cod, Flounder, Haddock, Halibut, Perch, Pickerel, Pike, Salmon, Shad, Sole, Trout Whitefish	1 piece, 6 cm x 2 cm x 2 cm (2¹/₂"x ³/₄" x ³/₄")
30 g	Herring	1/3 fish
30 g	Sardines	2 medium or 3 small

30 g	Smelts	2 medium

Shellfish

30 g	Clams, Mussels, Oysters, Scallops, Snails	3 medium
30 g	Crab, Lobster, flaked	50 mL (1/4 cup)
30 g	Shrimp – fresh	5 large
30 g	– frozen	10 medium
30 g	– canned	18 small

Meat and Poultry
e.g. Beef, Chicken, Ham, Lamb, Pork, Turkey, Veal, Wild Game:

25 g	Back Bacon	3 slices, thin
35 g	Chop	1/2 chop, with bone
25 g	Minced or ground, lean	30 mL (2 tbsp)
25 g	Sliced, lean	1 slice 10 cm x 5 cm x 5 mm (4"x2"x $^1/_4$")
25 g	Steak, lean	1 piece, 4 cm x 3 cm x 2 cm (1$^1/_2$" x 1$^1/_4$" x $^3/_4$")

Organ Meats

25 g	Heart, Liver	1 slice, 5 cm x 5 cm x 1 cm (2" x 2" x $^1/_2$")
25 g	Kidney, Sweet Breads, chopped	50 mL (1/4 cup)

Soybean

70 g	Bean Curd or Tofu, 1 block = 6 cm x 6 cm x 4 cm (2 $^1/_2$" x 2 $^1/_2$" x 1 $^1/_2$")	1/2 block

The following choices contain extra fat, so use them less often.
Cheese

25 g	Cheese, all types, made from whole milk, e.g. Brick, Brie, Camembert, Cheddar, Edam, Tilsit	1 piece, 5 cm x 2 cm x 2 cm (2" x $^3/_4$" x $^3/_4$")
25 g	Cheese, coarsely grated, e.g. Cheddar	75 mL (1/3 cup)
15 g	Cheese, Dry, finely grated, e.g. Parmesan	45 mL (3 tbsp)
55 g	Cheese, Ricotta	50 mL (1/4 cup)

Egg

50 g	Egg, in shell, raw or cooked	1 medium
55 g	Egg, scrambled	50 mL (1/4 cup)

Meat

40 g	Bologna, Summer Sausage or Salami	1 slice, 5 mm, 10 cm (1/4", 4") diameter
40 g	Canned Luncheon Meat	1 slice, 9 cm x 4.5 cm x 1 cm (3½" x 1¾" x ½")
25 g	Ground Beef, medium fat	30 mL (2 tbsp)
25 g	Sausage, Pork, Link	1 link
65 g	Spareribs or Shortribs, with bone	10 cm x 6 cm (4" x 2½")
25 g	Stewing Beef	1 cube, 2.5 cm (1")
25 g	Wiener	1/2 medium

Miscellaneous

15 g	Peanut Butter, all kinds	15 mL (1 tbsp)

Fats & Oils ▲

This group includes a variety of high-fat foods such as vegetable oil, salad dressings, nuts, margarine and butter. All fats are a concentrated source of energy. Be especially careful to measure fats and oils if weight loss is necessary. If you have been advised to use polyunsaturated fats, choose oils such as, canola, safflower, sunflower, corn and soybean. Soft margarines in a tub with a label statement of "Polyunsaturated Fat 35%-55%, Saturated Fat 18%-25% are recommended in preference to solid fats.

One Choice from the Fats and Oils Group ▲ contains approximately 5 g of fat and yields an energy value of about 190 kilojoules (45 calories).

5 g	Bacon, side, crisp	1 slice
5 g	Butter, Margarine	5 mL (1 tsp)
30 g	Cream — Half and Half (cereal) 10%	30 mL (2 tbsp)
35 g	— Sour 12-14%	45 mL (3 tbsp)
15 g	Cream Cheese, Cheese Spread	15 mL (1 tbsp)
5 g	Lard, Salt Port, raw or cooked	5 mL (1 tsp)
20 g	Nuts, shelled — Almonds	8 nuts
5 g	— Brazil Nuts	2 nuts
10 g	— Cashews, Filberts, Hazelnuts	5 nuts
10 g	— Peanuts	10 nuts
5 g	— Pecans	5 halves
10 g	— Walnuts	4 halves
5 g	Oil, cooking and salad	5 mL
15 g	Pâté, Liverwurst, Meat Spreads	15 mL (1 tbsp)
10 g	Salad Dressing — Blue, French, Italian	10 mL (2 tsp)
5 g	— Mayonnaise, Thousand Island	5 mL (1 tsp)

The **complete** *Good Health Eating Guide Food Groups* in color, and other information about diabetes, is available from the Canadian Diabetes Association. For a price list, contact your local Branch or Division of the Canadian Diabetes Association.

Reprinted by permission from CHOICE COOKING, 1983, Canadian Diabetes Association, published by NC Press, Toronto.

Appetizers and Small Snacks

Appetizers tease the taste buds and wake up the appetite for the rest of the meal. Many are tiny tidbits of food such as dips and vegetables, saucy meatballs or light soups, crisp salads, chilled juices and juicy fruit that can be eaten without forks or spoons. These are called 'finger foods'. They can be eaten hot or cold and are often served in a casual manner in the living room or family room before dinner. Dips and vegetables, saucy meatballs or light soups, crisp salads, chilled juices and juicy fruit are also just right as the starter of a meal, and are usually served at the table. When the appetizer is the first course of a meal, it should be light and go with the foods that follow. For a snack party, serve an assortment of appetizers or bite-size foods.

When a small meal is what you fancy, and as long as it fits into your meal plan, one or two of these small snacks will fit the bill.

Bunch of Crunch

On a tray or platter, set out an assortment of the following vegetables: Whole green beans, broccoli and cauliflower florets, celery and sweet red and green pepper sticks, cucumber and zucchini slices, and red radishes.

Each serving:

1 ▪▪ Extra

Consider a handful ▪▪ Extra Vegetables. These are the right kind of vegetables to serve with a dip like Basil Cheese Dip (recipe, p. 37) All you will need to count is the Choice Value of the dip.

Keep in the refrigerator in plastic containers. Any or all of the vegetables are great for nibbling when you feel like an extra snack that's not included in your meal plan.

Melba Toast

Preparation Time: *5 minutes*
Cooking Time: *10 minutes*

Call this 'crisp bread' if you wish. It is like the melba toast served in top-notch restaurants and dining rooms. The thoroughly dry, crisp triangles keep beautifully in a container with a loose fitting lid. They are great to have on hand to serve with soups and salads.

4	slices whole wheat bread	4

Each serving: 4 triangles (1 slice bread)

1 ▫ Starchy Choice

*15 g carbohydrate
3 g protein*

*300 kilojoules
(72 Calories)*

- Toast bread.

- Place each slice on a bread board. Cut off crusts and reserve for making bread crumbs. With a bread knife, holding the toast in place with the palm of the hand, carefully cut each slice in half horizontally to make 2 thin slices. Cut each thin slice in half, corner to corner, to form 2 triangles.

- Place triangles toasted side down on oven racks or nonstick cookie sheets.

- Bake in a 180ºC (350ºF) oven for 10 minutes or until triangles are dry and turn golden brown.

Makes 16 triangles, 4 servings

Mini Meatballs

You might like to plan a meatball making session as a evening or Saturday activity. Stash them away in the freezer where they will be ready and waiting to be cooked up for snacks, stews or in a sauce for spaghetti. Use them for Meatball Ragout (recipe p. 77)

Preparation Time: *30 minutes*
Baking Time: *10 minutes*

500 g	lean ground beef	1 lb
50 mL	fine dry bread crumbs	1/4 cup
50 mL	water	1/4 cup
25 mL	chopped fresh chives OR green onion	2 tbsp
5 mL	Dijon mustard	1 tsp
5 mL	Worcestershire sauce	1 tsp
2 mL	salt	1/2 tsp
1 mL	freshly ground pepper	1/4 tsp

Each serving: 4 meatballs

1 ◻ Protein Choice

2 g carbohydrate
7 g protein
3 g fat

260 kilojoules
(63 Calories)

- In a large bowl, combine ground beef, bread crumbs, water, chives, mustard, Worcestershire sauce, salt and pepper. Mix well to blend flavors.

- With hands, roll 15 mL (1 tbsp) at a time into balls.

- Place on a broiler pan to allow fat to drain off.

- Bake in a 200ºC (400ºF) oven for 10 minutes or until lightly browned.

Makes 48 meatballs, 12 servings

❖ **Timely Tip:**

Both uncooked and cooked meatballs freeze well. To freeze meatballs, place them in a single layer on a baking sheet. Place in freezer for 1 hour. (This prefreezing prevents balls from sticking together.) Remove and, working quickly, place in plastic bags, dividing into single-serving size portions or desired meal size. Close and fasten bags, pushing out all air. Label with name, date and instructions for using. Immediately store in freezer for up to 4 months. To cook frozen meatballs, place on rack in broiler pan and bake in a 200ºC (400ºF) oven for 15 to 20 minutes for raw meatballs, 10 to 12 minutes for precooked.

Microwave Directions:
Reduce water to 25 mL (2 tbsp). Microwave meatballs in two batches. Place 24 balls on a microwave safe rack; cover with waxed paper. Microwave on High (100%) for 3 minutes until meat just loses its pinkness. Remove to paper towel-lined plate. Let stand for 1 minute. Repeat with remaining meatballs.

Potted Cheese

Preparation Time: *5 minutes*

This mildly sharp smoothy is so easy to make you will always want to keep a 'pot' in your refrigerator.

250 mL	2% cottage cheese	1 cup
50 mL	shredded old Cheddar cheese	$^1/_4$ cup
50 mL	cubed blue cheese	$^1/_4$ cup
5 mL	Dijon mustard	1 tsp

Each serving: 45 mL (3 tbsp)

1 ⬧ Protein Choice

1 g carbohydrate
6 g protein
3 g fat

230 kilojoules
(55 Calories)

- In a food processor or blender, combine cottage cheese, Cheddar cheese, blue cheese and musatrd; process until smooth.

- Spoon into a small crock or dish.

- Cover and refrigerate until serving time. (Will keep up to 7 days in refrigerator.)

Makes 325 mL (1-$^1/_3$ cups), 7 servings

Variations:
Potted Caraway Cheese
Add 5 mL (1 tsp) caraway seed to the above mixture.

Curried Potted Cheese
Use 5 mL (1 tsp) curry powder and 2 mL ($^1/_2$ tsp) sugar substitute, equivalent to 2 mL ($^1/_2$ tsp) sugar in place of the Dijon mustard in the above mixture.

Cheese Chips

Not only are these crisp, cheesy crackers good on their own, they are excellent with soups or salads. Consider them for rounding out a meal.

Preparation Time: *5 minutes*
Baking Time: *15 minutes*

125 mL	all-purpose flour	$^1/_2$ cup
125 mL	whole wheat flour	$^1/_2$ cup
125 mL	freshly grated Parmesan cheese	$^1/_2$ cup
2 mL	baking powder	$^1/_2$ tsp
Pinch	each white pepper, curry powder & salt	Pinch
25 mL	margarine	2 tbsp
1	egg, lightly beaten	1
25 mL	water	2 tbsp

- Reserve 15 mL (1 tbsp) of the all-purpose flour for flouring board.

- In a bowl, combine remaining all-purpose flour, whole wheat flour, cheese, baking powder, pepper, curry and salt.

- With 2 knives, cut in margarine until mixture resembles coarse crumbs.

- Combine egg and water; stir into flour mixture until mixture can be gathered into a ball of dough.

- Knead dough on a lightly floured board 5 to 6 strokes. Roll out to 3 mm (1/8 in) thickness. Cut into 5 cm (2 in) triangles.

- Bake in a 180ºC (350ºF) oven for 12 to 15 minutes or until lightly browned.

Makes 36 chips, 6 servings

Each serving: 6 chips

1 ☐ Starchy Choice

1 ◩ Protein Choice

15 g carbohydrate
6 g protein
6 g fat

580 kilojoules
(138 Calories)

Cornmeal Tortillas (Cornmeal Pancakes)

Preparation Time: *5 minutes*
Standing Time: *10 minutes*
Cooking Time: *15 minutes*

Using cornmeal in this batter results in pancakes very similar to the Mexican tortilla. Crispy Corn Chips (see variation below) can be made when the pancakes are cut up and dried out in a hot oven.

1	egg	1
250 mL	water	1 cup
125 mL	all-purpose flour	1/2 cup
75 mL	cornmeal	1/3 cup
2 mL	baking powder	1/2 tsp
2 mL	salt	1/2 tsp

Each serving: 2 tortillas

1 ▢ Starchy Choice

13 g carbohydrate
3 g protein
1 g fat

310 kilojoules
(73 Calories)

- In a bowl, combine egg and water. Stir in flour, cornmeal, baking powder and salt; beat well, then allow to stand for 5 to 10 minutes.

- Heat a nonstick frypan over medium heat. Brush very lightly with vegetable oil. Stir batter, then pour batter, 25 mL (2 tbsp) at a time, into frypan to make very thin pancakes.

- Cook until just dry on top. Do not turn. Stack until all pancakes are cooked. Stir batter as it is being used.

Makes 12 tortillas (pancakes), 6 servings

Each serving: 12 corn chips
Calculations as above

Variation:
Crispy Corn Chips
Cut pancakes into 6 wedges. Lay wedges in single layers on nonstick baking sheets. Bakes in 190ºC (375ºF) oven for about 10 to 12 minutes or until lightly browned, crisp and dry. (Some pieces may be damper than others and may require a few more minutes baking.) Cool and pack into airtight bags.
Makes 72 corn chips, 6 servings.

Roasted Potato Skins

My kids and their friends love these snacks. They disappear before I can say "roasted potato skins". Fortunately, the leftover cooked pulp that I tuck in the refrigerator is excellent cold for salad or rewarmed for the potato part of a meal.

Preparation Time: *15 minutes*
Baking Time: *1 hour*

6	medium baking potatoes	6
5 mL	vegetable oil	1 tsp
10 mL	margarine, softened	2 tsp
	Garlic powder OR grated Parmesan cheese OR salt and freshly ground pepper	

- Scrub potatoes. Place a few drops of oil in palm of hand and rub it over potatoes. Prick each potato with a fork to allow steam to escape during baking.

- Place oiled potatoes on oven rack. Bake in a 200ºC (400ºF) oven for 40 minutes or until tender.

- Remove from oven and cut each one in half crosswise. Let cool until they can be handled. Scoop out potato pulp, leaving about 3 mm (1/8 in) flesh clinging to skin. Cut each skin into 4 pieces. Reserve scooped out potato pulp for dishes like Cheesy Chive Potatoes (recipe, p. 112). If not using immediately, wrap in plastic wrap and keep in refrigerator for up to 4 days.

- Dip a small pastry or paint brush into the soft margarine. Brush inside of each potato piece very sparingly with margarine.

- Sprinkle very lightly with garlic powder or Parmesan or just salt and pepper.

- Place potato pieces skin side down on nonstick baking sheets. Bake in a 180ºC (350ºF) oven for 15 to 20 minutes or until browned and crisp around edges.

- Serve hot or at room temperature. Store in covered container or plastic bags in refrigerator if some of the potato pulp is still moist, or in cupboard if skins and flesh are completely dry.

Makes 48 pieces, 6 servings

Each serving: 8 pieces

$^{1}/_{2}$ ▲ Fats & Oils Choice

2 g carbohydrate
1 g protein
2 g fat

130 kilojoules
(30 Calories)

Falafel

Preparation Time: *10 minutes*
Standing Time: *1 hour*
Cooking Time: *15 minutes*

In the Middle East, street vendors sell pita bread stuffed with Falafel and garnished with greens and yogurt. As well, try Falafel Patties in a hamburger bun to make a great vegetarian burger. Dress it with your favourite ■■■ *Extra relishes.*

1	can (540 mL/19 oz) chick peas	1
50 mL	finely chopped celery	1/4 cup
50 mL	finely chopped onion	1/4 cup
15 mL	chopped fresh parsley OR 5 mL (1 tsp) dried	1 tbsp
1 mL	baking powder	1/4 tsp
10 mL	sesame seed	2 tsp
1 mL	ground turmeric	1/4 tsp
1 mL	ground cumin	1/4 tsp
1	egg	1
1	clove garlic, finely chopped	1

Each serving: 6 Falafel balls

1 ▢ Starchy Choice

1 ▨ Protein Choice

16 g carbohydrate
7 g protein
3 g fat

500 kilojoules
(119 Calories)

- Drain and rinse chick peas.
- In a bowl, mash chick peas with back of large spoon or potato masher. Stir in celery, onion, parsley and baking powder; mix well. (Do not purée in blender or processor.)

- In a separate bowl, place sesame seed, turmeric, cumin, egg and garlic. Blend or whisk together until well blended. Pour into chick pea mixture; stir until well blended.

- Cover and let stand 1 hour.

- With wet hands, shape unto 2.5 cm (1 in) balls. Flatten slightly and place on lightly greased nonstick baking sheet. Bake in 180ºC (350ºF) oven for 15 minutes or until lightly browned. Serve warm with Nippy Yogurt Sauce (recipe, p 62).

Makes 30 Falafel balls, 5 servings

Each serving: 1 patty

Calculations as above

Variation:
Falafel Patties: Form Falafel mixture into 5 patties. Bake as for Falafel. Serve in pita pockets, remembering to count their Choice value.

Makes 5 patties, 5 servings

Basil Cheese Dip

*Prepare and serve an assortment of crisp vegetables — celery,
cucumber and zucchini sticks, broccoli and cauliflower florets,
ivory mushrooms, ruby radishes — to use for dipping. Arrange
them in cartwheel fashion around a bowl of dip set on a round plate
or platter.*

Preparation Time: *5 minutes*

250 mL	2% cottage cheese	1 cup
50 mL	finely chopped fresh basil OR 15 mL (1 tbsp) dried	1/4 cup
1	small clove garlic crushed & chopped	1
25 mL	freshly grated Parmesan cheese	2 tbsp
2 mL	salt	1/2 tsp
Pinch	freshly ground pepper	Pinch

Each serving: 45 mL (3 tbsp)

1 ◪ Protein Choice

*1 g carbohydrate
7 g protein
1 g fat*

*170 kilojoules
(41 Calories)*

- In the container of food processor or blender, combine
  cottage cheese, basil, garlic, Parmesan cheese, salt and
  pepper. Process for 1 to 2 minutes, stopping machine and
  scraping down side of container once or twice. (If machines
  are not available, with wooden spoon, press cottage cheese
  through a sieve into a bowl; stir in remaining ingredients in
  order, making sure basil and garlic are very finely
  chopped.)

- Transfer dip to a small dish.

Makes 250 mL, 1 cup

Helpflu Hint:
Instead of 1 fresh garlic clove, you can use 2 mL (1/2 tsp) garlic
powder for about the same flavor.

Appetizers

Recipe	Food Choices per Serving		Energy per Serving		
			kiljoules	Calories	
Bunch of Crunch	1 ⊞	Extra Vegetables			p.30
Melba Toast	1 ◻	Starchy	300	72	p.30
Mini Meatballs	1 ⊘	Protein	260	63	p.31
Potted Cheese	1 ⊘	Protein	230	55	p.32
Potted Caraway Cheese	1 ⊘	Protein	230	55	p.32
Curried Potted Cheese	1 ⊘	Protein	230	55	p.32
Cheese Chips	1 ⊘	Protein; 1 ◻ Starchy	580	138	p.33
Crispy Corn Chips	1 ◻	Starchy	310	73	p.34
Corn Tortillas	1 ◻	Starchy	310	73	p.34
Roasted Potato Skins	½ ▲	Fats & Oils	130	30	p.35
Falafel	1 ⊘	Protein; 1 ◻ Starchy	500	119	p.36
Falafel Patties	1 ⊘	Protein; 1 ◻ Starchy	500	119	p.36
Basil Cheese Dip	1 ⊘	Protein	170	41	p.37

Hot and Cold Drinks

Frosty lemonade, frothy hot chocolate, steaming cider or creamy eggnog are all refreshing. Quick-to-fix beverages like these cheer you up, pick you up, cool you off or warm you up. They are wonderful to share with friends.

Keep the instant mixes on hand for quick-to-fix sodas and shakes. Some are energy-free and simply thirst quenchers. Others are more nutritious and yield energy indicated in the calculations, so make sure they fit into your meal plan before you make them.

Look through this section. You will find drinks for casual as well as more formal occasions, for kids and adults, for winter and summer. Have fun fixing them and drinking them!

Eggnog

Preparation Time: *2 minutes*

An eggnog makes a good breakfast in a hurry. This version is far less rich than the traditional one often served as a festive holiday treat.

1	egg	1
250 mL	skim milk	1 cup
5 mL	vanilla	1 tsp
	Sugar substitute equivalent to 5 mL (1 tsp) sugar	
Pinch	nutmeg	Pinch

Each serving: 250 mL (1 cup)

1   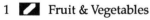   Protein Choice

2   ◆   Milk Choices (2%)

12 g carbohydrate
14 g protein
6 g fat

660 kilojoules
(158 Calories)

- Combine egg, milk, vanilla and sugar substitute in a blender; process until smooth. (Alternatively, beat egg with whisk or hand beater, then beat in remaining ingredients.)

- Pour into a glass and sprinkle lightly with nutmeg.

Makes 250 mL (1 cup), 1 serving

Fruit Flip

Preparation Time: *5 minutes*

Not only is this flip a smooth, fruity snack that will pacify hunger pangs, it is also worth considering as a dessert.

175 mL	2% milk	$^2/_3$ cup
75 mL	2% yogurt	$^1/_3$ cup
1	small peach, peeled, pitted & sliced	1
5 mL	vanilla	1 tsp
	Sugar substitute equivalent to 10 mL (2 tsp) sugar	

Each serving: 250 mL (1 cup)

1   ▨   Fruit & Vegetables

2   ◆   Milk Choices (2%)

22 g carbohydrate
9 g protein
2 g fat

600 kilojoules
(142 Calories)

- In container of blender or food processor, combine skim milk, yogurt, peach slices, vanilla and sugar substitute. Process until smooth. (Alternatively, in a bowl, mash peach until slushy. Stir in remaining ingredients; mix well.)

- Serve in a tall glass.

Makes 250 mL (1 cup), 1 serving

Lemonade Syrup

It's worth squeezing the lemons for this concentrate. Keep it bottled in the refrigerator as an instant mix for long refreshing coolers in summertime and for piping hot drinks in the winter.

Preparation Time: *10 minutes*

	Thin outer yellow rind of 1 lemon	
250 mL	lemon juice (5 to 6 lemons)	1 cup
125 mL	water	1/2 cup
	Sugar substitute equivalent to 250 mL (1 cup) sugar	

Each serving: 15 mL (1 tbsp) concentrate, enough for 250 mL (1 cup) lemonade

- With a vegetable peeler or sharp knife, peel yellow rind from lemon in thin strips.

- In a saucepan, combine rind, juice and water; bring to a boil, reduce heat and simmer for about 3 minutes.

1 **++** Extra

- Cool, strain and stir in sugar substitute. Store in glass jar or bottle in refrigerator.

Makes 375 mL (1-1/2 cups) concentrate, enough for 25 drinks

1 g carbohydrate

20 kilojoules
(4 Calories)

Variations:

Lemon-Limeade Syrup:
Replace 125 mL (1/2 cup) of the lemon juice with lime juice.

Lemonade Drinks:

Lemonade:
For each glass of lemonade, combine 15 mL (1 tbsp) Lemonade Syrup with 250 mL (1 cup) ice water. Add an ice cube or two, if desired.

Calculations as above

Hot Lemonade:
Place 15 mL (1 tbsp) Lemonade Syrup in cup. Pour in 250 mL (1 cup) hot water.

Lemon Tea:
For each cup, place 10 mL (2 tsp) Lemonade Syrup in tea cup. Pour over 200 mL (3/4 cup) weak tea.

Iced Lemon Tea:
For each glass, place 15 mL (1 tbsp) Lemonade Syrup in glass. Add 2 to 3 ice cubes and metal spoon. Pour weak tea over spoon. Stir. Add more ice, if desired. Garnish with thin lemon slice.

Instant Chocolate Syrup

Preparation Time: *10 minutes*

Another versatile concentrate, this instant syrup is simple to make and easy to use. Keep it on hand to make Chocolate Banana Shake below.

Each serving: 15 mL (1 tbsp)

1 **++** Extra

    2 g carbohydrate
    1 g protein

200 mL	dry unsweetened cocoa	$^3/_4$ cup
Pinch	cinnamon	Pinch
300 mL	water	$1^1/_4$ cup
5 mL	vanilla	1 tsp
	Sugar substitute equivalent to 125 mL ($^1/_2$ cup) sugar	

50 kilojoules
(12 Calories)

Microwave Directions:
In a 1 L (4 cup) microwave-proof measuring cup or bowl, combine cocoa, cinnamon and water. Microwave at High (100%) for 2 minutes; stir well. Microwave at High (100%) for 2 minutes longer. Cool for 5 minutes. Stir in vanilla and sweetener.

- In a heavy saucepan, combine cocoa, cinnamon and water; stir or whisk until there are no dry lumps of cocoa. Stir and cook over medium heat until mixture comes to a boil. Reduce heat; boil gently, stirring often, for 5 minutes or until mixture is thick and smooth. Cool slightly. Stir in vanilla and sugar substitute.

- Pour into a container or jar with lid. Cover and store in refrigerator for up to 3 weeks.

Makes 250 mL (1 cup) syrup

Chocolate Banana Shake

Preparation Time: *2 minutes*

The banana turns choclate milk into a shake that's dairy bar thick, creamy and delicious.

Each serving: 250 mL (1 cup)

1 **◢** Fruits & Vegetables

1 **◆** Milk Choice (Skim)

$^1/_2$	small banana, cut in pieces	$^1/_2$
125 mL	skim milk	$^1/_2$ cup
10 mL	Instant Chocolate Syrup	2 tsp
1	ice cube	1

17 g carbohydrate
5 g protein

370 kilojoules
(88 Calories)

- In container of blender ot food processor combine banana, skim milk, Instant Chocolate Syrup and ice cube. Process until banana is puréed and mixture is smooth. (Alternatively, in a bowl, mash banana. Stir in remaining ingredients; mix well.) Serve immediately.

Makes 250 mL (1 cup), 1 serving

Frothy Rich Hot Chocolate

Hot chocolate is on my list of 'comfort foods'. Is it on yours?
Whisking creates a frothy top which is special.

Preparation Time: *2 minutes*

200 mL	skim milk	³/₄ cup
25 mL	Instant Chocolate Syrup (recipe, p. 42)	2 tbsp
2 mL	vanilla	¹/₂ tsp
1	dollop whipped topping, optional	1
Pinch	ground cinnamon, optional	Pinch

Each serving: 200 mL(³/₄ cup)

2 ◆ Milk Choices (skim)

- In a small saucepan, heat milk to simmering.

- Remove from heat; with a whisk, briskly beat in Instant Chocolate Syrup and vanilla. Pour into mug.

- Top with whipped topping and sprinkle with cinnamon, if desired.

13 g carbohydrate
8 g protein

350 kilojoules
(84 Calories)

Makes 200 mL (³/₄ cup), 1 serving

Spicy Mulled Cider

Mulled cider is a wonderfully warm, comforting brew that will
make coping with a cold, blustery day a little easier.

Preparation Time: *5 minutes*
Simmering Time: *20 minutes*

500 mL	unsweetened cider or apple juice	2 cups
500 mL	weak tea	2 cups
5 mL	lemon juice	1 tsp
2 mL	whole allspice	¹/₂ tsp
2 mL	whole cloves	¹/₂ tsp
1	stick (5 cm/2 in) cinnamon	1
	Sugar substitute equivalent to 50 mL (¹/₄ cup) sugar	
	Ground nutmeg	

Each serving: 175 mL(²/₃ cup)

1 ▨ Fruits & Vegetables

- In a saucepan, combine cider, tea, lemon juice, allspice, cloves and cinnamon stick. Heat to boiling. Reduce heat, cover and simmer for 20 minutes to infuse the spices.

- Strain. Stir in sugar substitute. Taste; add a little more sugar substitute if desired.

- Serve in hot mugs. Sprinkle with nutmeg.

10 g carbohydrate

170 kilojoules
(40 Calories)

Makes 1 L (4 cups), 6 servings

Hot and Cold Drinks

Recipe	Food Choices per Serving	Energy per Serving kilojoules Calories		
Eggnog	1 ▨ Protein; 2 ◆ Milk (2%)	660	158	p. 40
Fruit Flip	1 ▨ Fruits & Vegetables; 2 ◆ Milk (2%)	600	142	p. 40
Lemonade Syrup	1 ✚✚ Extra	20	4	p. 41
Lemon-Limeade Syrup	1 ✚✚ Extra	20	4	p. 41
Lemonade	1 ✚✚ Extra	20	4	p. 41
Hot Lemonade	1 ✚✚ Extra	20	4	p. 41
Lemon Tea	1 ✚✚ Extra	20	4	p. 41
Iced Lemon Tea	1 ✚✚ Extra	20	4	p. 41
Instant Chocolate Syrup	1 ✚✚ Extra	50	12	p. 42
Chocolate Banana Shake	1 ▨ Fruits & Vegetables; 1 ◆ Milk (skim)	370	88	p. 42
Frothy Rich Hot Chocolate	2 ◆ Milk (skim)	350	84	p. 43
Spicy Mulled Cider	1 ▨ Fruits & Vegetables	170	40	p. 43

Super Soups

Everyone loves a bowlful of soup. There is nothing like it — it's appetizing, comforting and satisfying.

Choose light, small servings, steamed or chilled, as a dinner starter, a planned snack between meals, or part of a salad and soup lunch. Or, make a heartier, stew-type soup or chowder for a meal-in-a-bowl — smooth or chunky, clear or creamy, hot or cold. My recipe collection includes all of these. Most of them are economical and easy to make.

Yes, one of the real joys of cooking is making soups. Once you have put all the ingredients in the pot and set it over the heat, enjoy the fragrant aroma as it brews and the flavors mingle. Soups look great with a simple garnish. Try a sprinkling of chopped parsley, green onions, or even paprika or curry powder.

Some vegetables are high in dietary fibre and low in available carbohydrate. They may be counted as **+++** Extra Vegetables if they are eaten in the portion size indicated with the recipe, because only part of the stated carbohydrate is actually available as blood sugar.

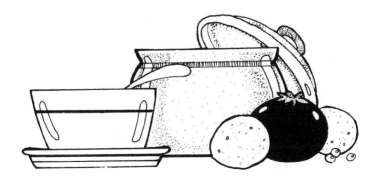

Q & E Vegetable Soup

Preparation Time: *5 minutes*
Cooking Time: *20 minutes*

Q and E stands for quick and easy. It only takes 20 minutes for this soup to cook — just enough time to set the table and make a sandwich.

Each serving: 250 mL (1 cup)

1 ☐   Starchy Choice

1 ▰   Fruits & Vegetables

26 g carbohydrate
5 g protein

520 kilojoules
(124 Calories)

3	stalks celery, thinly sliced	3
2	medium potatoes, peeled and finely chopped	2
2	leeks OR 1 medium onion, chopped	2
1	medium (15 cm/6 in) zucchini, cut in half lengthwise and sliced	1
250 mL	frozen green peas	1 cup
750 mL	chicken broth	3 cups
250 mL	shredded spinach OR leaf lettuce	1 cup
	Freshly ground pepper	

- In a large saucepan, combine celery, potatoes, leeks, zucchini and peas. Pour in broth.
- Bring to a boil, reduce heat and simmer for 15 minutes or until potatoes are tender.
- Stir in spinach and pepper to taste. Cook for 1 minute longer.
- Ladle into warm soup tureen or bowls.

Makes 1 L (4 cups), 4 servings

Microwave Directions:
In 2 L (8 cup) microwaveable container, combine celery, potatoes, leeks, zucchini, peas and 250 mL (1 cup) hot broth. Cover with vented plastic wrap. Microwave at High (100%) for 14 minutes, stirring halfway through cooking and giving container a quarter turn. Add spinach and remaining hot broth. Microwave at High (100%) for 3 minutes longer or until steaming. Stir well and let stand for 3 minutes before serving.

Each serving: 175 mL(²/₃ cup)

1 ▰   Fruits & Vegetables

1 ◆   Milk Choice (skim)

15 g carbohydrate
4 g protein
1 g fat

360 kilojoules
(85 Calories)

Variation:

Creamy Vegetable Soup
- Pour 125 mL (¹/₂ cup) milk in the container of blender or processor.
- Add 500 mL (2 cups) Q and E Vegetable Soup.
- Purée until smooth
- Heat to serve or refrigerate and serve chilled.

Makes 625 mL (2-¹/₂ cups), 4 servings.

Bacon and Bean Soup

When the vegetables are finely chopped it takes only a short simmering time to develop and blend the flavors of the bacon and assorted winter vegetables. The beans add character, dietary fibre and a heartiness that is satisfying. And an added plus — the soup is better a day or two after it is made. Store it in a covered container in the refrigerator.

3	slices back bacon	3
3	stalks celery, chopped	3
2	medium carrots, chopped	2
1	medium onion, chopped	1
250 mL	chopped turnip	1 cup
750 mL	beef broth	3 cups
1	bay leaf	1
2 mL	dried thyme	1/2 tsp
1	can (540 mL/19 oz) kidney OR pinto beans, drained and rinsed	1

- Cut bacon into thin slivers. In a 3 L (12 cup) saucepan, combine bacon, celery, carrots, onion, turnip, beef broth, bay leaf and thyme.

- Bring to a boil; reduce heat, cover and simmer for 15 minutes or until vegetables are tender.

- Add beans and continue to simmer 5 to 10 minutes or until hot, and flavors are blended.

- Remove the bay leaf and ladle into warm soup tureen or soup bowls.

Makes 1.5 L (6 cups), 8 servings

Preparation Time: *25 minutes*

Each serving: 200 mL(³/₄ cup)

1 ☐ Starchy Choice

1 ⊘ Protein Choice

15 g carbohydrate
7 g protein
2 g fat

450 kilojoules
(106 Calories)

Microwave Directions:
In 2 L (8 cup) microwaveable container, combine, bacon, celery, carrots, onion, turnip, 250 mL (1 cup) hot broth, bay leaf and thyme. Cover with vented plastic wrap. Microwave at High (100%) for 14 minutes, stirring halfway through cooking and giving container a quarter turn. Stir in beans and remaining hot broth. Microwave at High (100%) for 3 minutes or until steaming. Stir well and let stand for 3 minutes before serving.

Clamato Chowder

Preparation Time: *10 minutes*
Cooking Time: *25-30 minutes*

2	medium potatoes, peeled & chopped	2
1	medium onion, chopped	1
1	stalk celery, chopped	1
1	can (540 mL/19 oz) tomatoes	1
1	can (142 g/5 oz) clams	1
250 mL	water	1 cup
250 g	fresh or frozen fish fillets (cod, halibut, haddock or flounder)	$1/_2$ lb
2 mL	salt	$1/_2$ tsp
Dash	hot pepper sauce	Dash
15 mL	chopped fresh parsley	1 tbsp

Each serving: 125 mL($1/_2$ cup)

$1/_2$ ▫ Starchy Choice

1 ▨ Protein Choice

8 g carbohydrate
8 g protein
3 g fat

380 kilojoules
(91 Calories)

- In a 3 L (12 cup) saucepan, combine potatoes, onion, celery, tomatoes, liquid from clams, (reserving clams for later), and water.

- Bring to a boil, reduce heat and simmer about 15 minutes or until potatoes are tender.

- Cut fish into bite-size pieces. Add clams, fish, salt and hot pepper sauce to potato mixture. Simmer for about 10 minutes or until fish is opaque and flakes easily with a fork. (If cut-up fish is still frozen or has ice crystals, add about 5 more minutes to cooking time.)

- Ladle into warm tureen or soup bowls and sprinkle with parsley.

Makes 1.25 L (5 cups), 10 servings

Microwave Directions:
In 2 L (8 cup) microwaveable container, combine potatoes, onion, celery and tomatoes. Cover with vented plastic wrap. Microwave at High (100%) for 12 minutes. Stir in clams with liquid, hot water, fish and hot pepper sauce. Microwave at High (100%) for 5 minutes or just until fish flakes easily with a fork. Season with salt. Stir and let stand for 3 minutes before serving.

Salmon Carrot Bisque

Classic bisques are usually thickened with a flour paste. Here the vegetables and salmon cook together for a soup light enough to start a meal or satisfying enough to make a main course when double portions are served.

Preparation Time: *7 minutes*
Cooking Time: *30-35 minutes*

1	medium potato, diced	1
1	carrot, diced	1
1	onion, chopped	1
1	stalk celery, diced	1
500 mL	chicken or fish broth	2 cups
1	can (106g/3³/₄ oz) salmon	1
10 mL	lemon juice	2 tsp
2 mL	salt	¹/₂ tsp
2 mL	dried dillweed	¹/₂ tsp
Pinch	dried rosemary	Pinch
Pinch	freshly ground pepper	Pinch
25 mL	chopped fresh parsley(optional)	2 tbsp

Each serving: 250 mL (1 cup)

¹/₂ ☐ Starchy Choice

1 ⬤ Protein Choice

7 g carbohydrate
7 g protein
3 g fat

350 kilojoules
(83 Calories)

- In saucepan over medium heat, combine potato, carrot, onion and celery.

- Add broth; bring to a boil and cook, stirring, for 5 minutes.

- Stir in salmon, lemon juice, salt, dill, rosemary and pepper. Simmer for 20 minutes or until vegetables are tender.

- Add parsley, if desired, and simmer for 5 minutes.

Makes 1 L (4 cups), 4 servings

Microwave Directions:
In 2 L (8 cup) microwaveable container, combine potato, carrot, onion, celery and 250 mL (1 cup) hot broth. Cover with vented plastic wrap. Microwave at High (100%), stirring once, for 4 minutes. Stir in salmon, lemon juice, salt, dillweed, rosemary, pepper and remaining broth. Microwave at High (100%) for 3 minutes or until nearly boiling. Stir in parsley; microwave at High (100%) for 1 minute. Stir and let stand for 3 minutes before serving.

Curried Cucumber and Tomato Soup

Preparation Time: *10 minutes*
Chilling Time: *1 hour*

This cool, crisp soup is best made in summer when the tomatoes and cucumbers are in season, but make sure they are peeled because their peel will be too bitter in this combination.

1	medium seedless cucumber, peeled	1
1	medium ripe tomato, peeled	1
15 mL	chopped onion	1 tbsp
1	small clove garlic, chopped	1
1 mL	curry powder	1/4 tsp
Pinch	each nutmeg, salt and pepper	Pinch
125 mL	water	1/2 cup
15 mL	cider or wine vinegar	1 tsp
2 to 4	drops of hot pepper sauce	2 to 4
	Sugar substitute equivalent to 10 mL (2 tsp) sugar	
	Chopped, fresh parsley, optional	

Each serving: 250 mL(1 cup)

1 ++ Extra Vegetables

3 g carbohydrate
1 g protein

70 kilojoules
(16 Calories)

- Chop cucumber and tomato into medium-size chunks.

- In container of blender or food processor (fitted with metal blade), combine cucumber, tomato, onion, garlic, curry, nutmeg, salt, pepper, water, vinegar, hot pepper sauce and sugar substitute. Purée until smooth.

- Pour into a large bowl or pitcher. Chill at least 1 hour. Pour into soup bowls or mugs. Garnish with chopped parsley, if desired.

Makes 1 L (4 cups), 4 servings

Orange Tomato Bouillon

To warm up the taste buds on a cold day, you can heat this made-in-a-minute soup. Hot or cold, it can also be served as a beverage.

Preparation Time: *3 minutes*

250 mL	tomato juice	1 cup
125 mL	chicken broth	$^1/_2$ cup
125 mL	unsweetened orange juice	$^1/_2$ cup
5 mL	Worcestershire sauce	1 tsp
2 mL	soy sauce	$^1/_2$ tsp
2	drop hot pepper sauce	2
	Grated orange rind, optional	

- In a pitcher or glass container, combine tomato juice, chicken broth, orange juice, Worcestershire, soy sauce and hot pepper sauce. Mix well.

- Pour over ice cubes in a wine glass or tumbler. Garnish with grated orange rind, if desired.

Makes 500 mL (2 cups), 2 servings

Each serving: 250 mL (1 cup)

1   **◢**   Fruits & Vegetables

12 g carbohydrate
2 g protein

240 kilojoules
(56 Calories)

Broccoli Soup

This soup is also good chunky. If you prefer it chunky, just chop the vegetables a little finer than you need to when you're planning to purée them for a smoother soup. For a pale cream-colored soup, use caulifower instead of broccoli.

Preparation Time: *10 minutes*
Cooking Time: *30 minutes*

1	bunch broccoli, chopped(1 L/4 cups)	1
1	medium potato, peeled & chopped	1
250 mL	chopped celery	1 cup
750 mL	water	3 cups
1	bay leaf	1
1	cube or packet instant chicken bouillon	1
2 mL	salt	$1/_2$ tsp
Pinch	each nutmeg and white pepper	Pinch

Each serving: 250 mL(1 cup)

1 ◨ Fruits & Vegetables

10 g carbohydrate
3 g protein

220 kilojoules
(52 Calories)

- In a large saucepan, combine combine broccoli, potato, celery, water, bay leaf, chicken bouillon cube and salt. Cover and bring to a boil. Reduce heat and simmer for 30 minutes.

- Remove bay leaf; transfer mixture to blender or processor fitted with metal blade. Add nutmeg and white pepper; process until smooth.

- To serve chilled or to store for later use, pour into bowl and refrigerate.

- To serve hot, return to saucepan; heat to simmering point.

- Ladle into soup bowls. Sprinkle lightly with paprika.

Makes 1 L (4 cups), 4 servings

Microwave Directions:
In 1 L (4 cup) microwaveable container, combine broccoli, potato, celery, bay leaf and 250 mL (1 cup) hot water. Cover with vented plastic wrap. Microwave at High (100%) for 10 minutes. Let stand for 2 minutes. Remove bay leaf. Stir in nutmeg and white pepper. Purée mixture. Dissolve bouillon in 500 mL (2 cups) boiling water. Stir into purée; mix well and serve.

Onion Soup

A hearty country-style soup, this pleasing combination of onions and cheese can be a meal in itself.

5 mL	corn oil	1 tsp
4	medium onions, thinly sliced	4
1	clove garlic, finely chopped	1
10 mL	all-purpose flour	2 tsp
1 L	beef broth	4 cups
2 mL	salt	$^1/_2$ tsp
Pinch	freshly ground pepper	Pinch
4	slices French loaf (1 cm/$^1/_2$" thick)	4
75 mL	grated Parmesan cheese	$^1/_3$ cup
125 mL	shredded Swiss cheese	$^1/_2$ cup

- In 3 L (12 cup) Dutch oven or saucepan over medium high heat, heat oil. Add onions and garlic; cook, stirring occasionally, for 10 minutes or until onions are transparent and tender.

- Stir in flour and continue to cook, stirring, 10 minutes longer or until mixture turns brown without burning.

- Stir in broth, salt and pepper; cover pan and simmer for 25 minutes.

- Meanwhile, toast bread slices.

- On a jelly-roll pan, place 4 (375 mL/$1^1/_2$ cup) ovenproof bowls or small crocks.

- Ladle 250 mL (1 cup) soup into each bowl.

- Sprinkle 5 mL (1 tsp) of the Parmesan cheese over each bowl of soup, then top with a slice of toast. Sprinkle equal amounts of Swiss cheese over bread, then remaining Parmesan.

- Bake in a 180°C (350°F) oven for 20 minutes or until cheese melts and begins to brown. Serve immediately.

Makes 1 L (4 cups), 4 servings

Preparation Time: *10 minutes*
Cooking Time: *1 hour*

Each serving: 250 mL (1 cup) soup and 1 slice of bread with cheese

1 ☐ Starchy Choice

2 ⊘ Protein Choices

18 g carbohydrate
14 g protein
8 g fat

840 kilojoules
(200 Calories)

Microwave Directions:
In 2 L (8 cup) microwaveable container, combine oil, onions, and garlic. Cover with plastic wrap. Microwave at High (100%) for 4 minutes, stirring once. Stir in flour. Microwave at High (100%) for 2 minutes longer. Stir in hot broth. Microwave at High (100%) for 4 minutes or until boiling. Stir well; season with salt and pepper. Continue as directed in recipe.

Super Soups

Recipe	Food Choices per Serving	Energy per Serving		
		kiljoules	Calories	
Q & E Vegetable Soup	1 ☐ Starchy; 1 ◪ Fruits & Vegetables	520	124	p. 46
Creamy Vegetable Soup	1 ◪ Fruits & Vegetables; 1 ◆ Milk (skim)	360	85	p. 46
Bacon & Bean Soup	1 ☐ Starchy; 1 ⊘ Protein	450	106	p. 47
Clamato Chowder	1 ☐ Starchy; 1 ⊘ Protein	380	91	p. 48
Salmon Carrot Bisque	½ ☐ Starchy; 1 ⊘ Protein	350	83	p. 49
Curried Cucumber & Tomato Soup	1 ✚✚ Extra Vegetables	70	16	p. 50
Orange Tomato Bouillon	1 ◪ Fruits & Vegetables	240	56	p. 51
Broccoli Soup	1 ◪ Fruits & Vegetables	220	52	p. 52
Onion Soup	1 ☐ Starchy; 2 ⊘ Protein	840	200	p. 53

Zesty Salads

Salad-making brings out the artist in both beginning and experienced cooks. That's because almost anything edible can go into a salad — vegetables, fruits, meats, cheeses, eggs, pasta, rice, beans, nuts and seasonings. The combinations are determined by the creative flair of the salad-maker and the use of the completed salad.

Light salads make colorful appetizing starters for a meal or refreshing small courses with a meal. In my home, I often make and serve cold, hearty salads with protein in them as the main course, for brunch, lunch or dinner, especially in the hot summertime. A warm bread and a dessert usually round out the meal.

Summer salads are best because garden-fresh vegetables and orchard-fresh fruits are in season. However, crunchy salads such as coleslaw, carrot and zucchini put zest into winter meal planning and add excitement to meals.

Note: Some vegetables are high in dietary fiber and low in available carbohydrate. They may be counted as ▪▪▪ Extra Vegetables if they are eaten in the portion size indicated with the recipe, because only part of the carbohydrate actually ends up as sugar in the blood.

Chick Pea & Tomato Salad

Preparation Time: *10 minutes*

For a complete protein meal, serve this hearty salad with grainy bread. Or try it tucked into pita bread for a superb sandwich.

1	can (540mL/19 oz) chick peas or white kidney beans	1
2	medium tomatoes	2
25 mL	chopped chives OR green onion tops	2 tbsp
10 mL	vegetable oil	2 tsp
25 mL	malt vinegar	2 tbsp
5 mL	turmeric	1 tsp
5 mL	dillweed	1 tsp
2 mL	salt	1/2 tsp
Pinch	freshly ground pepper	Pinch

Each serving:125 mL (¹/₂ cup)

1 ☐ Starchy Choice

1 ◩ Fruits & Vegetables

1 ▨ Protein Choice

24 g carbohydrate
8 g protein
4 g fat

690 kilojoules
(164 Calories)

- Drain and rinse beans, then drain well again. Place in a bowl.

- Peel tomatoes, if desired, and cut each tomato into 12 pieces. Remove seeds and place seeds in a sieve set over a bowl. Press to extract juice into bowl. Reserve juice.

- Add tomato pieces and chives to beans.

- Whisk oil, vinegar, turmeric, dillweed, salt and pepper into tomato juice. Pour over salad ingredients. Toss gently.

Makes 500 mL (2 cups), 4 servings

Greek-Style Salad

Feta cheese gives this salad a distinctive, salty, sharp burst of flavor.

Preparation Time: *15 minutes*

$^1/_2$	medium Romaine or iceberg lettuce	$^1/_2$
2	medium tomatoes	2
1	small cucumber	1
1	small red onion	1
125 mL	crumbled feta cheese OR cottage cheese (110 g)	$^1/_2$ cup
	Dressing:	
15 mL	olive oil	1 tbsp
15 mL	lemon juice	1 tbsp
5 mL	dried parsley OR 15 mL (1 tbsp) chopped fresh	1 tsp
2 mL	dried oregano	$^1/_2$ tsp
2 mL	garlic salt	$^1/_2$ tsp
Pinch	each thyme & freshly ground pepper	Pinch
6	pitted black olives (optional)	6

Each serving: 1/4 salad

1 ✚✚ Extra Vegetables

1 ◆ Milk Choice (skim)

1 ▲ Fats & Oils Choice

5 g carbohydrate
4 g protein
6 g fat

390 kilojoules
(94 Calories)

• Tear lettuce into bite-size pieces. Cut tomatoes, cucumber and onion into bite-size chunks.

• In a glass bowl, combine lettuce, tomatoes, cucumber, onion and cheese; cover and chill.

• **Dressing:** In a small bowl or cup, combine olive oil, lemon juice, parsley, oregano, garlic salt, thyme and pepper; beat together with fork or whisk.

• Pour dressing over salad; toss gently to coat ingredients with dressing.

• Slice olives; sprinkle over salad.

Makes 4 servings

Carrot and Zucchini Salad

Preparation Time: *10 minutes*
Chilling Time: *20 minutes*

Anyone counting calories will love this cool, colorful and crunchy salad.

2	medium carrots	2
2	medium zucchini (15 cm/6 in)	2
25 mL	orange juice	2 tbsp
15 mL	lemon juice	1 tbsp
	Sugar substitute equivalent to 10 mL (2 tsp) sugar	
5 mL	poppy seed	1 tsp
Pinch	each salt & freshly ground pepper	Pinch

Each serving:125 mL (¹/₂ cup)

1 ⊞ Extra Vegetables

4 g carbohydrate
1 g protein

80 kilojoules
(20 Calories)

- With a vegetable peeler, peel off and discard the rough outer skin of carrots. With vegetable peeler, continue paring the carrots into wafer-thin strips until as much of carrots as possible is used.

- With vegetable peeler, pare the zucchini into wafer-thin strips.

- Place carrot and zucchini strips in a bowl and cover with ice water; chill for 20 minutes.

- Drain vegetables well in sieve or strainer; transfer to salad bowl.

- Combine orange juice, lemon juice, sugar substitute, poppy seed, salt and pepper. Pour over vegetables. Toss well.

- Serve.

Makes 500 mL (2 cups), 4 salad servings

Chicken Salad Chinois

Chinois indicates a Chinese treatment, with the snappy flavor of ginger added to the finished dish — in this case an exciting cold chicken and vegetable combination.

Preparation Time: *10 minutes*
Chilling Time: *2 hours*

500 mL	cut-up cooked chicken	2 cups
125 mL	chopped zucchini	¹/₂ cup
125 mL	chopped radishes	¹/₂ cup
50 mL	2% yogurt	¹/₄ cup
15 mL	soy sauce	1 tbsp
	Sugar substitute equivalent to 2 mL (¹/₂ tsp) sugar	
2 mL	ground ginger	¹/₂ tsp
750 mL	shredded lettuce	3 cups

- In a bowl, combine chicken, zucchini and radishes.

- In a cup, combine yogurt, soy sauce, sugar substitute and ginger. Pour over chicken mixture; toss to coat evenly.

- Refrigerate at least 2 hours before serving, then toss well again.

- Place lettuce in salad bowl; spoon chicken mixture over; toss gently. Divide evenly into 4 portions.

Makes 1.25 mL (5 cups), 4 servings

Variation:

Chicken Salad in Pita Pockets: Cut 4 regular-size pita breads in half; open pockets and fill each pocket with one-eighth of Chicken Salad Chinois.

Each serving:300 mL(1¹/₄ cup)

2 ▨ Protein Choices

> *2 g carbohydrate*
> *15 g protein*
> *7 g fat*

> *550 kilojoules*
> *(131 Calories)*

Each serving: 2 Pita Pockets (1 Pita plus 300 mL (1¹/₄ cup) Chicken Salad Chinois)

2 ☐ Starchy Choices
2 ▨ Protein Choices

> *33 g carbohydrate*
> *20 g protein*
> *8 g fat*

> *1192 kilojoules*
> *(284 Calories)*

Pork, Vegetables and Grapefruit in Lettuce Leaves

Preparation Time: *20 minutes*
Cooking Time: *20 minutes*

The Vietnamese serve wonderful combinations of meats and vegetables and sometimes even noodles rolled up in lettuce leaves.

500 g	boneless pork shoulder or loin cut in 1 cm ($^1/_2$ in) slices	1 lb
250 mL	chicken broth	1 cup
10	fresh or defrosted medium shrimp, peeled and cleaned	10
1	small onion	1
1	medium carrot	1
$^1/_2$	seedless English cucumber	$^1/_2$
250 mL	bean sprouts	1 cup
1	small grapefruit	1
25 mL	sesame seeds	2 tbsp
25 mL	soy sauce	2 tbsp
	Sugar substitute equivalent to 5 mL (1 tsp) sugar	
12	small lettuce leaves	12

Each serving: 2 rolls (125 mL /1½ cup mixture and 2 lettuce leaves

$^1/_2$ ◪ Fruits & Vegetables

2 ◪ Protein Choices

6 g carbohydrate
17 g protein
7 g fat

650 kilojoules
(155 Calories)

- Trim pork of any visible fat.
- In a saucepan, combine pork and broth. Bring to a boil; reduce heat and simmer, uncovered, for 10 minutes.
- Add shrimp, cover and continue to simmer for 3 to 5 minutes longer or until pork is no longer pink and shrimp is cooked. Remove from heat and allow pork and shrimp to cool. Drain. Cut pork and cut shrimp into slivers.
- Cut onion in half lengthwise, then into thin crosswise slices.
- Shred carrot and cucumber as for cole slaw. Squeeze dry.
- Wash bean sprouts, removing bitter root ends, and chop.
- In a bowl or on a platter, pile ingredients in separate mounds, cover and refrigerate.
- Before serving, cut grapefruit in half. Scoop out pulp, reserving shells. Remove pulp from membranes, discarding membranes and seeds. Add pulp to vegetables and meat.
- Sprinkle sesame seeds, soy sauce and sugar substitute over mixture. Toss thoroughly to coat ingredients with dressing.
- Spoon into bowl or empty grapefruit shells, if desired, to serve. Place rinsed and dried lettuce leaves on plate. Have each diner spoon about 50 mL ($^1/_4$ cup) salad onto a lettuce leaf, then fold in sides and roll up leaves to eat by hand.

Makes 750 mL (3 cups) filling, 6 servings

Microwave Directions:
In microwaveable container, combine pork and hot broth. Cover with vented plastic wrap. Microwave at High (100%) for 2$^1/_2$ minutes. Add shrimp. Microwave at High (100%) for 2$^1/_2$ minutes longer or until pork is no longer pink and shrimp is curled and cooked. Set aside to cool in liquid. Continue as recipe directs.

Keeps-A-Week Coleslaw

Here's a salad that is best if made in advance. It stays crisp for a whole week, covered, in a cold corner of the refrigerator.

Preparation Time: *7 minutes*
Chilling Time: *1 hour*

1.5 L	shredded cabbage (about ¹/₂ medium head)	6 cups
1	medium onion, finely chopped	1
1	medium carrot, shredded	1
	Sugar substitute equivalent to 50 mL (10 tsp)	
50 mL	vinegar	¹/₄ cup
10 mL	vegetable oil	2 tsp
5 mL	Dijon mustard	1 tsp
2 mL	salt	¹/₂ tsp
2 mL	celery seed	¹/₂ tsp
2 mL	creamy horseradish	¹/₂ tsp
Pinch	freshly ground black pepper	Pinch

Each serving: 125 mL(¹/₂ cup)

1 **++** Extra Vegetables

3 g carbohydrate
1 g protein
1 g fat

110 kilojoules
(25 Calories)

- In a large bowl, combine cabbage, onion and carrot.

- In a small saucepan, combine sugar substitute, vinegar, oil, mustard, salt, celery seed, horseradish and pepper. Heat to boiling.

- Pour hot dressing immediately over cabbage mixture. Stir well.

- Cover and chill for 1 hour, stirring occasionally, then serve or keep in the refrigerator for up to 7 days. At serving time, spoon into salad bowls or onto salad plates.

Makes 1 L (4 cups), 8 servings

Variations:

Each serving: 125 mL(½ cup)

½ ▨ Fruits & Vegetables

   6 g carbohydrate
   1 g protein
   1 g fat

   160 kilojoules
   (37 Calories)

Raisin Slaw: Into 500 mL (2 cups) Keeps-A-Week Coleslaw, stir 50 mL (¼ cup) chopped raisins or whole currants. Makes 6 servings.

Each serving: 175 mL(⅔ cup)

1 ▨ Fruits & Vegetables

   9 g carbohydrate
   1 g protein
   1 g fat

   210 kilojoules
   (49 Calories)

Apple Yogurt Slaw: Into 500 mL (2 cups) Keeps-A-Week Coleslaw, stir 1 medium apple, cored and chopped, and 50 mL (¼ cup) 2% yogurt. Makes 4 servings.

Nippy Yogurt Dressing or Sauce

Preparation Time: 2 minutes

What a versatile sauce! Use it as a dip for hot meatballs or crisp vegetables, as a relish for meaty hamburgers or tuna sandwiches, and as a dressing for crisp greens or sliced tomatoes.

125 mL	2% yogurt	½ cup
25 mL	sweet green relish	2 tbsp
	Sugar substitute equivalent to 1 mL (¼ tsp) sugar	
5 mL	curry powder	1 tsp

Each serving: 15 mL (1 tbsp)

1 ++ Extra

   2 g carbohydrate
   1 g protein

   50 kilojoules
   (12 Calories)

- In a small mixing bowl, combine yogurt, relish, sugar substitute and curry powder; mix well.

Makes 175 mL (⅔ cup).

Tomato Tarragon Dressing

This fat-free dressing is as good as commercial French dressings but without the fattening salad oil.

Preparation Time: *5 minutes*

125 mL	canned tomato soup	¹/₂ cup
125 mL	tomato juice	¹/₂ cup
25 mL	wine vinegar	2 tbsp
25 mL	lemon juice	2 tbsp
15 mL	soy sauce	1 tbsp
15 mL	dried tarragon	1 tbsp
5 mL	Dijon mustard	1 tsp
1	clove garlic, mashed & chopped	1
	Sugar substitute equivalent to 10 mL (2 tsp) sugar	
2	drops hot pepper sauce	2

Each serving: 25 mL (2 tbsp)

1 ⊞ Extra

2 g carbohydrate

30 kilojoules
(8 Calories)

- In a blender, food processor or jar with screw-top lid, combine tomato soup, tomato juice, vinegar, lemon juice, soy sauce, tarragon, mustard, garlic, sugar substitute and hot pepper sauce.

- Process or shake for about 10 seconds.

- If processed, pour into jar with screw-top lid.

- Keep in refrigerator. Always shake before using.

Makes about 375 mL (1¹/₂ cups).

Zesty Salads

Recipe	Food Choices per Serving		Energy per Serving		
			kilojoules	Calories	
Chick Pea and Tomato Salad	1 ☐ Starchy; 1 ⊘ Protein 1 ◪ Fruits & Vegetables		690	164	p. 56
Greek-Style Salad	1 ⊞ Extra Vegetables; 1 ◆ Milk (skim) 1 ▲ Fats & Oils		390	94	p. 57
Carrot & Zucchini Salad	1 ⊞ Extra Vegetables		80	20	p. 58
Chicken Salad Chinois	2 ⊘ Protein		550	131	p. 59
Chicken Salad in Pita Pockets	2 ☐ Starchy; 2 ⊘ Protein		1192	284	p. 59
Pork, Vegetables & Grapefruit in Lettuce Leaves	½ ◪ Fruits & Vegetables; 2 ⊘ Protein		650	155	p. 60
Keeps-a-Week Coleslaw	1 ⊞ Extra Vegetables		110	25	p. 61
Raisin Slaw	½ ◪ Fruits & Vegetables		160	37	p. 62
Apple Yogurt Slaw	1 ◪ Fruits & Vegetables		210	49	p. 62
Nippy Yogurt Sauce	1 ⊞ Extra		50	12	p. 62
Tomato Taragon Dressing	1 ⊞ Extra		30	8	p. 63

Notes

over: *Coconut Bran Muffins*

Notes

over: *Pork Veronique*

Satisfying Snacks and Sandwiches

Burgers and pizzas are both in this section. And the Topless Burger is just that. It is open-faced with no bun on top.

Noon-time treats to eat at home or pack for lunch are planned to fit into the meal plans of young people with diabetes. Others are hot and hearty. They make great tasting supper specials that are fast to fix. Many of them can be made ahead to store in the refrigerator or freezer.

Few sandwich recipes have been included because I am sure you know how to make a regular sandwich. When you do, make sure you count all the Food Choices of both the bread and the filling you choose.

Tuna Melt

Preparation Time: *15 minutes*

Few can resist this combination and it is unbelievably easy to make. Call it fantastic and fast, if you like.

1	can (198 g/7 oz) chunk tuna rinsed and drained	1
25 g	mozzarella cheese, shredded	1 oz
125 mL	chopped celery	1/2 cup
25 mL	sweet pickle relish	1 tbsp
	freshly ground pepper	
6	slices whole wheat bread OR 3 English muffins, split in half	6

Each meal serving: 1 slice

1 ☐ Starchy Choice

1 ☑ Protein Choice

16 g carbohydrate
10 g protein
4 g fat

590 kilojoules
(140 Calories)

Each snack serving: 1/2 slice

1/2 ☐ Starchy Choice

1/2 ☑ Protein Choice

8 g carbohydrate
5 g protein
2 g fat

290 kilojoules
(70 Calories)

- In a bowl, combine tuna, mozzarella, celery and relish. Season with pepper to taste.

- Toast bread slices. Place on a baking sheet. Spread 125 mL (1/2 cup) tuna mixture on each slice.

- Bake in a 190ºC (375ºF) oven for 10 minutes or until cheese melts.

- Serve immediately. Cut in half for meal-size servings, in quarters or sixths for snack-size serving.

Makes 6 meal-size servings; 12 snack-size servings

Microwave Directions:
Spread toast with tuna mixture. Microwave on paper towel, 2 slices at a time, uncovered, at Medium (50%) for 2 minutes or until cheese begins to melt.

Basic Burgers

Now you can cook your own quarter pounder exactly the way you want it. Using lean ground beef means top-notch quality with less fat and shrinkage.

500 g	lean ground beef	1 lb
15 mL	finely chopped onions	1 tbsp
15 mL	cold water	1 tbsp
10 mL	Worcestershire sauce	2 tsp
5 mL	liquid beef bouillon concentrate	1 tsp
3	drops hot pepper sauce	3

- In a bowl, combine ground beef, onion, water, Worcestershire sauce, bouillon and hot pepper sauce; mix lightly.

- Divide into 4 equal portions, and shape each into a 2.5 cm (1 in) thick patty.

- Choose cooking method:

  Broil: Place burgers on broiler rack lightly oiled or sprayed with nonstick spray, 7.5 cm (3 in) from heat and broil for 4 minutes; turn and cook for 2 to 3 minutes on other side or to desired degree of doneness.

  Bake: Place burgers on rack in shallow roasting pan. Bake in160ºC (325ºF) oven for 7 to 8 minutes or to desired degree of doneness.

  Barbecue: Place burgers on a lightly oiled grill rack over medium heat, about 10 cm (4 in) from coals and grill for 4 minutes; turn and cook for 2 to 3 minutes on other side or to desired degree of doneness.

  Pan-cook: Place burgers in a nonstick or heavy skillet and cook over medium heat for 4 minutes; turn and cook to desired degree of doneness.

Makes about 4 burgers, 4 servings

Preparation Time: *5 minutes*
Cooking Time : *8 - 10 minutes*

Each serving: 1 burger

3 ⊘ Protein Choices

21 g protein
9 g fat

690 kilojoules
(165 Calories)

Microwave Directions:
Flatten burgers to 1 cm (1/2 in) thick; arrange on microwave safe rack. Cover with waxed paper. Microwave at High (100%) for 2 minutes; turn burgers over; rotate rack one quarter turn. Microwave at High (100%) for 2 minutes or until meat is no longer pink. Let stand for 2 minutes.

Topless B L T Burger

Preparation Time: *5 minutes*
Cooking Time: *8 - 10 minutes*

This open-faced burger, smothered in mushrooms and bacon, is attractive and tasty as a dinner burger.

1	recipe Basic Burgers (recipe p. 67)	1
5 mL	Dijon mustard	1 tsp
4	strips lean bacon, cut in pieces	4
8	small mushrooms, sliced	8
2	whole wheat hamburger buns	2
4	lettuce leaves	4
1	tomato, cut in 4 slices	1
2	green onions, sliced	2

Each serving: 1 burger

1 ☐ Starchy Choice

3 ⧄ Protein Choices

1 ▲ Fats & Oils Choice

17 g carbohydrate
25 g protein
14 g fat

1230 kilojoules
(294 Calories)

- Stir Dijon mustard into Basic Burger Mix.
- Shape into 4 patties; cook using method of choice.
- Meanwhile, in a skillet, cook bacon for 2 to 3 minutes or until crisp. Pour off excess drippings. Add mushroom slices to pan; stir-cook about 3 minutes or until there is no moisture in pan.
- For each burger, place lettuce leaf on half of each hamburger bun; top with burger, tomato slice, mushroom mixture and garnish with green onion.
- Serve on plates with knife and fork for eating.

Makes 4 burgers, 4 servings

Sunshine Burgers

Just looking at this burger combination will make you think of
California sunshine!

Preparation Time: *5 minutes*
Cooking Time : *8 - 10 minutes*

1	recipe Basic Burgers (recipe p. 67)	1
4	sesame burger buns	4
10 mL	margarine	2 tsp
	Spinach or lettuce leaves	
250 mL	alfalfa sprouts	1 cup
125 mL	cottage cheese, mashed	1/2 cup
1	small navel orange, peeled and cut in 8 slices	1
10 mL	sunflower seeds	2 tsp

Each serving: 1 burger

2 ☐ Starchy Choices

4 ☑ Protein Choices

- Shape Basic Burgers into 4 patties and cook using method of choice.

- Split and toast hamburger buns;spread lightly with margarine.

- For each burger, place spinach leaf on bottom half of roll; top with burger.

- Top burger with sprouts, cottage cheese, 2 orange slices, a few sunflower seeds, and the other half of roll.

Makes about 4 burgers, 4 servings

32 g carbohydrate
30 g protein
13 g fat

1530 kilojoules
(365 Calories)

Mini Pizzas

Preparation Time: *10 minutes*
Cooking Time: *15 minutes*

Making pizza at home is lots of fun. The Tomato Sauce has all the special spices that make pizza taste wonderful, so plan to make it ahead so it's ready when you are in the mood for this fast food.

4	English muffins, split in half	4
200 mL	Tomato Sauce (recipe, p. 113)	³/₄ cup
125 g	lean back bacon	¹/₄ lb
6	mushrooms, sliced	6
4	stuffed olives, thinly sliced	4
1	small onion, sliced	1
¹/₂	green pepper, seeded & sliced	¹/₂
125 g	mozzarella cheese, shredded	¹/₄ lb
75 mL	freshly grated Parmesan cheese	¹/₃ cup

Each serving: 1 mini pizza

1 ▢ Starchy Choice

1 ▨ Protein Choice

1 ▲ Fats & Oils Choice

18 g carbohydrate
10 g protein
7 g fat

740 kilojoules
(175 Calories)

- On each muffin half, spread 25 mL (2 tbsp) tomato sauce.
- Top each with one-eighth of back bacon, mushrooms, olives, onion and green pepper. Sprinkle each with mozzarella and Parmesan cheese, dividing evenly.
- Place on nonstick baking sheet. Bake in 180ºC (350ºF) oven for 10 to 15 minutes or until cheese melts and begins to brown.
- Serve immediately.

Makes 8 Mini Pizzas, 8 servings

Microwave Directions:
Microwave back bacon at High (100%) for 1¹/₂ minutes. Assemble pizzas. Microwave 4 assembled mini pizzas at a time at Medium High (70%) for 1¹/₂ minutes or until cheese melts. Repeat with remaining mini pizzas.

Sloppy Joes

Depend on the good old Sloppy Joe when you want a meal-in-minutes.
The beef bouillon adds an extra burst of meaty flavor to the sauce.

Preparation Time: *5 minutes*
Cooking Time : *20 minutes*

250 g	lean ground beef	$^1/_2$ lb
1	small onion, chopped	1
1	stalk celery, chopped	1
1	can (213 mL/7$^1/_2$ oz) tomato sauce or 250 mL (1 cup) Tomato Sauce (recipe p. 113)	1
1	packet or cube beef bouillon	1
2 mL	Worcestershire sauce	$^1/_2$ tsp
Pinch	freshly ground pepper	Pinch
2	hamburger buns, split & toasted	2

Each serving: 125 mL($^1/_2$ cup) meat mixture on $^1/_2$ bun

1 ☐ Starchy Choice
2 ⊘ Protein Choices
1 ⊞ Extra Vegetables

- In a skillet, combine ground beef, onion and celery. Stir-cook, breaking up meat, about 7 minutes or until beef begins to brown and onion is tender.

- Stir in tomato sauce, beef bouillon, Worcestershire sauce and pepper. Heat until mixture boils; cook, stirring, for 2 to 3 minutes longer or until mixture is thickened to spooning consistency.

- Place toasted bun halves on plates.

- Spoon 125 mL ($^1/_2$ cup) meat mixture over each. Serve immediately.

Makes 4 servings

20 g carbohydrate
15 g protein
5 g fat

780 kilojoules
(185 Calories)

Microwave Directions:
In microwaveable container, combine crumbled ground beef, onion and celery. Cover with waxed paper. Microwave at High (100%) for 2$^1/_2$ minutes, stirring once to break up meat. Stir in tomato sauce, beef bouillon, Worcestershire sauce and pepper. Cover with waxed paper. Microwave at High (100%) for 2$^1/_2$ minutes or until thoroughly heated through. Let stand for 3 minutes before serving. Stir well.

Sassy Chicken Fingers

Preparation Time: *15 minutes*
Cooking Time: *25 minutes*

Hot, moist chicken baked in a crusty crumb that makes finger-licking good eating when dipped in a cool, creamy sauce. The 'heat' in the sauce will depend on the amount of freshly ground pepper used.

Chicken Fingers

3	boneless and skinless chicken breasts (375g/3/4 lb in total)	3
25 mL	2% yogurt	2 tbsp
12	soda crackers, crushed	12
5 mL	dried thyme	1 tsp
2 mL	dried marjoram	1/2 tsp
1 mL	curry powder	1/4 tsp
	Salt	

Each serving: 8 Fingers, 60 mL (4 tbsp) sauce

1 ☐ Starchy Choice
3 ⬛ Protein Choices

   15 g carbohydrate
   22 g protein
   10 g fat

   1000 kilojoules
   (238 Calories)

Sauce

125 mL	2% yogurt	1/2 cup
25 mL	catsup	2 tbsp
25 mL	finely chopped celery	2 tbsp
10 mL	soy sauce	2 tsp
2 mL	minced garlic (optional)	1/2 tsp
	Freshly ground pepper	

Microwave Directions:
Arrange 12 chicken fingers in a circle around outside edge of microwave safe baking rack, tucking under any thin ends. Cover with waxed paper. Microwave on High (100%) for 3 minutes. Let stand for 2 minutes. Repeat with remaining chicken fingers. Chicken is melt-in-your-mouth tender and the crumb stays soft.

- **Chicken Fingers:** Trim breasts of any visible fat. Cut each breast into 8 even strips.

- In a bowl, combine chicken strips and yogurt. Stir gently to coat each piece of chicken with yogurt.

- In a shallow dish or plate, combine cracker crumbs, thyme, marjoram and curry.

- With a fork, place each chicken strip in crumbs and roll to coat with crumbs.

- Place on a cake rack set in a baking pan or dish. Repeat with remaining chicken strips until all are coated and lined up in a single layer on a rack.

- Bake in a 190°C (375°F) oven for 25 minutes or until crumbs are lightly browned and crisp. Remove from oven and sprinkle lightly with salt to taste.

- **Sauce:** Combine yogurt, catsup, celery, soy sauce, garlic, if desired, and pepper to taste. Serve as a dip for Chicken Fingers

Makes 24 Fingers, 3 servings, 8 Fingers each

Pizza Quiche

Enjoy the best of both; the flavor and texture of popular pizza toppings baked in a surprisingly good crustless quiche.

Preparation Time: *10 minutes*
Cooking Time: *35 minutes*

5 mL	margarine	1 tsp
50 mL	chopped onion	1/4 cup
1	clove garlic, finely chopped	1
2	slices whole wheat bread	2
200 mL	skim milk	3/4 cup
2	eggs	2
2	egg whites	2
5 mL	dried oregano	1 tsp
50 mL	catsup	1/4 cup
125 mL	shredded mozzarella cheese	1/2 cup
6	medium mushrooms, sliced	6
1	medium tomato, sliced	1
1	pepperette (thin pepperoni) sliced (about 25 g/1 oz)	1
1/2	small green pepper, in strips	1/2
	Freshly ground pepper	
50 mL	freshly grated Parmesan cheese	1/4 cup

Each serving: 1/6 of quiche

1/2 ☐ Starchy Choice
1 ◆ Milk Choice (2%)
1 ∅ Protein Choice

11 g carbohydrate
10 g protein

620 kilojoules
(147 Calories)

- In a small frypan, melt margarine. Add onion and garlic; cook for about 5 minutes or until soft.

- Break bread into small pieces and place in a bowl or container of food processor. Add milk, eggs and egg whites. Blend until bread is crumbly in mixture. Stir in oregano and sautéed onion and garlic.

- Pour in a lightly greased 23 cm (9 in) pie plate.

- Bake in a 180ºC (350ºF) oven for 25 minutes or until set.

- Remove from oven and spread with catsup. Sprinkle with mozzarella. Top with mushrooms, tomato and pepperette slices and green pepper strips. Sprinkle with pepper to taste and Parmesan cheese.

- Return to oven and bake for 10 minutes or until mozzarella melts and Parmesan begins to brown.

- Cut into 6 wedges to serve.

Makes 6 servings

Satisfying Snacks & Sandwiches

Recipe	Food Choices per Serving		Energy per Serving		
			kilojoules	Calories	
Tuna Melt - 1 slice	1 ☐ Starchy; 1 ⊘ Protein		590	140	
- ½ slice	½ ☐ Starchy; ½ ⊘ Protein		290	70	p. 66
Basic Burgers	3 ⊘ Protein		690	165	p. 67
Topless BLT Burger	1 ☐ Starchy; 3 ⊘ Protein;				
	1 ▲ Fats & Oils		1230	294	p. 68
Sunshine Burger	2 ☐ Starchy; 4 ⊘ Protein		1530	365	p. 69
Mini Pizzas	1 ☐ Starchy; 1 ⊘ Protein;		740	175	p. 70
	1 ▲ Fats & Oils				
Sloppy Joes	1 ☐ Starchy; 2 ⊘ Protein;		780	185	p. 71
	1 ✛ Extra Vegetables				
Sassy Chicken Fingers	1 ☐ Starchy; 3 ⊘ Protein		1000	238	p. 72
Pizza Quiche	½ ☐ Starchy; 1 ⊘ Protein;		620	147	p. 72
	1 ◆ Milk (2%)				

74

Make It Meat, Poultry or Fish

When I grew up in Saskatchewan, we had chicken nearly every Sunday in our house. My mom's roast chicken, with its sage dressing, was the best and it still is. When we did not have chicken, we had roast pork or beef.

Roasting, of course, is not the only way to cook meat and poultry. You can braise, boil, poach, stir-braise, barbecue and stew it. There are so many ways, there is no reason to ever fry it and add extra fat to your diet.

Fish is just as versatile and makes good light eating when it is not cooked in a batter in hot fat.

Supermarkets today offer an amazing assortment of meat: beef, pork, lamb and veal cuts, and chicken from roasting birds to boned breasts. You will find roasts, chops, steaks, cutlets, stewing meat and ground meat packaged in amounts to cook up for a whole family or a single serving.

Fish, from both saltwater and fresh, can also be purchased whole, in steaks or fillets. Like meats and poultry, it is available all through the year, fresh, frozen and smoked, cured and canned.

Meat, poultry and fish provide complete protein. They are also important sources of B vitamins and minerals in the diet. Select lean cuts of meat, poultry and fish when you shop, trim off any visible fat before and after cooking, and drain or skim off any fat that collects during cooking. If you do, you will reduce the amount of food energy provided by these foods. This is especially important for weight watchers.

Because these protein-packed foods are often the most costly part of a meal, they should be handled and cooked with care. Following recipe directions closely will help you do this. You will notice that I recommend using a roast meat thermometer. It takes the guesswork out of deciding when roast meat is done.

In my recipes, the seasoning (herbs and spices) and vegetables (onions, celery and green pepper) may be varied a bit to suit you and your family's taste without changing the amount of Choices.

Roast Beef

For the best roast beef, choose a tender cut of beef: rib, sirloin, eye of the round or rump. Other cuts, which are less tender, are better cooked in moisture by braising or stewing. Select a lean roast that is compact and evenly shaped, untied or tied. Roasts smaller than 1.5 kg (3 lbs) dry out when cooked and seem tough, so it is wise to select heavier cuts for roasting.

Each serving: 75 g (3 oz)
Lean Roast Beef

3 ☑ Protein Choices

21 g protein
9 g fat

690 kilojoules
(165 Calories)

Microwave Directions:
Place seasoned (no salt) roast, fat side down, on microwaveable rack in shallow microwaveable baking pan. Cover with waxed paper. Microwave at Medium Low (30%). Halfway through cooking time drain off melted fat and pan juices. Turn roast over and rotate dish. Shield ends of meat or exposed bone ends with foil. Microwave for the following times:
Boneless Beef
Rare - 31 to 38 min/ kg
14 to 17 min/lb
Medium
Rare - 36 to 40 min/kg
16 to 18 min/lb
Medium - 39 to 44 min/kg
18 to 20 min/lb
After microwaving, allow roast to stand, tented with foil, for 15 to 20 minutes to allow internal temperature to rise to temperature of doneness and to firm meat to make carving easier.

- Arrange roast, fat side up, on a rack in a shallow roasting pan.

- Sprinkle or rub your choice of seasonings on the outside of roast: mustard, garlic, rosemary, marjoram, pepper, Worcestershire sauce, but no salt. Salt tends to draw juices from the meat as it cooks.

- Insert a meat thermometer into the thickest part of the meat, making sure the tip does not rest on bone or in fat. Using a thermometer to register internal temperatures is the best way to check whether or not a roast is cooked to the desired degree of doneness.

- Roast uncovered, in a 160ºC (325ºF) oven until cooked to desired doneness.

Doneness	Time	Internal Temperature
Rare	45 min/kg (20 min/lb)	60ºC (140ºF)
Medium	55 min/kg (25 min/lb)	65ºC (150ºF)
Well-done	65 min/kg (30 min/lb)	70ºC (160ºF)

- Once roast is cooked, remove it from the oven and place it on a hot platter and allow it to stand tented with foil in a warm place about 15 minutes. This allows some of the juice to be reabsorbed, firms the meat and makes carving easier.

A boneless roast yields 7 to 8 servings per kilogram (3 to 4 servings per pound).

Meatball Ragout

Some chick peas are mashed to act as a thickener for this simple and satisfying one-pot meal.

Preparation Time: *8 minutes*
Cooking Time: *30 minutes*

1	can (398 mL/14 oz) tomatoes	1
1	medium onion, chopped	1
2	cloves garlic, mashed & chopped	2
1	packet or cube instant beef bouillon	1
1/2	sweet green or red pepper, seeded & sliced	1/2
20	Mini meatballs (recipe, p. 31)	20
250 mL	cooked chick peas, drained & rinsed	1 cup

- In saucepan or skillet, combine tomatoes, onion, garlic and beef bouillon. Bring to a boil; cook, stirring occasionally, about 4 minutes or until onion is translucent.

- Stir in sweet pepper and Mini Meatballs. Bring mixture back to a boil; reduce heat and simmer for 5 minutes.

- With a fork, mash half the chick peas and add to meatball mixture. Stir in remaining chick peas.

- Simmer for 5 to 10 minutes longer to heat thoroughly and until liquid evaporates enough to make a stew-like consistency.

- Divide equally into 4 bowls or deep plates and serve.

Makes 4 servings

Each serving: 1/4 Ragout

1 ▣ Starchy Choice
2 ▣ Protein Choices

18 g carbohydrate
14 g protein
5 g fat

730 kilojoules
(173 Calories)

Microwave Directions:
Drain tomatoes, reserving juice. In microwaveable container, combine tomatoes, onion, garlic and bouillon. Cover with lid or plastic wrap. Microwave at High (100%) for 3 minutes or until onions are translucent. Stir in reserved juice, pepper and meatballs. Microwave at High (100%), stirring halfway through, for 3 minutes. Stir in mashed and whole chick peas. Microwave at High (100%) for 2 minutes longer or until thoroughly heated.

Sukiyaki

Preparation Time: *15 minutes*
Cooking Time: *5-7 minutes*

Legends tell us that early Japanese peasants were forbidden to eat meat. However, they did anyway by cooking whatever game they could catch right on the spot, on the metal of their hoes (suki means hoes, yaki means to broil.)

500 g	flank steak	1 lb
2	medium carrots, sliced	2
1	medium onion, sliced OR 4 green onions, sliced	1
6	medium mushrooms, sliced	6
500 mL	shredded Chinese or regular cabbage	2 cups
250 g	snow peas OR green beans, trimmed	$^{1}/_{2}$ lb
250 g	bean sprouts	$^{1}/_{2}$ lb
125 mL	sliced bamboo shoots	$^{1}/_{2}$ cup

Warishita (Cooking Sauce)

50 mL	soy sauce	$^{1}/_{4}$ cup
50 mL	water	$^{1}/_{4}$ cup
10 mL	red wine vinegar	2 tsp
5 mL	liquid beef bouillon concentrate	1 tsp
	Sugar substitute equivalent to 10 mL (2 tsp) sugar	

Each serving: $^{1}/_{4}$ **of Sukiyaki (75g/3 oz meat)**

1 ▨ Fruits & Vegetables

3 ▨ Protein Choices

11 g carbohydrate
22 g protein
9 g fat

890 kilojoules
(213 Calories)

- Place steak in freezer for 1 hour before slicing. (It is much easier to slice if it is partially frozen.) Slice beef paper thin across the grain.)
- On a tray or platter, arrange beef and vegetables attractively in neat piles.
- **Warishita:** In a small pitcher or bowl, combine soy sauce, water, vinegar, bouillon concentrate and sugar substitute; reserve.
- Use electric nonstick skillet or sukiyaki pan on table over heat.
- Pour about 50 mL (1/4 cup) of the sauce into skillet; add slices of steak and cook at medium-high heat, stirring with spatula to cook slices quickly about 15 seconds on each side. Pour in a little more sauce and cook for 30 seconds longer, then move the steak to the side of the pan.
- Add carrots and onion to pan; cook, stirring, for 2 minutes. Move them to another side of the pan. Add remaining vegetables and pour over remaining sauce. Stir-cook for 2 to 3 minutes longer.
- Serve beef and vegetables separately from skillet or toss vegetables and meat together and serve.

Makes 4 servings

78

Variation
Chicken Sukiyaki: Substitute chicken for beef. Use 1 large whole chicken breast (500 g/1 lb) boned and skinned. (Also for ease in cutting, partially freeze the chicken for about 1 hour, then slice into fine thin pieces.) Use chicken bouillon instead of beef bouillon.
Makes 4 servings

Calculations as for Sukiyaki on preceding page.

Pork Veronique

When the term 'Veronique' is used, it means grapes are an ingredient in the finished dish.

Preparation Time: *10 minutes*
Cooking Time: *30 minutes*

250 mL	chicken broth	1 cup
500 g	pork tenderloin	1 lb
1	clove garlic, minced	1
2 mL	dried thyme	1/2 tsp
250 mL	green seedless grapes, cut in half	1 cup
10 mL	cornstarch	2 tsp
15 mL	cold water	1 tsp

Each serving: 1/4 **pork with sauce**

1 ▨ Fruits & Vegetables
3 ▨ Protein Choices

9 g carbohydrate
22 g protein
9 g fat

860 kilojoules
(205 Calories)

- Into a shallow baking dish, pour broth.

- Cut tenderloin crosswise into 12 medallions or rounds and pound with meat mallet gently until pieces are flat and round. Arrange in a single layer in broth. Sprinkle with garlic and thyme.

- Bake in a 180ºC (350ºF) oven for 15 minutes; add grapes and cook for 5 minutes longer. Transfer pork and grapes with slotted spoon to serving dish.

- Strain pan juices into small saucepan; bring to a boil and cook until reduced to half.

- Stir cornstarch into water; stir into pan juices. Stir and cook until thickened.

- Pour sauce over pork and grapes.

Makes 4 servings

Microwave Directions:
Use half the broth, pour it into microwaveable shallow dish. Arrange pork in dish. Cover with waxed paper. Microwave at Medium (50%) for 6 minutes, rotating dish at half time. Add grapes. Microwave at Medium (50%) for 1 minute. Transfer pork and grapes to serving dish. In glass measure or bowl, microwave pan juices and cornstarch mixture for 1-1/2 minutes or until thick. Continue as recipe directs.

Pork and Ratatouille

Preparation Time: *10 minutes*
Cooking Time: *30 minutes*

Cooks throughout Southern France have their own special recipes for ratatouille. That strange word is the name for a glorious vegetable stew made with late summer vegetables: tomatoes, onions, zucchini and eggplant, the egg-shaped purple one.

500 g	lean pork shoulder or loin of pork trimmed of all visible fat	1 lb
10 mL	soy sauce	2 tsp
	Sugar substitute equivalent to 5 mL (1 tsp) sugar	
5 mL	vinegar	1 tsp
500 g	eggplant, peeled & cubed	1 lb
1	medium onion, chopped	1
1	medium zucchini, sliced	1
1	clove garlic, finely chopped	1
5 mL	dried oregano	1 tsp
1	can (398 mL/14 oz) Italian tomatoes	1

Each serving: ¼ Pork and Ratatouille

1 🍎 Fruits & Vegetables
3 🥩 Protein Choices

12 g carbohydrate
21 g protein
9 g fat

890 kilojoules
(213 Calories)

- Cut pork into thin slivers, 5 x 1 x 1 cm (2 x ³/₄ x ³/₄ in).

- In a bowl, combine soy sauce, sugar substitute and vinegar; add pork and set aside to marinate.

- Meanwhile, in a skillet or large saucepan, combine eggplant, onion, zucchini, garlic, oregano and tomatoes; bring to a boil, stirring to break up tomatoes. Reduce heat and simmer, stirring occasionally, for 10 minutes.

- Stir in pork and marinade. Cook, stirring occasionally, about 20 minutes longer or until pork is no longer pink and excess moisture has evaporated.

Makes 4 servings

Microwave Directions:
In microwaveable container., combine eggplant, onion, zucchini, garlic, oregano and tomatoes. With fork, break up tomatoes. Cover with lid or waxed paper. Microwave at High (100%), stirring at halftime, for 10 minutes. Stir pork into vegetable mixture. Microwave at Medium High (75%) for 7 minutes or until pork is cooked and no longer pink.

Liver Creole

Liver is an excellent source of iron and should be included regularly in meal planning. Thin strips cooked quickly in tomato-green pepper sauce are always tender and full of flavor.

Preparation Time: *15 minutes*
Cooking Time: *25 minutes*

1	medium onion, chopped	1
1	small sweet green pepper, seeded and chopped	1
1	clove garlic, finely chopped	1
1	can (540 mL/19 oz) tomatoes	1
5 mL	dried basil	1 tsp
1 mL	ground cardamom	1/4 tsp
Pinch	ground cumin	Pinch
5 mL	vegetable oil	1 tsp
500 g	beef or pork liver	1 lb
15 mL	red wine vinegar	1 tbsp
	Sugar substitute equivalent to 10 mL (2 tsp) sugar	
2 mL	salt	1/2 tsp
1 mL	freshly ground pepper	1/4 tsp

Each serving: 1/4 of creole

1/2 🥗 Fruits & Vegetables

3 🍖 Protein Choices

7 g carbohydrate
23 g protein
10 g fat

880 kilojoules
(210 Calories)

- In a nonstick skillet, combine onion, green pepper and garlic; stir-cook for 2 to 3 minutes.

- Add tomatoes, basil, cardamom and cumin; simmer for 10 minutes.

- Brush separate nonstick skillet with oil. Sauté liver about 3 minutes on each side. Remove liver and cut into thin strips.

- Add liver strips, wine vinegar, sugar substitute, salt and pepper to tomato mixture; simmer for 3 to 4 minutes.

Makes 4 servings

Microwave Directions:
In microwaveable container, combine onion, pepper and garlic. Cover with lid or plastic wrap. Microwave at High (100%) for 2 minutes. Stir in tomatoes, basil, cardamom, cumin. Microwave at High (100%), stirring once, for 6 minutes. Cook liver in skillet as directed in recipe. Add liver strips, wine vinegar and pepper to tomato mixture. Microwave at High (100%) for 2 minutes. Stir in sweetener and salt.

Herb & Lemon Lamb Chops

Preparation Time: *5 minutes*
Marinating Time: *2 hours*
Cooking Time: *15-20 minutes*

The small amount of olive oil in the lemony, herb marinade is just enough to add flavor and help keep the chops from drying out when they cook.

4	shoulder lamb chops (500g/1 lb total)	4
	Juice of 1 lemon	
1	clove garlic, mashed & chopped	1
15 mL	chopped fresh rosemary OR 5 mL (1 tsp) dried	1 tbsp
15 mL	chopped fresh summer savory OR 5 mL (1 tsp) dried	1 tbsp
5 mL	olive oil	1 tsp
Pinch	freshly ground pepper	Pinch

Each serving: 1 lamb shoulder chop

2 ⊘ Protein Choices

1 g carbohydrate
14 g protein
7 g fat

520 kilojoules
(123 Calories)

- Trim visible fat from edges of chops. Discard trimmings. Place chops in a double plastic bag placed in a bowl.

- Combine lemon juice, garlic, rosemary, summer savory, olive oil and pepper. Pour over chops; close bag up tightly around chops with a wire twist-tie.

- Place in refrigerator to marinate at least 2 hours.

- Remove chops from marinade and pat dry with paper towels. Place on roasting rack or cake rack in a shallow pan.

- Bake in a 180ºC (350ºF) oven for 15 minutes for rare, 20 minutes for well-done.

Makes 4 servings

Microwave Directions:
After marinating and patting lamb chops dry, heat browning dish in microwave oven at High (100%). Arrange chops on very lightly oiled, hot browning dish. Microwave at Medium (50%) for 6 minutes, turning chops halfway through cooking time.

Chicken in a Package

Food cooked in a foil or parchment packet actually steams in its own juices. The result is exciting and succulent. The flavor is fresh and the aroma fragrant.

Preparation Time: *20 minutes*
Cooking Time: *15-20 minutes*

1	medium carrot	1
1	medium (15 cm/6 in) zucchini	1
2	stalks celery	2
2	green onions	2
125 mL	thinly sliced mushrooms	¹/₂ cup
125 mL	chicken broth	¹/₂ cup
	Foil or cooking parchment paper	
2	whole chicken breasts (375 g/³/₄ lb total) split, boned and skinned	2
5 mL	dried summer savory	1 tsp
Pinch	freshly ground pepper	Pinch

Each serving: 1 piece chicken breast with about 125 mL (¹/₂ cup) vegetables

3 🗹 Protein Choices

2 g carbohydrate
22 g protein
9 g fat

740 kilojoules
(177 Calories)

- Wash and peel carrot. Wash and trim zucchini. Wash celery. Cut each vegetable into 5 cm (2 in) shoestring pieces (often called julienne cut). Cut onions lengthwise into thin strips 5 cm (2 in) long.

- In a skillet, combine carrot, zucchini, celery, onions and mushrooms with chicken broth. Stir-cook over medium heat for 2 to 3 minutes. Set aside to cool.

- Cut foil or cooking parchment paper into four 25 cm (10 in) squares.

- Place a half a chicken breast diagonally near center of each sheet. Top each one with one-quarter of the braised vegetables and a pinch of summer savory and sprinkle of pepper. Fold other half of foil loosely over food to form a triangle. Fold edges together twice to seal securely. Place packages on a baking sheet. (Recipe can be prepared in advance to this point and refrigerated for up to 2 days.)

- Bake in a 160°C (325°F) oven for 15 minutes or until chicken is firm to the touch when pressed lightly with a finger. (To make this test for doneness, slit one package taking care not to spill juice, then press chicken.)

- To serve, slide each package onto a dinner plate, slit top and tear back foil to reveal chicken and vegetables. Slide out of foil package onto plate, if desired.

Makes 4 servings

Microwave Directions:
Prepare Chicken in a Packet in parchment paper. Arrange on large microwaveable plate with thickest end toward the outside. Microwave at High (100%), rotating halfway through cooking time, for 6 to 8 minutes or until chicken is no longer pink. Let stand for 3 minutes before opening packets and serving.

Lime-Broiled Chicken Breasts

Preparation Time: *5 minutes*
Marinating Time: *3 hrs*
Cooking Time: *10 minutes*

Marinating flavors the chicken. Plan so that the marinating is done ahead but leave the cooking until the last moment. Cook the chicken for the short time recommended, then serve it immediately. It is wonderful!

2	whole chicken breasts, boned, skinned & split (375 g/3/4 lb total)	2
	Juice of 1 lime	
25 mL	soy sauce	2 tbsp
1	clove garlic, minced	1
15 mL	grated fresh ginger root	1 tbsp
	Sugar substitute equivalent to 5 mL (1 tsp) sugar	
	Salt and freshly ground pepper	

Each serving: 1 chicken breast

3 🡵 Protein Choices

1 g carbohydrate
21 g protein
9 g fat

710 kilojoules
(169 Calories)

- Trim any visible fat from chicken breasts; place breasts in a glass bowl.

- Combine lime juice, soy sauce, garlic, ginger root and sugar substitute. Pour over chicken, coating each piece. Marinate in refrigerator, covered, for at least 3 hours or overnight.

- Preheat broiler.

- Broil about 10 cm (4 in) from heat for 10 minutes, brushing with remaining marinade if surface seems dry.

- Season with salt and pepper to taste. Serve.

Makes 4 servings

Microwave Directions:
Arrange marinated chicken breasts in microwaveable pie plate with thickest part to the outside. Cover with waxed paper. Microwave at High (100%), rotating pie plate once, for about 8 minutes or until chicken is no longer pink inside.

❖ **Helpful Hint:**

To barbecue chicken breasts, first marinate them as directed above. Preheat barbecue, then place chicken pieces on the barbecue grill about 10 to 12 cm (4 to 5 in) over medium-high heat. Barbecue for 10 minutes, turning once and brushing with marinade. Overcooked chicken will be dry and seem stringy.

Roast Chicken

For first-class, old-fashioned specialty, buy Grade A roasting chickens. Stewing quality, utility birds become tough when cooked by the dry heat roasting method.

| 1.5 kg | small roasting chicken | 3¹/₂ lb |

- Rinse and wipe chicken. Remove and discard any fat that can be pulled away from body cavity.
- Stuff bird, if desired. See Grandma's Bread Stuffing (recipe, p. 86).
  a) Prepare stuffing, Do not stuff bird until ready to cook.
  b) Fill neck cavity with dressing; pull neck skin over dressing to hold it. Secure flap of neck skin to back of bird with a skewer.
  c) Stuff vent end (back end) of bird, taking care not to pack stuffing too tightly.
  d) Skewer or sew the opening closed. (Use metal skewers or poultry pins or coarse thread on a darning needle.) If vent end is too large to close, cover opening and exposed dressing with piece of foil.
  e) Fold wing tips back under bird, then tie wings and legs close to body.
- Place bird breast side up on a rack in an open roasting pan.
- Brush skin with 1 or 2 drops of oil or margarine, if desired. (Do not add water to the pan.) Cover bird loosely with foil. Insert meat thermometer into thickest part of the thigh, not touching bone.
- Roast in a 160ºC (325ºF) oven about 2 to 2¹/₂ hours for a stuffed 1.5 kg (3¹/₂ lb) chicken. (If unstuffed, reduce roasting time slightly.) A half hour before cooking time is up, remove foil, and baste chicken with pan drippings to help brown.
- The chicken is cooked when internal temperature reaches 85ºC (190ºF), the leg joint moves when the drumstick is turned, the thickest part of the thigh feels tender and soft when pressed with a knife and juice runs clear and no longer pink.
- Place chicken on hot plate. Stand in a warm place for 15 to 20 minutes to allow juices to reabsorb and chicken to set. This makes the carving easier.

Makes 7 servings

Preparation Time: *15 minutes*
Cooking Time: *2 to 2½ hours*
(45 minutes per kg/ 20 minutes per lb)

Each serving: 75 g (3 oz) chicken, without stuffing

3 ☑ Protein Choices

21 g protein
9 g fat

690 kilojoules
(165 Calories)

Grandma's Bread Stuffing

Preparation Time: *5 minutes*

My mom made stuffing like this for roast chicken and so did her mom, so it seems natural for me to use it regularly.

10 mL	margarine or butter	2 tsp
125 mL	chopped onion	1/2 cup
125 mL	chopped celery	1/2 cup
2 mL	dried sage	1/2 tsp
2 mL	dried summer savory	1/2 tsp
4	slices stale bread	4
125 mL	chicken broth	1/2 cup
Pinch	Freshly ground pepper	Pinch

Each serving: 200 mL(3/4 cup)

1 ▢ Starchy Choice

1/2 ▲ Fats & Oils Choice

17 g carbohydrate
2 g protein
2 g fat

390 kilojoules
(94 Calories)

- In a medium saucepan, melt margarine. Add onion and celery; sauté about 5 minutes or until onion is translucent. Remove from heat.

- Stir in sage and savory.

- Cut bread into small cubes. Add to saucepan; toss with onion mixture.

- Sprinkle with chicken broth and mix until moistened. Season with pepper. Mix well.

- Stuff chicken, packing loosely because the stuffing will swell during cooking.

Makes 4 servings (enough for a 1.5 - 2 kg /3 1/2 - 4 1/2 lb chicken)

Microwave Directions:
In microwaveable container, combine margarine, onion and celery. Microwave at High (100%) for 2 1/2 minutes or until onion is translucent. Continue as recipe directs.

♣ **Timely Tip:**

Stuffed poultry (chicken, turkey, duck) should be roasted immediately after stuffing to prevent any chance of bacterial growth.

Chicken and Vegetable Stir-Fry

Chinese stir-fry cooking is certainly popular with busy cooks. It is no wonder! Fresh vegetables and cooked chicken go together for a nutritious meal-in-minutes. Or use cooked beef or pork .

Preparation Time: *10 minutes*
Cooking Time: *5 minutes*

125 mL	sliced carrots	¹/₂ cup
250 mL	unpeeled zucchini slices	1 cup
250 mL	diagonally cut celery slices	1 cup
1	medium onion, cut in half and sliced	1
15 mL	corn oil	1 tbsp
1	clove garlic, mashed & chopped OR 2 mL (¹/₂ tsp) garlic powder	1
125 mL	cold water	¹/₂ cup
15 mL	soy sauce	1 tbsp
10 mL	cornstarch	2 tsp
1 mL	ground ginger	¹/₄ tsp
250 mL	cut-up cooked chicken	1 cup

Each serving: ¹/₄ **vegetables and chicken**

1 ⊘ Protein Choice
¹/₂ ▲ Fats & Oils Choice
1 ⊞ Extra Vegetables

5 g carbohydrate
7 g protein
6 g fat

430 kilojoules
(102 Calories)

- Prepare carrots, zucchini, celery and onion; set aside.

- In wok or large skillet (electric one is perfect), heat oil; add garlic and cook about 30 seconds.

- Stir in vegetables in order listed; stir-fry over medium-high heat about 3 minutes.

- Stir in water; reduce heat, cover and steam vegetables for about 7 minutes or until tender-crisp.

- In a small dish, blend together soy sauce, cornstarch and ginger. Push vegetables to one side of pan. Stir cornstarch mixture into broth in pan and cook for about 1 minute or until mixture thickens.

- Add cooked chicken. Gently stir together vegetables, thickened broth and chicken until chicken is heated through.

Makes 4 servings

 Note: only part of the stated carbohydrate from the vegetables is actually available to affect the blood sugar. This has been considered in assigning the Food Choice Value.

Stir-Braised Scallops with Vegetables

Preparation Time: *15 minutes*
Cooking Time: *15 minutes*

Pearly white, tender scallops are low in fat, making the energy (kilojoules/Calories) value of each serving low.

2	medium carrots, cut in julienne	2
250 mL	broccoli florets	1 cup
1	green pepper, chopped	1
1	clove garlic, finely chopped	1
125 mL	chicken broth	1/2 cup
2	green onions, chopped	2
250 mL	shredded cabbage	1 cup
250 mL	bean sprouts	1 cup
1	pkg (396 g/14 oz) frozen scallops defrosted and cut in half crosswise	1
75 mL	water	1/3 cup
15 mL	soy sauce	1 tbsp
	Sugar substitute equivalent to 10 mL (2tsp) sugar	
10 mL	corn starch	2 tsp
25 mL	sliced almonds, toasted (8 almonds/20g)2 tbsp	

Each serving: 250 mL(1 cup)

1/2 ▨ Fruits & Veghetables

3 ▨ Protein Choices

9 g carbohydrate
23 g protein
2 g fat

610 kilojoules
(146 Calories)

- In a large skillet, combine carrots, broccoli, green pepper, garlic and broth. Stir-braise vegetables for 3 minutes.

- Add green onions, cabbage, bean sprouts and scallops; stir-cook for 5 minutes longer.

- Stir together water, soy sauce, sugar substitute and cornstarch; add to vegetables and scallops. Stir-cook about 3 minutes or until sauce thickens. Garnish with almonds and serve.

Makes 4 servings

Lemon Fish Fillets in a Packet

Fish is easy to cook. It does not take long because it is tender and has little connective tissue. Please watch cooking time, and do not overcook fish. Overcooking causes flavor and moisture loss. Perfectly cooked fish is opaque throughout, still springy when touched, and flakes easily when tested with a fork. For this recipe use cod, flounder, haddock, halibut, Boston blue fish, salmon or sole.

Preparation Time: *10 minutes*
Cooking Time: *25 minutes*

2	squares (30 cm/12 in) heavy foil	2
10 mL	margarine	2 tsp
250 g	fresh or frozen (thawed) fish fillets	$^1/_2$ lb
25 mL	finely chopped celery	2 tbsp
10 mL	finely chopped onion	2 tsp
2	thin slices lemon OR 10 mL (2 tsp) lemon juice	2
Pinch	each salt and pepper	Pinch

Each serving: 90 g (3 to 4 oz)

3 ▨ Protein Choice

24 g protein
9 g fat

740 kilojoules
(177 Calories)

- Lay foil on work surface, dull side up. Brush 5 mL (1 tsp) margarine over each piece of foil, leaving 5 cm (2 in) border around all sides free of margarine. Pressing gently, fold each square in half, diagonally from corner to corner, to form a triangle, then open up pieces of foil again.

- Divide fish evenly into 2 portions and place one portion on each piece of foil to one side of the fold line.

- Top each portion of fish with half the celery, half the onion and 1 slice lemon. Season with salt and pepper.

- Fold half of foil diagonally over fish and vegetables so that the two opposite edges and corners meet and form a triangle. Fold edges together twice and pinch to seal edges. Place packages on a baking sheet.

- Bake in a 200ºC (400ºF) oven for 25 minutes or until fish is springy when touched and flakes easily with a fork.

- To serve, place packages on dinner plate, cut an X through top of each package and eat fish right from the package, or, transfer it with the juice to the plate.

Makes 2 servings

Microwave Directions:
Use parchment paper instead of foil to wrap fish, vegetables and lemon as directed in recipe. Place packets on microwaveable plate. Microwave at High (100%), turning plate halfway through cooking time, for 6 minutes or until fish is opaque and just flakes with a fork.

Variation:
Tomato Fish Fillets In a Packet: In place of lemon slices, use tomato slices, cut 1 cm (1/2 in) thick.

Microwave Tomato Fish Fillets as above.
Serving and calculations as above

Baked Fish Fillets with Walnuts

Preparation Time: *3 minutes*
Cooking Time: *12 minutes*

The growing popularity of fish and seafood is not surprising. Both cook quickly and go well with many different flavors.

500 g	fish fillets (cod, flounder, haddock or sole) fresh or frozen (thawed)	1 lb
1 mL	salt	$1/_4$ tsp
Pinch	freshly ground pepper	Pinch
20 mL	chopped walnuts	4 tsp
4	lemon wedges	4

Each serving: 75 g (3 oz)

3 ⧄ Protein Choices

   24 g protein
   7 g fat

   670 kilojoules
   (159 Calories)

Microwave Directions:
In microwaveable baking dish, arrange fillets in a single layer. Sprinkle with pepper and walnuts. Cover with waxed paper. Microwave at High (100%), rotating dish twice, for 6 minutes or until fish is opaque and just flakes with a fork. Let stand, covered, 4 minutes.

- In a nonstick baking dish, place fillets in a single layer. Sprinkle evenly with salt, pepper and walnuts (5 mL/1 tsp) per 125 g ($1/_4$ lb) fillet.

- Bake, uncovered, in a 200ºC (400ºF) oven, basting once or twice, for 12 minutes or just until fish is opaque and flakes easily when tested with a fork.

- Serve on warm plates. Garnish each serving with a wedge of lemon.

Makes 4 servings

Each serving: 75 g (3 oz)

3 ⧄ Protein Choices

   25 g protein
   5 g fat

   610 kilojoules
   (145 Calories)

Microwave as above

Variation:

Baked Fish Fillets Parmesan: In place of walnuts, sprinkle 20 mL (4 tsp) grated Parmesan cheese evenly over fish fillets before baking.

♣ **Slick Trick:**

For one serving, place fish fillet on ovenproof plate, if one is available, and cook fish right on plate. Make sure oven mitts are standing by to handle the hot plate.

Crisp Fish Sticks

These are better than the packaged frozen ready-to-heat ones and have very little added fat.

Preparation Time: *10 minutes*
Cooking Time: *12 minutes*

500 g	fish fillets(flounder, whitefish, haddock, cod) fresh or frozen (thawed)	1 lb
125 mL	2% yogurt or milk	$^1/_2$ cup
5 mL	Worcestershire sauce	1 tsp
5 mL	soy sauce	1 tsp
12	soda crackers, finely crushed	12
250 mL	cornflakes, crushed	1 cup
Pinch	freshly ground pepper	Pinch
10 mL	margarine, melted OR corn oil	2 tsp
	Salt, optional	

Each serving: 2 fish fillets

1 ▢ Starchy Choice
4 ▨ Protein Choices

14 g carbohydrate
27 g protein
9 g fat

1030 kilojoules
(245 Calories)

- Cut fish into 8 even pieces (about 60 g/2 oz each).

- In a shallow dish or pie plate, combine yogurt, Worcestershire and soy sauce.

- In a second shallow dish or pie plate, combine crushed cracker, corn flake crumbs and pepper. With fingers, rub margarine into crumbs until evenly distributed.

- Dip each piece of fish into yogurt mixture, then into crumbs to coat completely. (If milk is used, you might have to dip fish twice, first into milk, then crumbs, then milk again and crumbs again.)

- Place fish 2.5 cm (1 in) apart on nonstick or lightly greased baking sheets. (Pieces should not touch.)

- Bake in a 225ºC (450ºF) oven for 6 minutes; turn and bake for 5 to 6 minutes longer or until crumb coating is crisp and fish flakes easily when tested with a fork. Salt lightly after baking, if desired.

Makes 4 servings, 2 pieces 100 g (4 oz) per serving

Variation:
Dilly Crisp Fish Sticks: Add 5 mL (1 tsp) dried dill to crumb mixture in the above recipe.

Microwave Directions:
Microwave browning dish at High (100%) for 5 minutes or according to manufacturer's directions. Brush dish with margarine. Arrange prepared fish sticks on dish to look like spokes of a wheel. Microwave at High (100%) for 2 minutes. Turn fish sticks. Microwave at High (100%) for 2-1/2 minutes or until fish just flakes with a fork. OR arrange fish sticks in spoke-like fashion on microwave roasting rack. Microwave at High (100%), rotating rack once, for 5 to 6 minutes or until fish just flakes with a fork.

Serving and calculations as above.

Make It Meat, Poultry or Fish

Recipe	Food Choices per Serving	Energy per Serving kilojoules	Calories	
Roast Beef	3 ⊘ Protein	690	165	p. 76
Meatball Ragout	1 ☐ Starchy; 2 ⊘ Protein	730	173	p. 77
Sukiyaki	1 ◢ Fruits & Vegetables; 3 ⊘ Protein	890	213	p. 78
Chicken Sukiyaki	1 ◢ Fruits & Vegetables; 3 ⊘ Protein	890	213	p. 79
Pork Veronique	1 ◢ Fruits & Vegetables; 3 ⊘ Protein	860	205	p. 79
Pork & Ratatouille	1 ◢ Fruits & Vegetables; 3 ⊘ Protein	890	213	p. 80
Liver Creole	¹/₂ ◢ Fruits & Vegetables; 3 ⊘ Protein	880	210	p. 81
Herb and Lemon Lamb Chops	2 ⊘ Protein	520	123	p. 82
Chicken in a Package	3 ⊘ Protein	740	177	p. 83
Lime-Broiled Chicken Breasts	3 ⊘ Protein	710	169	p. 84
Roast Chicken	3 ⊘ Protein	690	165	p. 85
Grandma's Bread Stuffing	1 ☐ Starchy; ¹/₂ ▲ Fats & Oils	390	94	p. 86
Chicken & Vegetable Stir-Fry	1 ⊞ Extra Vegetables; 1 ⊘ Protein ¹/₂ ▲ Fats & Oils	430	102	p. 87
Stir-Braised Scallops with Vegetables	¹/₂ ◢ Fruits & Vegetables; 3 ⊘ Protein	610	146	p. 88
Lemon Fish Fillets in a Packet	3 ⊘ Protein	740	177	p. 89
Tomato Fish Fillets in a Packet	3 ⊘ Protein	740	177	p. 89
Fish Fillets with Walnuts	3 ⊘ Protein	670	159	p. 90
Fish Fillets Parmesan	3 ⊘ Protein	610	145	p. 90
Crisp Fish Sticks	1 ☐ Starchy; 4 ⊘ Protein	1030	245	p. 91
Dilly Crisp Fish Sticks	1 ☐ Starchy; 4 ⊘ Protein	1030	245	p. 91

Make It Meatless

After my first trip to Mexico, I came back with a new recipe for beans. They had appeared in my meals every day while I was away and they were very good.

Now I plan many menus featuring beans and find they make some of the most economical meatless meals. And, as well as being relatively inexpensive as compared to meat meals, they are nutritious and provide dietary fibre.

Legumes, like beans, and lentils, provide nutritious but incomplete vegetable protein, not complete animal protein like that found in meat, milk, eggs and cheese. However, when two vegetable proteins, such as beans and rice or legumes and grains, are eaten together, the quality of protein is improved and the combination becomes a complete protein that is essential in our diets.

Other combinations that work are rice and lentils, corn and beans, rice and peas, pasta and beans, and brown bread and beans. The nutritional quality of vegetable protein is often improved by a little animal protein and the two then provide complete protein. Macaroni and cheese, or rice pudding containing rice, egg, and milk, are examples of this.

Pasta and rice dishes also fit into this meatless section. Both are types of starchy carbohydrate and a 125 mL (1/2 cup) serving can replace a slice of bread as 1 ▫ Starchy Choice in a meal.

Lentil Curry with Cucumbers and Bananas

Preparation Time: *5 minutes*
Cooking Time: *10-15 minutes*

Curries are often eaten with simply prepared fruits and vegetables to lessen and cool the 'heat' of the spice combination. A side dish of cucumbers with yogurt, and sliced bananas, serve that purpose here.

1	medium onion, chopped	1
1	small apple, cored & chopped	1
25 mL	water	2 tbsp
5-10 mL	curry powder	1-2 tsp
2 mL	salt	1/2 tsp
Pinch	freshly ground pepper	Pinch
1	can (540 mL/19 oz) lentils	1
250 mL	chopped cucumber	1 cup
50 mL	2% yogurt	1/4 cup
1/2	small banana, sliced	1/2
Dash	lemon juice	Dash

Each serving: 125 mL(1/2 cup) plus 1/4 cucumber and 1/4 banana

1 ☐ Starchy Choice
1 ◪ Fruits & Vegetables
1/2 ⊘ Protein Choice

24 g carbohydrate
7 g protein

520 kilojoules
(124 Calories)

- In a saucepan, combine onion, apple, water, curry to taste, salt and pepper.

- Stir-braise over medium-low heat, about 4 minutes or until onion is translucent and apple tender, adding a little more water if pan becomes dry.

- Drain and rinse lentils under cold running water; drain well. Stir into apple mixture. Cook, stirring occasionally, about 5 minutes or until heated through.

- In a small bowl, combine cucumber and yogurt.

- Slice banana; sprinkle with a few drops of lemon juice.

- Serve curry with cucumber and banana.

Makes 4 servings

Microwave Directions:
In microwaveable dish, layer onion and apple; sprinkle with 15 mL (1 tbsp) water, curry powder, salt and pepper. Cover tightly with lid or plastic wrap. Microwave at High (100%) for 3 minutes or until onion is translucent. Stir in rinsed and drained lentils. Microwave at High (100%) for 2 minutes or until heated through. Continue with recipe as directed.

Pasta E Fagioli – Pasta and Beans

When pasta and beans are eaten together, they complement each other and provide complete protein to the diet. You'll find this meal-in-a-pot is not only nutritious, it is economical too because both legumes (beans) and pasta are reasonably priced.

250 mL	macaroni or other small shell pasta	1 cup
1	can (398 mL/14 oz) kidney beans	1
1	can (398 mL/14 oz) tomatoes	1
250 mL	diced carrots	1 cup
2	stalks celery, diagonally sliced	2
1	medium onion, chopped	1
1	clove garlic, finely chopped	1
2 mL	dried thyme	$1/_2$ tsp
2 mL	dried fines herbes*	$1/_2$ tsp
2 mL	salt	$1/_2$ tsp
Pinch	freshly ground black pepper	Pinch

- In a large saucepan, in 1.5 L (6 cups) lightly salted boiling water, cook macaroni about 10 minutes or until *al dente* (tender but firm); place in strainer or sieve to drain. Pour beans over macaroni. Rinse well under cold running water; drain well.

- In the same saucepan, combine tomatoes, carrots, celery, onion, garlic, thyme, fines herbes, salt and pepper. Bring to a boil and cook for 3 minutes.

- Stir macaroni and beans into tomato mixture. Reduce heat; cover and simmer for 7 to 10 minutes or until vegetables are tender. Add a little water if liquid evaporates too quickly.

Makes 4 servings

♣ **Timely Tip**

Fines Herbes, a mixture of oregano, basil and parsley, can be found in supermarket herb racks.

Preparation Time: *20 minutes*
Cooking Time : *10 minutes*

Each Serving: 250 mL (1 cup)

2 ☐ Starchy Choices
1 ☑ Protein Choice

> *33 g carbohydrate*
> *8 g protein*
> *1 g fat*
>
> *730 kilojoules*
> *(173 Calories)*

Microwave Directions:
Prepare beans and macaroni as directed. In 1.5 L (6 cup) microwaveable container, combine remaining ingredients. Cover tightly with lid or plastic wrap. Microwave at High (100%) for 6 minutes. Stir in macaroni and beans. Cover with waxed paper. Microwave at High (100%) for 6 minutes or until vegetables are tender.

Twice Cooked Beans

Preparation Time: *5 minutes*
Cooking Time: *10 minutes*

Mexicans fry cooked beans with flavorings until they are pulpy but still moist. They call them 'Frijoles' which means refried beans. Mashed potatoes, move over! Refried beans are taking your place at many tables.

1	can (540 mL/19oz) pinto Romano or kidney beans	1
5 mL	corn oil	1 tbsp
125 mL	chopped onion	1/2 cup
Pinch	ground coriander	Pinch
Pinch	chili powder	Pinch

Each serving: 125 mL(1/2 cup)

2 ☐ Starchy Choices

1 ⊘ Protein Choice

29 g carbohydrate
11 g protein
3 g fat

790 kilojoules
(187 Calories)

- Drain beans, reserving liquid.
- In a saucepan or skillet, heat oil; add beans, onion, coriander and chili powder. Stir and mash with the back of a large spoon or potato masher until beans are partially mashed. Simmer, stirring frequently, for 5 to 10 minutes or until the beans are the desired consistency, adding a small amount of reserved bean liquid if necessary.

Makes 3 servings

Microwave Directions:
In microwaveable container, combine drained beans, onion, coriander and chili powder. Mash beans. Microwave at High (100%) for 4 minutes or until heated through and onions are translucent. Thin with a small amount of bean liquid, if desired.

Mexican Beans and Rice

When dried beans (legumes) and rice are combined and eaten together in a dish like this, they complement each other and provide complete protein that is equivalent to meat. Neither beans nor rice alone supply complete protein. If you prefer more 'heat' in the flavor of this Mexican-style hotpot, add a bit more chili powder and a few drops of hot pepper sauce.

Preparation Time: *20 minutes*
Cooking Time : *15 minutes*

1	medium onion, chopped	1
1	green pepper, seeded & chopped	1
1	can (540 mL/19 oz) tomatoes	1
2 mL	chili powder	$1/_2$ tsp
2 mL	Worcestershire sauce	$1/_2$ tsp
1 mL	celery seed	$1/_4$ tsp
1	can (540 mL/19 oz) kidney, pinto or Romano beans, drained and rinsed	1
250 mL	cooked brown or white long grain rice	1 cup
Pinch	freshly ground pepper	Pinch
75 mL	shredded Cheddar cheese	$1/_3$ cup

Each Serving: 200 mL($^3/_4$ cup)

1 ☐ Starchy Choice
1 ◨ Fruits and Vegetables
1 ⊘ Protein Choice

26 g carbohydrate
8 g protein
3 g fat

680 kilojoules
(163 Calories)

- In a 2L (8 cup) saucepan, combine onion, green pepper, tomatoes, chili powder, Worcestershire sauce and celery seed. Bring to a boil over medium heat; reduce heat and simmer for 5 minutes, stirring once or twice.

- Add rinsed beans, rice and pepper. Stir gently to combine. Continue to simmer 10 minutes longer for flavors to blend.

- Serve sprinkled with shredded cheese.

Makes 6 servings

Microwave Directions:
In 1.5 L (6 cup) microwaveable container, combine onion, green pepper, tomatoes, chili powder, Worcestershire sauce and celery seed. Cover tightly with lid or waxed paper. Microwave at High (100%) for 3 minutes. Stir in rinsed beans, rice and pepper. Microwave at High (100%), uncovered, stirring halfway through cooking time, for 7 minutes or until heated through. Sprinkle with cheese.

Quickest Ever Chili

Preparation Time: *10 minutes*
Cooking Time: *15 minutes*

If you have only an hour to make your meal, eat it and clean up afterward, then this is for you. All the ingredients simmer together for a few minutes, and a bowl of hot chili is ready. Tofu (soybean curd) adds protein to the mixture.

2	stalks celery, thinly sliced	2
1	medium onion, chopped	1
1	green pepper, chopped	1
125 mL	chicken broth	$^1/_2$ cup
1	can (213 mL/$7^1/_2$ oz) tomato sauce	1
10-15 mL	chili powder	2-3 tsp
1	can (540 mL/19 oz) Romano or pinto beans, drained and rinsed	1
1	block tofu (6 x 6 x 4 cm/ $2^1/_2$ x $2^1/_2$ x $1^1/_2$ in) (140 g)	1
Pinch	freshly ground pepper	Pinch

Each serving: 200 mL(³/₄ cup)

2 ▢ Starchy Choices
1 ▨ Protein Choice

28 g carbohydrate
11 g protein
4 g fat

810 kilojoules
(192 Calories)

- In a saucepan, combine celery, onion, green pepper, chicken broth, tomato sauce and chili powder.

- Cook over medium heat, stirring occasionally, for 5 minutes.

- Stir in beans.

- Press tofu between paper towels to remove some of the moisture. Cut into small cubes; stir into bean mixture. Simmer about 10 minutes.

- Serve in bowls or deep plates.

Makes 4 servings, 750 mL (3 cups)

Microwave Directions:
In 1.5 L (6 cup) microwaveable container, combine celery, onion, green pepper, 50 mL (1/4 cup) chicken broth, tomato sauce and chili powder. Cover tightly with lid or plastic wrap. Microwave at High (100%) for 6 minutes or until onion is translucent. Stir in beans, tofu and pepper. Cover and microwave at High (100%) for 5 minutes or until heated through.

Spanish Rice with Chick Peas

Rice and the legume, chick peas, complement each other to make this a combination that supplies complete protein . It rates with individuals practising a vegetarian routine.

Preparation Time: *10 minutes*
Cooking Time : *15 minutes*

2	stalks celery, chopped	2
1	medium onion, chopped	1
1	green pepper, chopped	1
1	clove garlic, chopped	1
1	can (540 mL/19 oz) tomatoes	1
2 mL	Worcestershire sauce	$^1/_2$ tsp
3	whole cloves	3
1	can (540 mL/19 oz) chick peas, drained and rinsed	1
250 mL	cooked long grain rice	1 cup
Pinch	freshly ground pepper	Pinch
50 g	shredded mozzarella cheese (125 mL/$^1/_2$ cup)	2 oz

Each Serving: 200 mL($^3/_4$ cup)

1 ☐ Starchy Choice
1 ◪ Fruits & Vegetables
1 ◪ Protein Choice

25 g carbohydrate
8 g protein
3 g fat

670 kilojoules
(159 Calories)

- In a 2L (8 cup) saucepan, combine celery, onion, green pepper, garlic, tomatoes, Worcestershire sauce and cloves.

- Bring to a boil over medium heat; reduce heat and simmer for 5 minutes, stirring once or twice.

- Stir in rinsed chick peas, rice and pepper. Continue to cook, stirring occasionally, for 10 minutes or until warmed through.

- Serve sprinkled with shredded cheese.

Makes 6 servings

Microwave Directions:
In 2 L (8 cup) microwaveable container, combine celery, onion, green pepper and garlic. Cover tightly with lid or plastic wrap. Microwave at High (100%) for 3 minutes or until onion is translucent. Stir in tomatoes, Worcestershire sauce and cloves. Cover and microwave at High (100%) for 3 minutes. Stir in chick peas, rice and pepper. Cover and microwave at High for 2 minutes or until heated through. Sprinkle with cheese.

Space-Age Barbecued Beans

Preparation Time: *10 minutes*
Cooking Time: *20-25 minutes*

When it is your turn to have the gang over after a football game or track meet, have a pot of these beans ready to reheat. With the beans, I like to serve Keeps-A-Week Coleslaw, (recipe, p. 61), which can also be made ahead.

125 mL	tubetti or macaroni	¹/₂ cup
1	can (540 mL/19 oz) red kidney beans	1
1	can (540 mL/19 oz) white kidney beans	1
125 mL	chicken broth	¹/₂ cup
2	medium zucchini (15 cm/6 in) chopped	2
1	medium onion, chopped	1
1	can (213 mL/7¹/₂ oz) tomato sauce	1
	Sugar substitute equivalent to 15 mL (1 tbsp) sugar	
10 mL	Dijon mustard	2 tsp
10 mL	vinegar	2 tsp
5 mL	horseradish	1 tsp

Each serving: 200 mL(³/₄ cup)

2 ▢ Starchy Choices

¹/₂ ▨ Protein Choice

28 g carbohydrate
8 g protein
2 g fat

680 kilojoules
(162 Calories)

- In a saucepan of rapidly boiling water, cook tubetti about 12 minutes or until *al dente* (tender but firm).

- Pour tubetti into a sieve or colander to drain; add both red and white kidney beans to drain, then rinse.

- In another saucepan, combine broth, zucchini, onion, tomato sauce, sugar substitute, mustard, vinegar and horseradish. Bring to a boil; reduce heat and simmer for 5 minutes.

- Stir in tubetti and beans. Continue to cook, stirring occasionally, for 15 minutes. Or, transfer mixture to a baking dish or casserole and bake in a 180ºC (350ºF) oven for 15 to 20 minutes or until warmed through.

Microwave Directions:
In 2L (8 cup) microwaveable container, combine broth, zucchini, onion, tomato sauce, mustard, vinegar and horseradish. Cover tightly with lid or plastic wrap. Microwave at High (100%) for 3 minutes or until onion is translucent. Stir in prepared tubetti and beans. Cover and microwave at High (100%) for 2 minutes or until heated through.

Makes 8 servings

Mushroom Lasagna

You can hardly tell there is no meat in this lasagna. It is a novel departure from the usual and is bound to be popular even for company dinners. A bonus — single portions can be frozen to be reheated later.

Preparation Time: *30 minutes*
Cooking Time: *1 hour*

15 mL	olive oil	1 tbsp
1	medium onion, chopped	1
1	clove garlic, minced	1
500 g	mushrooms, chopped	1 lb
2	stalks celery, chopped	2
$^1/_2$	sweet red or green pepper, chopped	$^1/_2$
1	can (398 mL/14 oz) Italian tomatoes	1
2 mL	each dried thyme, oregano & basil	$^1/_2$ tsp
Pinch	freshly ground pepper	Pinch
4	lasagna noodles	4
250 g	2% cottage cheese	$^1/_2$ lb
250 mL	shredded skim milk mozzarella cheese (100 g/4 oz)	1 cup
25 mL	freshly grated Parmesan cheese	2 tbsp

Each serving: 1/4 baking dish of lasagna

1 ☐ Starchy Choice
1 ▨ Fruits and Vegetables
3 ▨ Protein Choices

25 g carbohydrate
27 g protein
9 g fat

1210 kilojoules
(289 Calories)

- In a 2 L (8 cup) saucepan combine oil, onion and garlic. Stir-cook over medium heat about 3 minutes or until onion is limp. Stir in mushrooms, celery and sweet pepper. Continue to cook over medium-high heat, stirring, until liquid evaporates (this happens quickly).

- Add tomatoes, thyme, oregano, basil and pepper. Bring to a boil; reduce heat and simmer, stirring occasionally, for 15 to 20 minutes or until thickened and saucy.

- In a large saucepan, cook lasagna noodles in 3L (12 cups) rapidly boiling, lightly salted water, about 8 minutes or until *al dente* (tender but firm).

- To assemble lasagna, spread 125 mL (1/2 cup) of the sauce on bottom of a 20 cm (8 in) baking dish. Top with single layer of lasagna noodles cut to fit dish, using ends to fill spaces. Spread with half the cottage cheese and half the mozzarella, 250 mL (1 cup) sauce and another layer of noodles. Spread with remaining cottage cheese and sauce. Sprinkle with remaining mozzarella and Parmesan.

- Bake in a 180ºC (350ºF) oven for 30 minutes or until heated through.

Makes 4 servings

Cheese Zucchini Puff

Preparation Time: *10 minutes*
Cooking Time: *50 minutes*

Produce departments always seem to have zucchini available and gardens overflow with them when they are in season. And creative cooks are always coming up with new recipes for the vegetable. This innovative soufflé-like dish is one of them and it rates a 10 as a meatless lunch or supper dish.

Each serving: 200 mL(³/₄ cup)

1 🔲 Starchy Choice

1 🚫 Protein Choice

15 g carbohydrate
9 g protein
5 g fat

590 kilojoules
(141 Calories)

500 mL	shredded zucchini (2 medium, each 15 cm/6 in)	2 cups
1	medium onion, chopped	1
125 mL	dry bread crumbs	¹/₂ cup
125 mL	shredded Cheddar cheese	¹/₂ cup
15 mL	finely chopped fresh basil OR 5 mL (1 tsp) dried	1 tbsp
1	egg	1
125 mL	skim milk	¹/₂ cup
2 mL	salt	1 tsp
Pinch	freshly ground pepper	Pinch

- In a bowl, combine zucchini, onion, bread crumbs, cheese and basil.

- In a separate bowl, combine egg, milk, salt and pepper; beat lightly.

- Pour egg mixture into zucchini mixture; stir well. Spoon into a 1.5 L (6 cup) casserole or baking dish.

- Bake in a 180°C (350°F) oven for 50 minutes or until top is lightly browned and tester, inserted halfway between outside and centre of dish, comes out clean.

Makes 4 servings

Crustless Spinach Quiche

Boys and men like this spinach, cheese and egg 'pie' and don't even miss the crust. A wedge or two makes a meal. A bunch of crunchy pieces of ▦ *Extra Vegetables is all that is needed as an accompaniment.*

Preparation Time: *15 minutes*
Cooking Time : *45 minutes*

5 mL	margarine	1 tsp
1	pkg (300 g) frozen chopped spinach	1
50 mL	chopped onion	$^1/_4$ cup
250 mL	2% cottage cheese	1 cup
175 mL	shredded Edam cheese (125 g/5 oz)	$^2/_3$ cup
125 mL	freshly grated Parmesan cheese	$^1/_2$ cup
125 mL	skim milk	$^1/_2$ cup
2	eggs	2
75 mL	whole wheat flour	$^1/_3$ cup
5 mL	baking powder	1 tsp
5 mL	dried sweet basil	1 tsp
1 mL	ground nutmeg	$^1/_4$ tsp
2 mL	salt	$^1/_2$ tsp
Pinch	freshly ground pepper	Pinch

Each Serving: $^1/_8$ **of spinach pie**

$^1/_2$ ▢ Starchy Choice

2 ▨ Protein Choices

7 g carbohydrate
14 g protein
7 g fat

620 kilojoules
(147 Calories)

- Grease a 23 cm (9 in) pie plate with margarine.

- Squeeze moisture out of spinach.

- In a bowl, combine spinach, onion, cottage cheese, Edam and Parmesan cheeses.

- In a blender or food processor, combine milk, eggs, flour, baking powder, basil, nutmeg, salt and pepper. Process at high speed for 1 minute. (Alternatively, in a bowl, whisk ingredients together vigorously.)

- Pour egg mixture over vegetable mixture; mix well. Pour into prepared pie plate.

- Bake in a 180°C (350°F) oven for 45 minutes or until knife inserted near center comes out clean. Let stand for 5 minutes before serving.

Makes 8 servings

Microwave Directions:
Cover filled, microwaveable pie plate with parchment or waxed paper. Microwave, turning pie plate every 3 minutes, at Medium High (70%) for 12 minutes or until knife inserted near center comes out clean. Let stand for 5 minutes before serving.

Make It Meatless

Recipe	Food Choices per Serving		Energy per Serving kilojoules Calories		
Lentil Curry with Cucumber & Bananas	1 ☐ Starchy; ½ ▨ Protein; 1 ▨ Fruits & Vegetables		520	124	p. 94
Pasta E Fagioli (Pasta & Beans)	2 ☐ Starchy; 1 ▨ Protein		730	173	p. 95
Twice Cooked Beans	2 ▲ Starchy; 1 ▨ Protein		790	187	p. 96
Mexican Beans & Rice	1 ☐ Starchy; 1 ▨ Protein; 1 ▨ Fruits & Vegetables		680	163	p. 97
Quickest Ever Chili	2 ☐ Starchy; 1 ▨ Protein		810	192	p. 98
Spanish Rice with Chick Peas	1 ☐ Starchy; 1 ▨ Protein; 1 ▨ Fruits & Vegetables		670	159	p. 99
Space Age Barbecued Beans	2 ☐ Starchy; ½ ▨ Protein		680	162	p. 100
Mushroom Lasagna	1 ☐ Starchy; 3 ▨ Protein; 1 ▨ Fruits & Vegetables		1210	289	p. 101
Cheese Zucchini Puff	1 ☐ Starchy; 1 ▨ Protein		590	141	p. 102
Crustless Spinach Quiche	½ ☐ Starchy; 2 ▨ Protein		620	147	p. 103

Vegetable Variations

It puzzles me when I realize some people think vegetables are blah and boring.

Every time I visit a farmer's market or walk down the fresh produce aisle of the super market I feel excited. What an array! Every color of the rainbow is there before my eyes along with every shape imaginable. Red round tomatoes, orange pointed carrots, green leafy lettuce, purple plump eggplant, yellow stringy beans. And there is just as fabulous a selection along the aisles of the canned goods and frozen packages.

Vegetables do add assorted colors, flavors, shapes and textures. A dinner without them would be boring and unbalanced. And it is the vegetables in our diet that supply us with carbohydrates, important vitamins and minerals plus dietary fibre. The only vegetables I find blah are the ones that are overcooked. They are dull and lifeless.

My rule with vegetables is to cook them only until tender-crisp. They are best that way, and more tasty than when they are flabby and mushy.

If you choose canned vegetables for your meals, remember they just have to be warmed; processing has already cooked them. Following the recipes here you can select a few new and tasty vegetable dishes, everything from a colorful mixture to a blend of two together.

Note: Some vegetables are high in dietary fibre and low in available carbohydrate. They may be counted as **+** *Extra Vegetables if they are eaten in the portion size indicated with the recipe, because only part of the carbohydrate actually ends up as sugar in the blood.*

Baked Asparagus

Preparation Time: *10 minutes*
Cooking Time: *15 minutes*

Each serving: 5 stalks

1 ➕ Extra Vegetables

3 g carbohydrate
1 g protein

70 kilojoules
(16 Calories)

Asparagus really does have the color and taste of Spring if you steam it in just the water clinging to it after being rinsed.

20	stalks asparagus	20
Pinch	freshly ground pepper	Pinch
1/2	lemon, cut into 4 wedges	1/2

Microwave Directions:
Layer asparagus in microwaveable dish. Sprinkle with pepper and lemon juice. Cover tightly with lid or plastic wrap. Microwave, rotating dish halfway through cooking time, at High (100%) for 4 minutes or until just tender. Let stand for 2 minutes.

- Rinse asparagus stalks, place them in a single or double layer in a 20 cm (8 in) baking dish or covered casserole. Sprinkle with pepper and the juice from 1 lemon wedge.

- Cover dish tightly with foil or its own cover. Bake in a 180ºC (350ºF) oven for 15 minutes or until tender-crisp.

- Serve 1 wedge lemon with each 5 stalks of asparagus.

Makes 4 servings

Parmesan Tomatoes

Preparation Time: *5 minutes*
Cooking Time : *7 minutes*

Each Serving: 1 tomato half

1 ➕ Extra Vegetables

2 g carbohydrate
1 g protein

50 kilojoules
(12 Calories)

Hot, juicy baked tomatoes that hold their shape are as pretty as a picture served beside a barbecued or baked steak, chop or chicken breast.

2	medium tomatoes	2
10 mL	freshly grated Parmesan cheese	2 tsp
2 mL	dried basil	1/2 tsp
Pinch	freshly ground pepper	Pinch

Microwave Directions:
In microwaveable pie plate, place tomato halves. Cover with vented plastic wrap. Microwave at High (100%) for 1 minute. Sprinkle cheese mixture over tomatoes. Cover with waxed paper. Microwave at High (100%) for 30 seconds or until cheese just starts to melt.

- Cut tomatoes in half. Place in a small baking dish cut side up.

- Combine cheese, basil and pepper. Sprinkle over tomatoes.

- Bake in a 180ºC (350ºF) oven for about 7 minutes or until heated through.

Makes 4 servings

Ginger Orange Carrots

My family loves these spicy and sweet carrots and so will yours.

300 g	carrots, thinly sliced (500 mL/2 cups)	10 oz
1	small orange	1
1 mL	ground ginger	1/4 tsp
5 mL	unsalted butter	1 tsp

- Scrub carrots. Peel if outside peel is coarse. Cut into very thin slices to make about 500 mL (2 cups).
- Grate orange rind to measure 5 mL (1 tsp). Squeeze juice from orange; reserve.
- In saucepan, combine carrot slices, orange rind, half the orange juice, ginger and butter. Braise, covered, over medium heat for 12 minutes.
- Add remaining orange juice; cook, uncovered, just until carrots are tender and juice has evaporated.

Makes 4 servings

Preparation Time: *5 minutes*
Cooking Time : *15-20 minutes*

Each Serving: 125 mL(1/2 cup)

1 ◢ Fruits & Vegetables

11 g carbohydrate
1 g protein
1 g fat

240 kilojoules
(57 Calories)

Microwave Directions:
In microwaveable container, combine carrot slices, orange rind, juice, ginger and butter. Cover tightly with lid or plastic wrap. Microwave at High (100%) for 4¹/₂ minutes or until carrots are just tender. Let stand for 2 minutes.

Steamed Leeks and Zucchini

Leeks look like very large green onions. They are milder than regular or green onions.

3	medium leeks	3
3	medium zucchini (each 15 cm/6 in)	3
Pinch	each ground cumin and nutmeg	Pinch
50 mL	chopped sweet red pepper OR seeded chopped tomato (optional)	1/4 cup

- Trim coarse green leaves from leeks; rinse under cold running water. Cut into 1 cm (1/2 in) slices.
- Rinse zucchini. Remove stem and flower ends. Cut into 1 cm (1/2 in) slices.
- In a steamer basket or perforated pan, combine leeks and zucchini; sprinkle with cumin and nutmeg. Place over saucepan of boiling water. Cover and steam for 4 to 5 minutes or until leeks are transparent and zucchini is tender-crisp. Add chopped pepper, if desired. Toss gently and serve.

Makes 4 servings

Preparation Time: *5 minutes*
Cooking Time: *5 minutes*

Each serving: 125 mL(1/2 cup)

1 ✚✚ Extra Vegetables

4 g carbohydrate
1 g protein

80 kilojoules
(20 Calories)

Braised Vegetable Medley

Preparation Time: *7 minutes*
Cooking Time: *15 minutes*

Each serving: 125 mL(¹/₂ cup)

¹/₂ ▟ Fruits & Vegetables
 6 g carbohydrate
 1 g protein

 120 kilojoules
 (28 Calories)

Microwave Directions:
On a microwaveable plate,
arrange squash and carrots
around outside edge. Place
zucchini, onion and celery in
the center. Pour on chicken
broth; sprinkle with pepper.
Cover with plastic wrap.
Microwave at High (100%)
for 10 minutes. Let stand for
5 minutes.

When an assortment of vegetables cooks together in the braising liquid the flavors mingle.

250 mL	chopped onion (¹/₂ Spanish onion)	1 cup
250 mL	cubed zucchini	1 cup
250 mL	cubed butternut squash	1 cup
250 mL	cubed carrot (3 medium)	1 cup
250 mL	sliced celery (3 stalks)	1 cup
125 mL	chicken broth	¹/₂ cup
Pinch	freshly ground pepper	Pinch

- In a 2 L (8 cup) saucepan, combine onion, zucchini, squash, carrot, celery, chicken broth and pepper. Bring to a boil over medium heat; reduce heat, cover and simmer over medium-low heat about 12 minutes or until carrots and celery are tender-crisp, and zucchini and squash are tender.
- Remove cover and if there is liquid in bottom of pan, continue to cook, stirring occasionally, for 1 to 2 minutes to allow most of liquid to evaporate.

Makes 6 servings

Braised Sweet Peppers

Preparation Time: *5 minutes*
Cooking Time : *7 minutes*

**Each Serving: 1/2 large
 pepper in strips**

1 ✚✚ Extra Vegetables
 3 g carbohydrate
 1 g protein

 50 kilojoules
 (12 Calories)

Microwave Directions:
In microwaveable container,
combine peppers and onion
in 2 to 3 layers. Add only 50
mL (¹/₄ cup) chicken broth,
ginger and pepper. Cover
tightly with lid or plastic
wrap. Microwave at High
(100%) for 5 minutes or until
just tender. Let stand for 2
minutes.

Bright slivers of red and green peppers will definitely add sparkle to meals that might otherwise seem a little dull.

1	large sweet green pepper	1
1	large sweet red pepper	1
1	small onion, chopped	1
125 mL	chicken broth	¹/₂ cup
5 mL	grated fresh ginger root OR 1 mL (1/4 tsp) dried	1 tsp
Pinch	freshly ground pepper	Pinch

- Cut peppers in half and remove seeds. Cut into long thin strips.
- In a skillet or saucepan, combine pepper strips, onion and chicken broth.
- Bring to a boil, reduce heat, and stir-braise (braise while stirring occasionally) for 5 to 7 minutes or until peppers are just tender-crisp. Add a little extra water, if required, to prevent peppers from sticking.
- Sprinkle with ginger and pepper. Toss gently and serve.

Makes 4 servings

Braised Red Cabbage

Cabbage is at its best when it is quickly cooked before any strong flavors develop. If you have a processor, use it to shred the cabbage. If not, the shredding is done easily with a sharp knife. A dull one bruises the cabbage.

Preparation Time: *10 minutes*
Cooking Time : *15 minutes*

¹/₂	medium red cabbage, finely shredded (1 L/4 cups)	¹/₂
1	small onion, chopped	1
3	whole allspice berries	3
2	whole cloves	2
5 mL	grated orange rind	1 tsp
125 mL	water	¹/₂ cup
50 mL	orange juice	¹/₄ cup
10 mL	soy sauce	2 tsp
10 mL	vinegar	2 tsp
5 mL	cornstarch	1 tsp

Each Serving: 200 mL(³/₄ cup)

¹/₂ 🔳 Fruits & Vegetables

6 g carbohydrate

*100 kilojoules
(24 Calories)*

- In a large skillet or 2L (8 cup) saucepan, combine cabbage, onion, allspice, cloves, orange rind and water.

- Bring to a boil, reduce heat and stir-braise (braise while stirring occasionally) for 12 minutes or until cabbage is tender-crisp. Add a little extra water, if required, to prevent cabbage from sticking to the bottom of the pan.

- In a small dish, combine orange juice, soy sauce and vinegar. Stir in cornstarch until smooth.

- Stir into cabbage mixture, continuing to cook and stirring until a thin sauce coats cabbage.

Makes 4 servings

Turnip Cubes

Preparation Time: *5 minutes*
Cooking Time: *12 minutes*

Each serving: 125 mL(¹/₂ cup)

¹/₂ ◢ Fruits & Vegetables

5 g carbohydrate

80 kilojoules
(20 Calories)

Microwave Directions:
In microwaveable container, layer turnip cubes. Sprinkle with 50 mL (¹/₄ cup) water, cumin and pepper. Cover tightly with lid or plastic wrap. Microwave, turning container halfway through cooking time, at High (100%) for 8 minutes or until just tender. Let stand for 4 minutes.

Both the purple-tipped, small white turnip and the yellow rutabaga are known as turnips. Either one cooks up quickly cut into small cubes.

500 g	white turnip or rutabaga	1 lb
Pinch	mace or powdered cumin	Pinch
Pinch	freshly ground pepper	Pinch

- Peel turnips and cut into small 1 cm (¹/₂ in) cubes.

- In a saucepan, combine turnips with enough water to cover. Bring to a boil, cover and cook about 12 minutes or until fork-tender.

- Drain and sprinkle with mace and pepper. Toss gently

Makes 4 servings

Squash and Potato Purée

Preparation Time: *7 minutes*
Cooking Time: *10 minutes*

Each serving: 125 mL(¹/₂ cup)

1 ◢ Fruits & Vegetables

11 g carbohydrate
2 g protein

220 kilojoules
(52 Calories)

Microwave Directions:
In small microwaveable container, arrange squash and potato into layers. Add clove and cumin. Cover with lid or plastic wrap. Microwave at High (100%) for 7 minutes or until soft. Let stand for 3 minutes. Continue as recipe directs.

I often vary the flavor of vegetables by puréeing or mashing two or three of them together as in this squash and potato combo. It is just another way to show that vegetables never should be boring.

¹/₂	butternut or acorn squash, 250 g(¹/₂ lb)	¹/₂
1	medium potato	1
1	whole clove	1
1 mL	ground cumin	¹/₄ tsp

- Peel squash and potato; dice or slice.

- In a saucepan, combine vegetables with clove and enough water to cover. Bring to a boil; reduce heat; cover and cook for 7 to 10 minutes or until soft.

- Drain; remove and discard clove.

- Mash by hand, or purée in food processor. Add cumin.

Makes 4 servings

Baked Potato Chips

Potato lovers and others will adore these. It's amazing how far just a little margarine will go when a small brush is used for spreading it on the potato slices. Yes, there is enough to give all the potato slices a light glaze of buttery flavor.

Preparation Time: *10 minutes*
Cooking Time : *20-30 minutes*

2	baking potatoes	2
15 mL	melted margarine	2 tsp
	Salt and freshly ground pepper	

- Scrub potatoes well, but do not peel.

- Place one oven rack in upper third of oven, the second one in the lower third of oven. Preheat oven to 250ºC (500ºF).

- Lightly brush about 5 mL (1 tsp) melted margarine on 2 nonstick baking sheets.

- Cut potatoes crosswise into 3 mm (1/8 in) think slices, 12 per half potato. Rinse with cold water, drain, and pat dry with paper towels.

- Arrange in single layer on prepared baking sheets. Brush remaining margarine very lightly across top of each potato slice.

- Place one baking sheet on each rack. Bake for 10 minutes. Switch pan positions and bake about 10 minutes longer or until potatoes are crisp and browned around edges.

- Transfer to serving platter. Sprinkle with little bit of salt and pepper. Serve immediately.

Makes 4 servings

Each Serving: ½ **potato**
(12 chips)

1 ☐ Starchy Choice

½ ▲ Fats & Oils Choice

12 g carbohydrate
2 g protein
3 g fat

350 kilojoules
(83 Calories)

Cheesy Chive Potatoes

Preparation Time: *20 minutes*

Each serving: 125 mL(¹/₂ cup)

1 ☐ Starchy Choice

    12 g carbohydrate
    4 g protein

    270 kilojoules
    (64 Calories)

Cooked potatoes are more exciting when dressed up a bit with cottage cheese and chives.

3	medium potatoes, boiled or baked* and peeled	3
125 mL	2% cottage cheese	¹/₂ cup
15 mL	fresh or frozen chopped chives	1 tbsp
1 mL	salt	¹/₄ tsp
Pinch	freshly ground pepper	Pinch

Microwave Directions:
In microwaveable container, roughly mash potatoes; stir in cottage cheese, chives, salt and pepper. Cover with lid. Microwave at High (100%), rotating halfway through cooking time, for 5 minutes.

- If potatoes have been refrigerated, place them in a steamer over boiling water for about 10 minutes.
- In a warm ovenproof bowl, roughly mash potatoes; stir in cottage cheese, chives, salt and pepper.
- Serve immediately or keep warm in 100ºC (200ºF) oven.

Makes 6 servings

Schnippled Green Beans

Preparation Time: *10 minutes*

This snappy salad is similar to the one made by Mennonite cooks in the Kitchener-Waterloo area of Ontario.

1	pkg (300 g) cut or frenched frozen green beans (375 mL/1¹/₂ cups)	1
2	green onions, sliced	2
25 mL	2% yogurt	2 tbsp
10 mL	vinegar	2 tsp
	Sugar substitute equivalent to 5 mL (1 tsp) sugar	
Pinch	freshly ground pepper	Pinch

Each serving: 125 mL(¹/₂ cup)
++

1   Extra Vegetables

    4 g carbohydrate
    1 g protein

    80 kilojoules
    (20 Calories)

- Defrost beans ahead (or place frozen beans in a sieve and pour boiling water over, then cool under cold running water; drain well).
- In a bowl, combine beans and green onions.
- In a small dish, combine yogurt, vinegar, sugar substitute and pepper; mix well. Pour yogurt sauce over beans. Toss to coat.

Makes 3 serving

Tomato Sauce

For a rich, tomatoey sauce, I always use pulpy, plum tomatoes. This one keeps well, so it is smart to make it up ahead on an evening or Saturday set aside for cooking. Then all you have to do at mealtime is cook the pasta and heat the sauce. Complete the meal with a salad of crispy greens.

Preparation Time: *10 minutes*
Cooking Time: *30-45 minutes*

1	can (540mL/19 oz) Italian plum tomatoes	1
1	packet or cube beef bouillon	1
2	cloves garlic, finely chopped	2
2	stalks celery, chopped	2
1	medium onion, chopped	1
1/2	green pepper, seeded & chopped	1/2
25 mL	chopped fresh parsley OR 10 mL (2 tsp) dried	2 tbsp
15 mL	chopped fresh basil OR 5 mL (1 tsp) dried	1 tbsp
2 mL	salt	1/2 tsp
2 mL	each thyme and oregano	1/2 tsp
Dash	hot pepper sauce	Dash

- In a saucepan, combine all ingredients. Stir, breaking up tomatoes.

- Bring to a boil; reduce heat and simmer for 30 to 45 minutes or until vegetables are tender. Purée if desired. Refrigerate or freeze.

Makes 375 mL (1¹/₂ cups)

Each serving: 25 mL (2 tbsp)

1 ▉ Extra

 3 g carbohydrate
 1 g protein

 70 kilojoules
 (16 Calories)

Each serving: 75 mL (¹/₃ cup)

1 ▉ Fruits & Vegetables

 10 g carbohydrate
 2 g protein

 200 kilojoules
 (48 Calories)

❖ Timely Tip:

Store tomato sauce in a covered jar or plastic container in the refrigerator for up to 10 days or freeze it for up to 4 months. Remember to label with name, date and instructions for use, just in case you forget what it is.

Vegetable Variations

Recipe	Food Choices per Serving		Energy per Serving		
			kiljoules	Calories	
Baked Asparagus	1 ++	Extra Vegetables	70	16	p. 106
Parmesan Tomatoes	1 ++	Extra Vegetables	50	12	p. 106
Ginger Orange Carrots	1 ◨	Fruits & Vegetables	240	57	p. 107
Steamed Leeks and Zucchini	1 ++	Extra Vegetables	80	20	p. 107
Braised Vegetable Medley	¹/₂ ◨	Fruits & Vegetables	120	28	p. 108
Braised Sweet Peppers	1 ++	Extra Vegetables	50	12	p. 108
Braised Red Cabbage	¹/₂ ◨	Fruits & Vegetables	100	24	p. 109
Turnip Cubes	¹/₂ ◨	Fruits & Vegetables	80	20	p. 110
Squash and Potato Purée	1 ◨	Fruits & Vegetables	220	52	p. 110
Baked Potato Chips	1 ☐	Starchy; ¹/₂ ◣ Fats & Oils	350	83	p. 111
Schnippled Green Beans	1 ++	Extra Vegetables	80	20	p. 112
Cheesy Chive Potatoes	1 ☐	Starchy	270	64	p. 112
Tomato Sauce	1 ◨	Fruits & Vegetables	200	48	p. 113

Bake It Fresh

Baked goods seem to please everyone — seniors, the middle-aged, yuppies, teenagers and kids.

Kneading real bread dough made with yeast is pleasant, relaxing and fascinating as you feel it become elastic under your hands. Watching quick breads — muffins, scones — plump up as they bake and brown is also exciting.

There is no reason to exclude these breads or cakes, cookies and bars from a balanced diet. Eating them in moderation is the secret to helping control energy intake.

I've created these recipes using the bare minimum of sugar and fat. When sugar (or molasses) is called for, it's there to enhance both the flavor and texture of the baked product.

One of the challenges I set for myself in developing these recipes was to come up with a real cake using as little sugar as possible. The angel cake and chiffon cakes are light and airy. Neither they nor the squares are sugary sweet.

So, now you can have your cake and eat it too. But, it's important to make the exact number of cookies and cut the same number of pieces of cake or bars as indicated in the recipe because the calculations are based on this yield.

Auntie Kay's Magic Bread

Preparation Time: 1½ hours
Baking Time: 30-40 minutes

A good yeast dough can be made into all sorts of bread. This one is one of the simplest but still the best that I have ever made and that is why it is the only one in the book. Bread freezes well, so while you are at it, make a double batch by simply multiplying all the ingredients by two. If you shape the loaves as I suggest, they can bake on a baking sheet and there will be no need for loaf pans. Better than that, make one or two loaves and a couple of other shapes — a pizza crust, or buns.

5 mL	granulated sugar	1 tsp
50 mL	warm water	¼ cup
1	pkg active dry yeast OR 15 mL (1 tbsp)	1
250 mL	water	1 cup
500 mL	all-purpose flour	2 cups
250 mL	whole wheat flour	1 cup
5 mL	salt	1 tsp
5 mL	corn oil	1 tsp
25 mL	corn meal	2 tbsp

- In a small bowl or measure, combine sugar and 50 mL (¼ cup) warm water. Sprinkle yeast over the top and let stand for 10 minutes or until frothy. (This activates the yeast.)
- In a large mixing bowl, combine 250 mL (1 cup) water and yeast mixture.
- Stir in half the all-purpose and half the whole wheat flours, and the salt. Beat vigorously about 30 strokes.
- Stir in the remaining flour, a little at a time, first stirring with spoon, then working it in with hands to form a rough dough.
- Turn out onto a lightly floured work surface, countertop or bread board.
- Knead dough, turning with fingers and pressing with the heel of the hand about 10 minutes or until the dough is smooth, satiny, elastic, and feels alive under the hands.
- Brush oil on bottom of clean bowl. Place dough in bowl, turn to coat dough very slightly with oil.
- Cover and let rise in a draft-free place about 1 hour or until it is double its original size.
- Push down and knead again for a few minutes.

- Sprinkle cornmeal on a lightly greased or nonstick baking sheet or jelly roll pan.

- With a sharp knife, cut dough into two equal portions. Shape each into a ball and let rest for 3 to 4 minutes under a towel. If necessary, lightly flour work surface to prevent dough from sticking.

- Form each ball into a loaf by pressing it into a 20 cm (8 in) square. Fold it in half lengthwise; pinch seam tightly to seal. Tuck ends under, pressing firmly. Place ovals on prepared pan, seam side down.

- Place pan in warm place. Lightly cover with a cloth. Let rise for 30 to 45 minutes or until loaves are nearly double in size.

- Bake in a 190ºC (375ºF) oven 35 minutes or until browned and loaves sound hollow when tapped.

- Remove from oven. Turn loaves out, top crust up, onto wire racks to cool.

Makes 2 loaves, 9 slices each

❖ **Timely Tip:**

To freeze bread in any of its various shapes, first allow it to cool to room temperature. Sometimes I slice it before I freeze it. Wrap it in airtight freezer wrap, plastic wrap or foil. Seal package, label it and store it in the freezer. It will keep its fresh-baked goodness in the freezer up to 3 months. Thaw at room temperature. Frozen slices can be popped into the toaster without being thawed.

Each Serving: 1 slice

1 ☐ Starchy Choice

15 g carbohydrate
2 g protein

290 kilojoules
(68 Calories)

Scones

Preparation Time: *5 minutes*
Baking Time: *30 minutes*

Scones are very British and usually make their appearance at teatime in England. I like them instead of bread at breakfast, lunch or dinner.

250 mL	all-purpose flour	1 cup
125 mL	whole wheat flour	$1/2$ cup
7 mL	baking powder	1-$1/2$ tsp
2 mL	baking soda	$1/2$ tsp
2 mL	salt	$1/2$ tsp
125 mL	buttermilk or sour skim milk*	$1/2$ cup
1	egg	1
15 mL	melted margarine	1 tbsp

Each serving: 1 wedge,
1/8 of scone

Plain Scones:

1 ☐ Starchy Choice

$1/2$ ▲ Fats & Oils Choice

 16 g carbohydrate
 4 g protein
 2 g fat

 410 kilojoules
 (98 Calories)

Cheese and Chive Scones:

1 ☐ Starchy Choice

$1/2$ ▲ Fats & Oils Choice

 16 g carbohydrate
 5 g protein
 3 g fat

 470 kilojoules
 (111 Calories)

Raisin and Lemon Scones:

1 ☐ Starchy Choice

$1/2$ ◪ Fruits & Vegetables

$1/2$ ▲ Fats & Oils Choice

 20 g carbohydrate
 4 g protein
 2 g fat

 480 kilojoules
 (114 Calories)

- In a mixing bowl, combine flours, baking powder, soda and salt.
- In a small bowl, whisk together buttermilk, egg and margarine; stir into dry ingredients just until mixed. Do not overmix.
- On a lightly floured surface, knead dough for 6 to 8 strokes and form into a 4 cm (1$1/2$ in) thick round biscuit.
- Place on a lightly greased or nonstick baking sheet. Pat down and cut slashes across the top in the form of an X.
- Bake in a 180ºC (350ºF) oven for 30 minutes or until golden brown.
- Cut into 8 wedges to serve.

Makes 8 servings

Variations:
Cheese and Chive Scones: Add 25 mL (2 tbsp) grated Parmesan cheese and 25 mL (2 tbsp) fresh or frozen chopped chives to the dry ingredients.

Raisin and Lemon Scones: Add 50 mL $1/4$ cup) chopped raisins and 5 mL (1 tsp) grated lemon rind to the dry ingredients.

♣ **Timely Tip:**

*To make sour skim milk, add 5 mL (1 tsp) lemon juice or vinegar to 125 mL ($1/2$ cup) skim milk. Let stand for 5 to 10 minutes at room temperature, then use.

Blueberry Scones

*If you ever serve these to your friends at tea-time or snack-time,
they'll probably ask for the recipe.*

Preparation Time: *10 minutes*
Baking Time : *20 minutes*

250 mL	all-purpose flour	1 cup
125 mL	whole wheat flour	$^1/_2$ cup
10 mL	baking powder	2 tsp
10 mL	granulated sugar*	2 tsp
2 mL	salt	$^1/_2$ tsp
125 mL	2% milk	$^1/_2$ cup
1	egg	1
25 mL	margarine, melted	2 tbsp
250 mL	blueberries	1 cup

Each Serving: 1 scone

1 ☐ Starchy Choice
1 ▲ Fats & Oils Choice

17 g carbohydrate
3 g protein
4 g fat

490 kilojoules
(116 Calories)

** The added sugar in the recipe has been included in the carbohydrate
and Food Choice Values.*

- In mixing bowl, combine flours, baking powder, sugar and
  salt.

- In small bowl, whisk together milk, egg and margarine.

- Make a well in flour mixture; pour in milk mixture. Add
  blueberries.

- Stir quickly just until dry ingredients are moistened. Do not
  overmix or beat. Batter should be rough and lumpy.

- Drop by 125 mL ($^1/_2$ cup) portions onto lightly buttered or
  nonstick baking sheet, to make 10 scones. Flatten slightly
  with back of spoon.

- Bake in 200ºC (400ºF) oven for 20 minutes or until golden
  brown.

Makes 10 scones

Apricot Coconut Bran Muffins

Preparation Time: *15 minutes*
Baking Time: *20 minutes*

Every time I make basic bran muffins I can't resist embellishing them with fruits, nuts and spices. Now I make this version regularly because I like the addition of coconut and apricots.

250 mL	all-purpose flour	1 cup
250 mL	natural bran	1 cup
50 mL	lightly packed brown sugar*	1/4 cup
10 mL	baking powder	2 tsp
2 mL	ground coriander or nutmeg	1/2 tsp
2 mL	salt	1/2 tsp
250 mL	2% milk	1 cup
1	egg	1
25 mL	margarine, melted	2 tbsp
15 mL	molasses*	1 tbsp
5 mL	vanilla	1 tsp
125 mL	unsweetened dessicated coconut	1/2 cup
50 mL	chopped dried apricots	1/4 cup

Each serving: 1 muffin

1 ☐ Starchy Choice
1 ▨ Fruits & Vegetables
1 ▲ Fats & Oils Choice

24 g carbohydrate
4 g protein
7 g fat

690 kilojoules
(164 Calories)

*The added sugar in the recipe has been included in the carbohydrate and Food Choice Values

- Lightly grease muffin cups, or spray with low-calorie nonstick vegetable coating or line with paper cups.

- In mixing bowl, combine flour, bran, brown sugar, baking powder, coriander and salt.

- In small bowl, beat together milk, egg, margarine, molasses and vanilla.

- Make a well in flour mixture; pour in milk mixture. Add coconut and apricots.

- Stir quickly just until lightly mixed. Do not overmix or beat. Batter should be rough and lumpy.

- Divide evenly among prepared muffin cups, filling each 2/3 full. Bake in 200°C (400°F) oven for 20 minutes or until golden brown.

Makes 10 muffins

Microwave Directions:

Spoon batter into paper cup-lined microwaveable muffin pan. Microwave at High (100%) for 2 1/2 minutes or just until tops are no longer moist. Let stand for 2 minutes. Remove from muffin pan to wire rack. Repeat with remaining batter.

Spicy Oat Bran Muffins

These have become favorite breakfast muffins. They're great split and toasted under the broiler.

Preparation Time: *10 minutes*
Baking Time: *20 minutes*

250 mL	all-purpose flour	1 cup
250 mL	oat bran cereal	1 cup
25 mL	lightly packed brown sugar *	2 tbsp
12 mL	baking powder	2¹/₂ tsp
5 mL	ground cinnamon	1 tsp
2 mL	ground nutmeg	¹/₂ tsp
2 mL	salt	¹/₂ tsp
250 mL	2% milk	1 cup
1	egg	1
50 mL	margarine, melted	¹/₄ cup
5 mL	vanilla	1 tsp

Each serving: 1 muffin

1 ☐ Starchy Choice
1 ▲ Fats & Oils Choice

15 g carbohydrate
4 g protein
5 g fat

The added sugar in the recipe has been included in the carbohydrate and Food Choice Values

540 kilojoules
(128 Calories)

- Lightly grease muffin cups, spray with low-calorie vegetable coating or line with paper cups.

- In mixing bowl, combine flour, bran, brown sugar, baking powder, cinnamon, nutmeg and salt.

- In small bowl, beat together milk, egg, margarine and vanilla.

- Make a well in flour mixture; pour in milk mixture.

- Stir quickly just until lightly mixed. Do not overmix or beat. Batter should be rough and lumpy.

- Divide evenly among prepared muffin cups, filling each 2/3 full.

- Bake in 200ºC (400ºF) oven for 20 minutes or until golden brown.

Makes 12 muffins

Microwave Directions:

Add an additional 2 mL (¹/₂ tsp) cinnamon to dry ingredients. Spoon batter into paper cup-lined microwaveable muffin pan. Sprinkle tops with about 2 mL (¹/₂ tsp) cinnamon. Microwave, 6 at a time, at High (100%) for 2¹/₂ minutes or just until tops are no longer moist. Let stand for 2 minutes. Remove from muffin pan to wire rack. Repeat with remaining batter.

Raisin Oat Bran Muffins

Preparation Time: *10 minutes*
Baking Time: *20-25 minutes*

Chopping the raisins releases some of their natural sweetness and spreads them more evenly through the batter.

250 mL	all-purpose flour	1 cup
175 mL	oat bran	$^2/_3$ cup
	Sugar substitute equivalent to 15 mL (1 tbsp) sugar	
10 mL	baking powder	2 tsp
2 mL	baking soda	$^1/_2$ tsp
2 mL	ground cardamom	$^1/_2$ tsp
2 mL	salt	$^1/_2$ tsp
200 mL	buttermilk or sour skim milk*	$^3/_4$ cup
1	egg, lightly beaten	1
15 mL	canola oil	1 tbsp
15 mL	molasses	1 tbsp
5 mL	vanilla	1 tsp
50 mL	raisins, finely chopped	$^1/_4$ cup

Each serving: 1 muffin

1 ⬜ Starchy Choice

$^1/_2$ ◢◣ Fats & Oils Choice

13 g carbohydrate
3 g protein
2 g fat

340 kilojoules
(82 Calories)

- Lightly grease muffin cups, spray with low-calorie vegetable coating or line with paper muffin cups.

- In a bowl, combine flour, oat bran, sugar substitute, baking powder, baking soda, cardamom and salt.

- In a separate small mixing bowl, combine buttermilk, egg, canola oil, molasses and vanilla.

- Make a well in dry ingredients; pour in buttermilk mixture and add raisins. Mix just until dry ingredients are moistened.

- Fill muffin cups $^2/_3$ full.

- Bake in a 200ºC (400ºF) oven for 20 minutes or until lightly browned.

Makes 12 muffins

* See Timely Tip, p. 118

Microwave Directions:
Spoon batter into paper cup-lined microwaveable muffin pan. Sprinkle tops with about 2 mL ($^1/_2$ tsp) cinnamon. Microwave, 6 at a time, at High (100%) for $2^1/_2$ minutes or just until tops are no longer moist. Let stand for 2 minutes. Remove from muffin pan to wire rack to cool. Repeat with remaining batter.

Orange Cornmeal Muffins

Orange brings out the crunchy sweetness of the cornmeal. Serve these golden gems with Quickest Ever Chili (recipe, p. 98) or Mexican Beans and Rice (recipe, p. 97) or as an energizing snack.

Preparation Time: *10 minutes*
Standing Time : *10 minutes*
Baking Time : *20 minutes*

75 mL	cornmeal	1/3 cup
125 mL	skim milk	1/2 cup
75 mL	orange juice	1/3 cup
15 mL	corn syrup	1 tbsp
5 mL	vanilla	1 tsp
250 mL	all-purpose flour	1 cup
	Sugar substitute equivalent to 15 mL (1 tbsp) sugar	
10 mL	baking powder	2 tsp
10 mL	grated orange rind	2 tsp
2 mL	baking soda	1/2 tsp
2 mL	salt	1/2 tsp
1	egg, lightly beaten	1
125 mL	grated carrot	1/2 cup
15 mL	margarine, melted	1 tbsp

Each Serving: 1 muffin

1 ☐ Starchy Choice

13 g carbohydrate
2 g protein
1 g fat

290 kilojoules
(69 Calories)

- Lightly grease muffin cups, spray with low calorie vegetable coating or line with paper muffin cups.

- In a bowl, combine cornmeal, skim milk, orange juice, corn syrup and vanilla; let stand for 10 minutes.

- In a separate bowl, combine flour, sugar substitute, baking powder, orange rind, soda and salt.

- Stir egg, carrot and margarine into cornmeal mixture.

- Add cornmeal mixture to dry ingredients; stir just until all dry ingredients are moistened.

- Fill muffin cups 2/3 full.

- Bake in a 200ºC (400ºF) oven for 20 minutes or until golden brown.

Makes 12 medium muffins

Microwave Directions:
Spoon batter into paper cup-lined microwaveable muffin pan. Sprinkle tops with about 2 mL (1/2 tsp) cinnamon. Microwave, 6 at a time, at High (100%) for 21/2 minutes or just until tops are no longer moist. Let stand for 2 minutes. Remove from muffin pan to wire rack to cool. Repeat with remaining batter.

Banana Nut Muffins

Preparation Time: *10 minutes*
Baking Time: *20-25 minutes*

Surprise your friends with muffin cakes. Drop the batter by the spoonful into 12 mounds on a lightly greased baking sheet. It is easier than using muffin cups. The result is muffins that look like big cookies.

250 mL	all-purpose flour	1 cup
125 mL	whole wheat flour	1/2 cup
	Sugar substitute equivalent to 15 mL (1 tbsp) sugar	
7 mL	baking powder	1-1/2 tsp
2 mL	baking soda	1/2 tsp
2 mL	salt	1/2 tsp
125 mL	buttermilk or sour skim milk	1/2 cup
1	banana, mashed	1
1	egg, lightly beaten	1
5 mL	vanilla	1 tsp
15 mL	melted margarine	1 tbsp
25 mL	chopped walnuts	2 tbsp

Each serving: 1 muffin

1 ⬜ Starchy Choice

1/2 ▲ Fats & Oils Choice

13 g carbohydrate
3 g protein
2 g fat

340 kilojoules
(82 Calories)

- Lightly grease muffin cups, spray with low-calorie vegetable coating or line with paper muffin cups.

- In a bowl, combine flours, sugar substitute, baking powder, baking soda and salt.

- In a separate bowl, combine buttermilk with mashed banana, egg, vanilla and margarine. Make a well in dry ingredients; pour in banana mixture and add nuts.

- Mix just until dry ingredients are moistened.

- Fill muffin cups 2/3 full.

- Bake in a 200ºC (400ºF) oven for 20 minutes or until lightly browned.

Makes 12 muffins

* See Timely Tip, p. 118

Microwave Directions:
Spoon batter into paper cup-lined microwaveable muffin pan. Sprinkle tops with about 2 mL (1/2 tsp) cinnamon. Microwave, 6 at a time, at High (100%) for 2 1/2 minutes or just until tops are no longer moist. Let stand for 2 minutes. Remove from muffin pan to wire rack to cool. Repeat with remaining batter.

Apricot Loaf

This moist, fruity loaf mellows after being stored for a few days, so make it several days before you plan to serve it. Wrap it in plastic wrap once it has cooled, then keep it in the bread box or refrigerator. The whole loaf or portions of it freeze well. Slices, wrapped in plastic and stashed in the freezer, are handy for dropping into the lunch box.

Preparation Time: *10 minutes*
Standing Time : *10 minutes*
Baking Time : *1 hour*

50 mL	chopped dried apricots (about 6)	¹/₄ cup
125 mL	100% bran cereal	¹/₂ cup
25 mL	lightly packed brown sugar	2 tbsp
	Sugar substitute equivalent to 40 mL (8 tsp) sugar	
250 mL	skim milk	1 cup
1	egg	1
10 mL	canola oil	2 tsp
375 mL	all-purpose flour	1¹/₂ cups
10 mL	baking powder	2 tsp

Each Serving: 1 slice

1 ☐ Starchy Choice

16 g carbohydrate
3 g protein
1 g fat

360 kilojoules
(85 Calories)

- In mixing bowl, combine apricots, bran cereal, sugar, sugar substitute and milk. Let stand about 10 minutes.

- Beat in egg and oil.

- Stir in flour and baking powder; stir until all dry ingredients are moistened.

- Spoon into lightly greased and floured 1.5 L (8 x 4 in) loaf pan.

- Bake in 190ºC (375ºF) oven for 1 hour or until firm to touch and tester inserted in center comes out clean. Let stand for 5 minutes. Remove from pan; cool on wire rack. Wrap and store for a couple of days.

Makes 1 loaf, cut into twelve 2 cm (³/₄ in) slices

Microwave Directions:
Pour batter into lightly greased and floured microwaveable 1 L (4 cup) ring mould. Sprinkle top lightly with cinnamon. Cover with waxed paper. Microwave, rotating every 3 minutes, at Medium (50%) for 6 minutes, then microwave at High (100%) for 4¹/₂ minutes longer or until top no longer looks wet and tester inserted near the center comes out clean. Let stand for 10 minutes to cool.

Apple Spice Squares

Preparation Time: *15 minutes*
Baking Time: *50 minutes*
Standing Time: *15 minutes*

Tangy apple butter, sandwiched between crumb layers, makes these squares sweet and chewy. One of the best — my family's favorite.

125 mL	all-purpose flour	1/2 cup
125 mL	quick-cooking rolled oats	1/2 cup
5 mL	baking powder	1 tsp
50 mL	unsalted margarine or butter	1/4 cup
50 mL	water	1/4 cup
1	egg, separated	1
	Sugar substitute equivalent to 125 mL (1/2 cup) sugar	
5 mL	vanilla	1 tsp
250 mL	Apple Butter (recipe, p. 226)	1 cup
1 mL	cream of tartar	1/4 tsp
15 mL	brown sugar	1 tbsp
125 mL	unsweetened shredded coconut	1/2 cup
125 mL	bran flakes, crushed	1/2 cup

Each serving: 2 squares

1 ▢ Starchy Choice

1 ▲ Fats & Oils Choice

13 g carbohydrate
2 g protein
5 g fat

440 kilojoules
(105 Calories)

- Lightly grease a 20 cm (8 in) square cake pan.

- In a bowl, combine flour, rolled oats and baking powder. With a pastry blender or two knives, cut in margarine or butter until mixture is crumbly.

- In a small bowl, beat together water, egg yolk and sugar substitute. Stir into crumbly dry mixture. Press onto bottom of cake pan.

- Stir vanilla into Apple Butter; spread over crumb layer in pan.

- In a bowl, beat egg white with cream of tartar until frothy. Add sugar gradually and beat until soft peaks form. Fold in coconut and bran flakes. Spread carefully and evenly over Apple Butter layer. Press down lightly with a fork.

- Bake in a 180ºC (350ºF) oven for 30 minutes or until top is lightly browned. Cool and cut into 25 squares.

Makes 25 squares, each 4 x 4 cm (1 1/2 in x 1 1/2 in)

Snacking Cake

When the cake comes out of the oven it seems dry and firm; however, it acts as a sponge when the syrup is poured over it. It soaks up the liquid. You can see it swell as it becomes moist and fluffy.

Preparation Time: *10 minutes*
Baking Time : *30 minutes*

200 mL	all-purpose flour	³/₄ cup
5 mL	baking powder	1 tsp
2 mL	cinnamon	¹/₂ tsp
2 mL	salt	¹/₂ tsp
1 mL	ground nutmeg	¹/₄ tsp
50 mL	melted margarine	¹/₄ cup
75 mL	granulated sugar	¹/₃ cup
2	eggs	2
50 mL	skim milk	¹/₄ cup
5 mL	grated lemon rind	1 tsp
125 mL	chopped walnuts	¹/₂ cup
Syrup		
250 mL	water	1 cup
	Sugar substitute equivalent to 175 mL (²/₃ cup) sugar	
25 mL	lemon juice	2 tbsp
1	stick (5 cm/2 in) cinnamon	1
4	whole cloves	4

Each Snack-size Serving:
¹/₂₀ of cake

¹/₂ ☐ Starchy Choice
1 ▲ Fats & Oils Choice

8 g carbohydrate
2 g protein
5 g fat

360 kilojoules
(85 Calories)

- In a small bowl, combine flour, baking powder, cinnamon, salt and nutmeg.
- In a second larger bowl, beat together margarine, sugar, eggs, skim milk and lemon rind.
- Stir in dry ingredients and fold in walnuts.
- Pour into a lightly greased 20 cm (8 in) square baking pan.
- Bake in a 180ºC (350ºF) oven for 25 to 30 minutes or until a tester inserted in the center comes out clean. Cool in pan.
- Syrup: In a saucepan, combine water, sugar substitute, lemon juice, cinnamon stick and cloves. Bring to a boil.
- Prick cake in many places with a fork and pour syrup over cake. Allow to sit 5 to 10 minutes for cake to absorb syrup.
- Cut into pieces and serve.
- Store cake, covered, in the refrigerator.

Makes 20 snack-size pieces, 9 dessert-size pieces

Each Dessert-size Serving:
¹/₉ of cake

1 ☐ Starchy Choice
2 ▲ Fats & Oils Choices

17 g carbohydrate
4 g protein
10 g fat

730 kilojoules
(174 Calories)

Apricot Almond Bars

Preparation Time: *20 minutes*
Baking Time: *25 minutes*

Fruity and chewy with a bit of crunch is how I describe these bars.

Crust

125 mL	all-purpose flour	1/2 cup
75 mL	whole wheat flour	1/3 cup
75 mL	oat bran	1/3 cup
	Sugar substitute equivalent to 25 mL (2 tbsp) sugar	
5 mL	baking powder	1 tsp
1 mL	salt	1/4 tsp
25 mL	margarine	2 tbsp
1	egg yolk	1
50 mL	water	1/4 cup

Filling

1	can (398 mL/14 oz) apricots, canned in juice	1
25 mL	cornstarch	2 tbsp
15 mL	granulated sugar*	1 tbsp
5 mL	vanilla	1 tsp
5 mL	almond extract	1 tsp

Topping

1	egg white	1
1 mL	cream of tartar	1/4 tsp
15 mL	icing sugar*	1 tbsp
175 mL	finely chopped unblanched almonds	2/3 cup

* The added sugar in the recipe has been included in the carbohydrate and Food Choice Values.

- **Crust:** In bowl, combine all-purpose and whole wheat flours, bran, sugar substitute, baking powder and salt.

- Cut in margarine until mixture is crumbly.

128

- With fork, beat together egg yolk and water. Stir into crumb mixture.

- Press mixture evenly onto bottom of nonstick or lightly greased 20 cm (8 in) square cake pan.

- **Filling:** Drain apricot juice into saucepan. Finely chop apricots.

- Stir chopped apricots into juice along with cornstarch and granulated sugar. Mix well.

- Cook over medium heat, stirring, for about 5 minutes or until mixture boils and thickens.

- Remove from heat. Stir in vanilla and almond extract.

- Pour over the prepared crust.

- **Topping:** Beat egg white with cream of tartar until frothy. Add icing sugar and beat until soft peaks form.

- Fold in chopped almonds.

- Spread evenly and carefully over apricot layer.

- Bake in 180ºC (350ºF) oven for 25 minutes or until top is golden brown.

- Cut evenly in 4 one way and in 5 the other way to make 20 bars.

Makes 20 bars

Each Serving: 1 bar

1   Fruits & Vegetables

1   Fats & Oils Choice

10 g carbohydrate
2 g protein
4 g fat

350 kilojoules
(83 Calories)

Raspberry Squares

Preparation Time: *25 minutes*
Baking Time: *25 minutes*

These squares look like little raspberry sandwiches. They're fruity and chewy.

250 mL	all-purpose flour	1 cup
125 mL	whole wheat flour	$^1/_2$ cup
50 mL	natural bran	$^1/_4$ cup
50 mL	granulated sugar*	$^1/_4$ cup
5 mL	baking powder	1 tsp
75 mL	cold margarine or butter	$^1/_3$ cup
1	egg	1
75 mL	water	$^1/_3$ cup
5 mL	almond extract	1 tsp
125 mL	raspberry dietetic fruit spread	$^1/_2$ cup

Each serving: 1 snack-size piece

1 ◢ Fruits & Vegetables

1 ▲ Fats & Oils Choice

10 g carbohydrate
1 g protein
3 g fat

290 kilojoules
(68 Calories)

Each serving: 1 dessert-size piece

1 ☐ Starchy Choice

1 ▲ Fats & Oils Choice

15 g carbohydrate
2 g protein
4 g fat

450 kilojoules
(107 Calories)

* The added sugar in the recipe has been included in the carbohydrate and Food Choice Values.

- In a bowl, combine all-purpose and whole wheat flours, bran, sugar and baking powder.

- With pastry blender or 2 knives, cut in margarine until mixture resembles fine crumbs.

- Beat together egg, water and almond extract. Stir into crumb mixture to form dough.

- Lightly press half of the dough onto bottom of nonstick or lightly greased 20 cm (8 in) square baking dish.

- Spread raspberry spread evenly over dough.

- Break remaining dough into small pieces and scatter evenly on top of spread.

- Bake in 180º (350ºF) oven for 25 to 30 minutes or until golden.

- For snack-size servings, cut evenly in 5 one way and 5 the other way.

- For dessert-size servings, cut evenly in 4 one way and in 4 the other way.

Makes 25 snack-size servings or 16 dessert-size servings

Coconut Orange Hermits

Hermits are soft cookies that look like little rugged hills. Fruit, nuts and spices are usually mixed into the batter.

Preparation Time: *10 minutes*
Baking Time : *15 minutes*

175 mL	all-purpose flour	$^2/_3$ cup
175 mL	whole wheat flour	$^2/_3$ cup
7 mL	baking powder	1-$^1/_2$ tsp
50 mL	margarine or butter	$^1/_4$ cup
15 mL	grated orange rind(1 small orange)	1 tbsp
50 mL	shredded unsweetened coconut	$^1/_4$ cup
25 mL	currants or chopped raisins	2 tbsp
25 mL	lightly packed brown sugar	2 tbsp
1	egg	1
50 mL	orange juice	$^1/_4$ cup
	Sugar substitute equivalent to 30 mL (6 tsp) sugar	

Each Serving: 2 Hermits

1 ☐ Starchy Choice

1 ▲ Fats & Oils Choice

14 g carbohydrate
2 g protein
5 g fat

460 kilojoules
(109 Calories)

- In mixing bowl, combine flours and baking powder.

- With a pasty blender or two knives, cut in margarine to form a crumbly mixture.

- Stir in orange rind, coconut, raisins and brown sugar.

- Whisk egg with orange juice and sugar substitute. Stir into flour mixture; mix until all dry ingredients are just moistened.

- Drop 15 mL (1 tbsp) batter at a time onto lightly greased or nonstick baking sheets about 4 cm (1$^1/_2$ in) apart.

- Bake in 190ºC (375ºF) oven for 12 to 15 minutes or until lightly browned.

Makes 24 Hermits

Butterscotch Peanut Cookies

Preparation Time: *15 minutes*
Baking Time: *18 minutes*

Each serving: 2 cookies

$^1/_2$ ▢ Starchy Choice

1 ▲ Fats & Oils Choice

7 g carbohydrate
2 g protein
6 g fat

380 kilojoules
(90 Calories)

Flattening each cookie with a fork ensures a crispy texture. Use chunky peanut butter for extra crunch and real peanut flavor.

250 mL	quick-cooking rolled oats	1 cup
250 mL	all-purpose flour	1 cup
125 mL	whole wheat flour	$^1/_2$ cup
10 mL	baking powder	2 tsp
175 mL	chunky peanut butter	$^2/_3$ cup
125 mL	margarine	$^1/_2$ cup
125 mL	water	$^1/_2$ cup
10 mL	vinegar	2 tsp
1	egg yolk	1
	Sugar substitute equivalent to 175 mL ($^2/_3$ cup) sugar	
5 mL	vanilla	1 tsp

- In a bowl, combine rolled oats, flours and baking powder. With a pastry blender or 2 knives, cut in peanut butter and margarine until mixture is crumbly.

- In a small bowl, beat together water, vinegar, egg yolk, sugar substitute and vanilla. Stir into crumbly dry mixture; mix well.

- Form 15 mL (1 tbsp) batter at a time into small balls. Place balls 2.5 cm (1 in) apart on a nonstick baking sheet.

- With the tines of a fork, flatten each ball by pressing in several directions until each cookie is a circle 6 cm ($2^1/_2$ in) wide.

- Bake in a 180ºC (350ºF) oven for 15 to 18 minutes or until lightly browned. Let cool.

- Store in a tightly covered cookie jar or container.

Makes 60 cookies

Oatmeal Chocolate Chip Cookies

Crisp, light and chocolaty – these cookies score high points with chocolate lovers

Preparation Time: *35 minutes*
Baking Time: *10 minutes*

75 mL	margarine	¹/₃ cup
75 mL	lightly packed brown sugar*	¹/₃ cup
50 mL	water	¹/₄ cup
1	egg white	1
300 mL	quick-cooking rolled oats	1¹/₄ cups
200 mL	all-purpose flour	³/₄ cup
5 mL	ground cinnamon	1 tsp
2 mL	baking soda	¹/₂ tsp
125 mL	mini-chocolate chips	¹/₂ cup

Each serving: 2 cookies

1 ☐   Starchy Choice
1 ▲   Fats & Oils Choice

The added sugar in the recipe has been included in the carbohydrate and Food Choice Values

> 14 g carbohydrate
> 2 g protein
> 6 g fat

> 470 kilojoules
> (112 Calories)

- In mixing bowl, cream together margarine and sugar until light and fluffy.

- Beat in water and egg white.

- Combine rolled oats, flour, cinnamon and soda. Stir into creamed mixture until well mixed.

- Stir in chocolate chips.

- Drop 15 mL (1 tbsp) at a time, about 5 cm (2 in) apart, onto nonstick or brown paper-lined baking sheets, to make 36 equal mounds.

- Bake in 200ºC (400ºF) oven for 10 to 12 minutes or until golden brown. Remove from pan to cake rack and let cool.

Makes 36 cookies

Double Chocolate Oatmeal Cookies

Preparation Time: *15 minutes*
Baking Time : *18 minutes*

For real chocolate lovers — a crunchy cookie under the easiest frosting ever!

250 mL	quick-cooking rolled oats	1 cup
250 mL	all-purpose flour	1 cup
250 mL	whole wheat flour	1 cup
25 mL	dry unsweetened cocoa	2 tbsp
10 mL	baking powder	2 tsp
125 mL	margarine or butter	$1/_2$ cup
125 mL	water	$1/_2$ cup
2	egg yolks	2
	Sugar substitute equivalent to 250 mL (1 cup) sugar	
5 mL	almond extract	1 tsp
125 mL	chocolate chips	$1/_2$ cup

Each Serving: 3 cookies

1 ☐ Starchy Choice

$1^1/_2$ ▲ Fats & Oils Choice

15 g carbohydrate
3 g protein
7 g fat

570 kilojoules
(135 Calories)

- In a bowl, combine oats, flours, cocoa and baking powder. With a pastry blender or 2 knives, cut in margarine until mixture is crumbly.

- In a small bowl, beat together water, egg yolks, sugar substitute and almond extract. Stir into crumbly mixture; mix well.

- Form 15 mL (1 tbsp) batter at a time into small balls. Place balls 2.5 cm (1 in) apart on a nonstick baking sheet.

- With the times of a fork, flatten each ball by pressing in several directions until each cookie is a circle 6 cm ($2^1/_2$ in) wide.

- Bake in a 180ºC (350ºF) oven for 15 to 18 minutes or until lightly browned.

- As soon as cookies are removed from the oven, immediately place 2 chocolate chips in the centre of each cookie. Let stand 1 minute. With the back of a spoon, spread or swirl chocolate chips (which are hot and soft) on top of each cookie to partly frost each cookie. Let cool.

- Store in a tightly covered cookie jar or container.

Makes 60 cookies

Carrot Raisin Cookies

When you prefer soft cookies, these are the ones to bake.

250 mL	all-purpose flour	1 cup
250 mL	natural bran	1 cup
50 mL	lightly packed brown sugar*	1/4 cup
10 mL	baking powder	2 tsp
5 mL	ground cinnamon	1 tsp
2 mL	salt	1/2 tsp
125 mL	grated carrot	1/2 cup
50 mL	chopped raisins	1/4 cup
1	egg	1
175 mL	2% milk	2/3 cup
25 mL	margarine or butter, melted	2 tbsp
15 mL	molasses*	1 tbsp
5 mL	vanilla	1 tsp

* The added sugar in the recipe has been included in the carbohydrate and Food Choice Values.

- Lightly oil 2 baking sheets or spray with low-calorie vegetable spray. Or use nonstick baking sheets.

- In mixing bowl, combine flour, bran, brown sugar, baking powder, cinnamon and salt. Stir in carrot and raisins.

- In small bowl, beat together egg, milk, margarine, molasses and vanilla.

- Make a well in dry ingredients. Pour in milk mixture and mix just until dry ingredients are moistened. Batter will be rough and lumpy.

- Drop by rounded 15 mL (1 tbsp) spoonfuls, about 5 cm (2 in) apart, onto prepared baking sheets, to make 26 equal mounds.

- Bake in 180ºC (350ºF) oven for 18 minutes or until browned.

Makes 26 cookies

Preparation Time: *25 minutes*
Cooking Time: *18 minutes*

Each serving: 2 cookies

1 ▢ Starchy Choice

1 ▲ Fats & Oils Choice

18 g carbohydrate
3 g protein
3 g fat

440 kilojoules
(105 Calories)

Crisp Grainy Wafers

Preparation Time: *10 minutes*
Baking Time: *30 minutes*

The two-step process of first baking these cookies, then drying them out, guarantees their crispness.

125 mL	all-purpose flour	1/2 cup
125 mL	whole wheat flour	1/2 cup
10 mL	baking powder	2 tsp
50 mL	margarine or butter	1/4 cup
250 mL	bran flakes	1 cup
125 mL	quick-cooking rolled oats	1/2 cup
50 mL	unsweetened shredded coconut	1/4 cup
50 mL	chopped nuts	1/4 cup
25 mL	lightly packed brown sugar	2 tbsp
1	egg	1
125 mL	water	1/2 cup
5 mL	vanilla	1 tsp
	Sugar substitute equivalent to 40 mL (8 tsp) sugar	
2 mL	cinnamon	1/2 tsp

Each serving: 4 cookies

1 ☐ Starchy Choice

1 ▲ Fats & Oils Choice

12 g carbohydrate
2 g protein
5 g fat

420 kilojoules
(101 Calories)

- In a mixing bowl, combine flours and baking powder.
- With a pastry blender or two knives, cut in margarine until mixture is crumbly.
- Stir in bran flakes, rolled oats, coconut, nuts and brown sugar.
- Whisk egg with water, vanilla, sugar substitute and cinnamon. Stir into flour mixture; mix just until all ingredients are moistened.
- Drop 5 mL (1 tsp) batter at a time onto lightly greased or nonstick baking sheet 4 cm (1 1/2 in) apart.
- Bake in a 180°C (350°F) oven for 12 minutes or until lightly browned.
- After all the cookies have baked, arrange them in layers on a single cookie sheet and return cookies to oven; immediately turn off heat. Allow cookies to stay in for 10 to 15 minutes to dry and crisp. Store in a covered container, with loose-fitting lid.

Makes 60 cookies

Pecan Crisps

Everyone loves these cookies. They are light and airy with a nutty crispness.

Preparation Time: *10 minutes*
Baking Time : *50 minutes*
Standing Time : *10 minutes*

2	egg whites	2
Pinch	cream of tartar	Pinch
50 mL	brown sugar, lightly packed	1/4 cup
2 mL	vanilla	1/2 tsp
75 mL	chopped pecans	1/3 cup
250 mL	rice crispy cereal	1 cup

- In bowl, beat egg whites with cream of tartar until soft peaks form. Add sugar gradually, then vanilla; beat until stiff peaks form.
- Fold in pecans and rice cereal.
- Drop 15 mL (1 tbsp) batter at a time 5 cm (2 in) apart onto non-stick or brown paper-lined baking sheets.
- Bake in a 160ºC (325ºF) oven for 20 minutes or until firm.
- Turn off oven and leave cookies for 1/2 hour longer to dry. Remove from oven and cool.

Makes 18 cookies

Each Serving: 3 cookies

1 ▢ Starchy Choice
1 ▲ Fats & Oils Choice

12 g carbohydrate
2 g protein
5 g fat

420 kilojoules
(101 Calories)

Macaroons

I'm tempted to call these sweetmeats, because they are like treats from a confectionery.

Preparation Time: *10 minutes*
Baking Time : *20 minutes*

2	egg whites	2
Pinch	salt	Pinch
75 mL	icing sugar*	1/3 cup
5 mL	vanilla	1 tsp
200 mL	unsweetened dessicated coconut	3/4 cup

- In bowl, beat egg whites with salt until soft peaks form. Gradually add sugar and vanilla; beating constantly until stiff peaks form. Fold in coconut.
- Drop by 15 mL (1 tbsp) portions, about 5 cm (2 in) apart, onto non-stick or brown paper-lined baking sheets to make 21 equal mounds.
- Bake in a 160ºC (325ºF) oven for 20 minutes or until lightly browned and firm. For chewy cookies, remove immediately; for crisp ones, turn off oven; let cookies dry as oven cools.

Makes 21 macaroons

Each Serving: 3 macaroons

1 ▰ Fruits & Vegetables
1 ▲ Fats & Oils Choice

8 g carbohydrate
2 g protein
6 g fat

390 kilojoules
(92 Calories)

Angel Cake

Preparation Time: *40 minutes*
Baking Time: *35 minutes*

A slice of this light, airy cake is wonderful on its own and superb when it accompanies a serving of fruit or sherbet

125 mL	fine granulated sugar*	¹/₂ cup
125 mL	icing sugar*	¹/₂ cup
375 mL	egg whites (approx 12)	1¹/₂ cups
5 mL	cream of tartar	1 tsp
5 mL	vanilla	1 tsp
250 mL	cake-and-pastry flour	1 cup
2 mL	salt	¹/₂ tsp

Each serving: ¹/₁₆ **of cake**

1 ☐ Starchy Choice

16 g carbohydrate
3 g protein

320 kilojoules
(77 Calories)

* *The added sugar in the recipe has been included in the carbohydrate and Food Choice Values.*

• Sift sugars into bowl. Stir to combine.

• In mixing bowl, beat egg whites and cream of tartar until soft peaks form. Add vanilla and 200 mL (³/₄ cup) of the combined sugars. Beat for 1 to 2 minutes or until stiff peaks form (peaks do not curl over when beaters are lifted).

• Into bowl containing remaining sugar, sift flour and salt. Stir to combine. Sift flour mixture over egg white mixture. With wire whisk, fold in flour mixture until no flour lumps are left.

• Spoon mixture into ungreased 3 L (10 in) tube pan. With knife, cut through batter to remove air bubbles. Smooth top.

• Bake in 180°C (350°F) oven for 35 minutes or until top is lightly browned and tester inserted in cake comes out clean.

• Invert pan and let cake cool before removing.

Makes one 3 L (10 in) angel cake, 16 servings

Chiffon Cake

This versatile cake has many delicious variations

250 mL	cake-and-pastry flour	1 cup
175 mL	granulated sugar (divided)*	2/3 cup
10 mL	baking powder	2 tsp
2 mL	salt	1/2 tsp
125 mL	water	1/2 cup
50 mL	oil	1/4 cup
2	egg yolks	2
4	egg whites	4
1 mL	cream of tartar	1/4 tsp

Preparation Time: *30 minutes*
Baking Time : *50 minutes*

Each Serving: 1/14 **of cake**

1 ▢   Starchy Choice
1 ▲   Fats & Oils Choice

16 g carbohydrate
2 g protein
5 g fat

480 kilojoules
(114 Calories)

- Into medium bowl, sift flour, 75 mL (1/3 cup) of the sugar, baking powder and salt. Stir to combine.

- Make a well in dry ingredients; pour in water, oil and egg yolks. Beat for 1 minute or until very smooth. Wash beaters.

- In large bowl, beat egg whites and cream of tartar until soft peaks form. Add remaining sugar and beat for 1 to 2 minutes longer or until stiff peaks form (peaks do not curl over when beaters are lifted).

- Pour egg yolk mixture evenly over entire surface of egg white mixture. Gently fold in by bringing wire whip or spatula through mixture, across bottom of bowl and back to top of mixture, rotating bowl after each motion. Fold just until blended and mixture is almost even-colored.

- Pour into ungreased 3L (10 in) tube pan. With knife, cut through batter to remove air bubbles. Smooth top.

- Bake in 160ºC (325ºF) oven for 50 minutes or until tester inserted in cake comes out clean.

- Invert pan and let cake cool before removing.

Makes one 3L (10 in) chiffon cake, 14 servings

Variation:
Cinnamon Chiffon: Add 10 mL (2 tsp) cinnamon and grated rind of 1 orange to dry ingredients.

Calculations as above.

Chocolate Chiffon Cake

Preparation Time: *30 minutes*
Baking Time: *50 minutes*

Here it is — a moist, chocolaty version of the Chiffon Cake (page 139)

200 mL	cake-and-pastry flour	³/₄ cup
175 mL	granulated sugar (divided)*	²/₃ cup
125 mL	unsweetened cocoa powder	¹/₂ cup
10 mL	baking powder	2 tsp
2 mL	salt	¹/₂ tsp
125 mL	water	¹/₂ cup
50 mL	oil	¹/₄ cup
2	egg yolks	2
4	egg whites	4
1 mL	cream of tartar	¹/₄ tsp

Each serving: ¹/₁₄ **of cake**

1 ⬜ Starchy Choice

1 🔺 Fats & Oils Choice

16 g carbohydrate
2 g protein
5 g fat

480 kilojoules
(114 Calories)

* *The added sugar in the recipe has been included in the carbohydrate and Food Choice Values.*

• Into medium bowl, sift flour, 75 mL (¹/₃ cup) of the sugar, cocoa, baking powder and salt. Stir to continue.

• Make a well in dry ingredients; pour in water, oil and egg yolks. Beat for 1 minute or until very smooth. Wash beaters.

• In large bowl, beat egg whites and cream of tartar until soft peaks form. Add remaining sugar and beat for 1 to 2 minutes longer or until stiff peaks form (peaks do not curl over when beaters are lifted).

• Pour egg yolk mixture evenly over entire surface of egg white mixture. Gently fold in by bringing wire whisk or spatula through mixture, rotating bowl after each motion. Fold just until blended and mixture is almost even-colored.

• Pour into ungreased 3 L (10 in) tube pan. With knife, cut through batter to remove air bubbles. Smooth top.

• Bake in 160ºC (325ºF) oven for 50 minutes or until tester inserted in cake comes out clean.

• Invert pan and let cake cool completely before removing.

Makes one 3L (10 in) chiffon cake, 14 servings.

Teddy Bear Cupcakes

Little people are bound to applaud when they see Teddy Bear Cupcakes standing in for a cake at a birthday party

Preparation Time: *30 minutes*
Baking Time: *25 minutes*
Assembling Time: *10 minutes*

	Batter for Chocolate Chiffon Cake (recipe, p. 140)	
200 mL	whipped dessert topping	³/₄ cup
28	mini-chocolate chips or dried currants	28

- Line 14 muffin cups with large paper liners

- Prepare Chocolate Chiffon Cake batter. Divide evenly among lined muffin cups, filling each about 3/4 full.

- Bake in 180ºC (350ºF) oven for 25 minutes or until tops spring back when touched. (Cupcakes will have more volume if muffin pans are placed in upper half of oven.)

- Remove from oven and let cool.

- Assemble up to 4 hours before serving. Remove paper from cupcakes. Cut top from each cupcake and cut each top in half to make 2 crescents. Place 15 mL (1 tbsp) whipped topping on each cupcake. Replace 2 crescents in topping to look like ears. Place 2 mini-chocolate chips on topping below ears to look like eyes and a third mini-chocolate chip or small piece of cupcake from one of the crescents for a nose.

- Refrigerate for up to 4 hours before serving.

Makes 14 servings

Each serving: 1 cupcake

1 ☐ Starchy Choice
1 ▲ Fats & Oils Choice

16 g carbohydrate
2 g protein
5 g fat

480 kilojoules
(114 Calories)

Microwave Directions:

Place large paper liners in microwaveable muffin pan (7 cups). Reduce water in recipe to 75 mL (¹/₃ cup). Spoon batter into paper liners, filling each about ³/₄ full. Microwave at High (100%) for 2¹/₂ minutes or until just dry on top. Let stand 2 minutes. Remove cupcakes from muffin pan. Repeat with remaining batter.

Apple Up and Down Cake

Preparation Time: *30 minutes*
Baking Time: *30 minutes*

Sweet and moist; this cake is best served warm.

15 mL	margarine	1 tbsp
25 mL	lightly packed brown sugar*	2 tbsp
2 mL	ground cinnamon	$1/2$ tsp
2 mL	ground nutmeg	$1/2$ tsp
3	medium apples, peeled, cored and sliced	3
200 mL	all-purpose flour	$3/4$ cup
5 mL	baking powder	1 tsp
2 mL	salt	$1/2$ tsp
75 mL	granulated sugar*	$1/3$ cup
1	egg	1
1	egg white	1
50 mL	oil	$1/4$ cup
50 mL	2% milk	$1/4$ cup
5 mL	vanilla	1 tsp
125 mL	dried currants	$1/2$ cup
1	medium apple, peeled, cored and grated	1

Each serving: 1/12 of cake

1 ▢ Starchy Choice
1 ◪ Fruits & Vegetables
1 ▲ Fats & Oils Choice

24 g carbohydrate
2 g protein
6 g fat

680 kilojoules
(161 Calories)

*The added sugar in the recipe has been included in the carbohydrate and Food Choice Values

- In deep 25 cm (10 in) skillet with ovenproof handle, melt margarine. Stir in brown sugar, cinnamon and nutmeg.
- Arrange apple slices on bottom of skillet in butter sauce. Remove from heat.
- In mixing bowl, combine flour, baking powder and salt.
- In second bowl, beat together sugar, egg, egg white, oil, milk and vanilla.
- Pour into dry ingredients. Stir just until blended.
- Fold in currants and grated apple.
- Pour into skillet over apple layer.
- Bake in 180º C (350ºF) oven for 25 to 30 minutes or until cake tester inserted in centre of cake comes out clean. Set aside to let cool
- Carefully invert pan and remove cake to serving plate.

Makes 12 servings

Microwave Directions:
In microwaveable 9-inch (23 cm) ring mould, melt butter in microwave at High (100%) for 30 seconds. Stir in brown sugar, cinnamon and nutmeg. Arrange apple slices on buttery layer. Cover mould tightly with microwave plastic wrap. Microwave at High (100%) for 2 minutes. Puncture plastic to allow steam to escape. Let stand while preparing batter. Spoon batter over apples. Cover with piece of waxed paper or parchment. Microwave at Medium High (70%) for 7 to 8 minutes or until top is no longer damp.
Let stand for 5 minutes.

Fruit Loaf with Brandy Sauce

You'll be tempted to try this as soon as it's out of the oven because the aroma is so tantalizing. But, it's best if you let it mellow for a day.

Preparation Time: *30 minutes*
Baking Time : *1 hour*
Standing Time : *24 hours*

Fruit Loaf

375 mL	all-purpose flour	1¹/₂ cups
50 mL	granulated sugar *	¹/₄ cup
10 mL	baking powder	2 tsp
2 mL	salt	¹/₂ tsp
25 mL	finely chopped dried apricots	2 tbsp
25 mL	finely chopped dried apple	2 tbsp
25 mL	dried currants	2 tbsp
15 mL	grated orange peel	1 tbsp
1	egg, beaten	1
200 mL	unsweetened white grape juice	³/₄ cup
10 mL	canola oil	2 tsp

Brandy Sauce

125 mL	apricot dietetic fruit spread	¹/₂ tsp
25 mL	brandy**	2 tbsp
25 mL	water	2 tbsp

The added sugar in the recipe has been included in the carbohydrate and Food Choice Values.

Each Serving: ¹/₁₂ **of cake**

1 ▢ Starchy Choice

1 ◪ Fruits & Vegetables

25 g carbohydrate
2 g protein
1 g fat

510 kilojoules
(122 Calories)

- **Fruit Loaf:** In mixing bowl, combine flour, sugar, baking powder and salt. Stir in apricots, apple, currants and orange peel.
- In small bowl, combine egg, grape juice and oil.
- Make a well in flour mixture; pour in juice mixture. Stir quickly just until ingredients are mixed and fruit is evenly distributed. Turn into waxed paper-lined 1.5 L (8 x 4 in) loaf pan.
- Bake in a 180ºC (350ºF) oven for 1 hour or until cake tester inserted in center comes out clean.
- **Brandy Sauce:** In small saucepan, combine apricot spread, brandy and water. Cook over medium heat until spread melts and mixture is warm. (**Most of the alcohol in this recipe evaporates.)
- With skewer, perforate loaf about 20 times. Pour Brandy Sauce over cake and let soak for 10 minutes.
- Remove loaf from pan. Wrap tightly in plastic wrap. Set aside to mellow for 24 hours.

Makes 12 servings

Microwave Directions:
Prepare loaf batter. Pour into a very lightly oiled 2 L (8 cup) microwaveable ring mould. Microwave, turning halfway through cooking time, at Medium (50%) for 5 minutes. Microwave at High (100%) for 2 minutes longer or until tester inserted in center of cake comes out clean. Let stand for 5 minutes. **Sauce:** In small microwaveable bowl, combine apricot spread, brandy and water. Microwave at High (100%) for 2 minutes or until spread melts. Continue as recipe directs.

Peach Upside-Down Cake

Preparation Time: *30 minutes*
Baking Time: *30 minutes*

Upside-Down Cake is one of my favorite desserts. My mom made it often when I was a child. Her peach one was the best and this one reminds me of it.

Peach Layer

8	medium peach halves or 14 peach halves canned in juice, drained	8
25 mL	lightly packed brown sugar*	2 tbsp
5 mL	ground nutmeg	1 tsp
5 mL	ground cinnamon	1 tsp
15 mL	water	1 tbsp

Cake Layer

125 mL	cake-and-pastry flour	$1/2$ cup
75 mL	granulated sugar*	$1/3$ cup
5 mL	baking powder	1 tsp
1 mL	salt	$1/4$ tsp
50 mL	water	$1/4$ cup
25 mL	oil	2 tbsp
1	egg, separated	1
1	egg white	1
1 mL	cream of tartar	$1/4$ tsp

* The added sugar in the recipe has been included in the carbohydrate and Food Choice Values.

- **Peach Layer:** Cut waxed paper to fit bottom of 20 cm (8 in) round cake pan. Grease bottom of pan only and fit in waxed paper.

- Peel and slice peaches. Arrange in even layer on waxed paper.

- Combine brown sugar, nutmeg and cinnamon. Reserve 15 mL (1 tbsp) and sprinkle remaining spice mixture over peaches. Sprinkle with water.

- **Cake Layer:** Into mixing bowl, sift flour, 15 mL (1 tbsp) of the sugar, baking powder, salt and reserved spice mixture.

144

- Combine water, oil and egg yolk. Stir into dry ingredients until just smooth.

- In mixing bowl, beat egg whites and cream of tartar until soft peaks form. Add remaining sugar and continue to beat until stiff peaks form.

- Drizzle egg yolk mixture over whites. Fold in until evenly distributed and even-colored.

- Pour over peach layer in pan. With fork, prick around edge of pan and in center to allow batter to flow between peaches.

- Bake in 160ºC (325ºF) oven for 30 minutes. Let cool for 5 minutes.

- Loosen edge with knife and invert warm cake onto serving plate.

Makes 10 servings

Each Serving: $\frac{1}{10}$ of cake

1 ☐ Starchy Choice

1 ▨ Fruits & Vegetables

1 ▲ Fats & Oils Choice

26 g carbohydrate
2 g protein
4 g fat

590 kilojoules
(141 Calories)

Bake It Fresh

Recipe	Food Choices per Serving		Energy per Serving		
			kilojoules	Calories	
Auntie Kay's Magic Bread	1 ☐ Starchy		290	68	p. 117
Scones	1 ☐ Starchy; ½ ▲ Fats & Oils		410	98	p. 118
Cheese & Chive Scones	1 ☐ Starchy; ½ ▲ Fats & Oils		470	111	p. 118
Raisin & Lemon Scones	1 ☐ Starchy; ½ ▲ Fats & Oils	½ ▨ Fruits & Vegetables	480	114	p. 118
Blueberry Scones	1 ☐ Starchy; 1 ▲ Fats & Oils		490	116	p. 119
Apricot Coconut Bran Muffins	1 ☐ Starchy; 1 ▨ Fruits & Vegetables	1 ▲ Fats & Oils	690	164	p. 120
Spicy Oat Bran Muffins	1 ☐ Starchy; 1 ▲ Fats & Oils		540	128	p. 121
Raisin Oat Bran Muffins	1 ☐ Starchy; ½ ▲ Fats & Oils		340	82	p. 122
Orange Cornmeal Muffins	1 ☐ Starchy		290	69	p. 123
Banana Nut Muffins	1 ☐ Starchy; ½ ▲ Fats & Oils		340	82	p. 124

Bake It Fresh

Recipe	Food Choices per Serving	Energy per Serving (kilojoules / Calories)		
Apricot Loaf	1 ☐ Starchy	360	85	p. 125
Apple Spice Squares	1 ☐ Starchy; 1 △ Fats & Oils	440	105	p. 126
Snacking Cake -snack	½ ☐ Starchy; 1 △ Fats & Oils	360	85	p. 127
— dessert	1 ☐ Starchy; 2 △ Fats & Oils	730	174	p. 127
Apricot Almond Bars	1 ◪ Fruits & Vegetables; 1 △ Fats & Oils	350	83	p. 128
Raspberry Squares	1 ◪ Fruits & Vegetables; 1 △ Fats & Oils	290	68	p. 130
— dessert	1 ☐ Starchy; 1 △ Fats & Oils	450	107	p. 130
Coconut Orange Hermits	1 ☐ Starchy; 1 △ Fats & Oils	460	109	p. 131
Butterscotch Peanut Cookies	½ ☐ Starchy; 1 △ Fats & Oils	380	90	p. 132
Oatmeal Chocolate Cookies	1 ☐ Starchy; 1 △ Fats & Oils	470	112	p. 133
Double Chocolate Oatmeal Cookies	1 ☐ Starchy; 1½ △ Fats & Oils	570	135	p. 134
Crispy Grainy Wafers	1 ☐ Starchy; 1 △ Fats & Oils	420	101	p. 136
Carrot Raisin Cookies	1 ☐ Starchy; 1 △ Fats & Oils	440	105	p. 135
Pecan Crisps	1 ☐ Starchy; 1 △ Fats & Oils	420	101	p. 137
Macaroons	1 ◪ Fruits & Vegetables; 1 △ Fats & Oils	390	92	p. 137
Angel Cake	1 ☐ Starchy	320	77	p. 138
Chiffon Cake	1 ☐ Starchy; 1 △ Fats & Oils	480	114	p. 139
Cinnamon Chiffon Cake	1 ☐ Starchy; 1 △ Fats & Oils	480	114	p. 139
Chocolate Chiffon Cake	1 ☐ Starchy; 1 △ Fats & Oils	480	114	p. 140
Teddy Bear Cupcakes	1 ☐ Starchy; 1 △ Fats & Oils	480	114	p. 140
Apple Up & Down Cake	1 ☐ Starchy; 1 ◪ Fruits & Vegetables; 1 △ Fats & Oils	680	161	p. 142
Fruit Loaf in Brandy Sauce	1 ☐ Starchy; 1 ◪ Fruits & Vegetables;	510	122	p. 143
Peach Up-side Down Cake	1 ☐ Starchy; 1 ◪ Fruits & Vegetables; 1 △ Fats & Oils	590	141	p. 144

Homey Puddings and Cool Pies

When I started thinking about puddings and pies for this book, I was filled with nostalgia. I closed my eyes and I could easily picture Mom's raisin-plumped bread puddings and mouth-watering baked fruit pies.

My memories inspired the down-home-style puddings in this section. Some of the pies, however, originated in my daughter Susan's 1980's kitchen.

Both the puddings and the pies are among the more hearty desserts in this cookbook and should be served with a light entrée.

If you plan to use one of them as part of a meal for a person with diabetes, it's wise to consider the Food Choice and energy value first. Then select other foods to complete the Choices allowed in the diabetic meal plan.

Vanilla Pudding

Preparation Time: *15 minutes*
Cooking Time: *5 minutes*

Pudding gives soup or salad suppers the perfect finishing touch.

500 mL	2% or skim milk	2 cups
75 mL	cornstarch	$^1/_3$ cup
2	egg yolks OR 1 whole egg	2
	Sugar substitute equivalent to 75 mL ($^1/_3$ cup) sugar	
10 mL	vanilla	2 tsp

Each serving: 125 mL($^1/_2$ cup)

$^1/_2$ ⬛ Starchy Choice

$1^1/_2$ ◆ Milk Choices (2%)

18 g carbohydrate
6 g protein
3 g fat

520 kilojoules
(123 Calories)

- In a heavy saucepan, combine 125 mL ($^1/_2$ cup) of the milk and cornstarch; mix well. Add remaining milk. Place over medium heat and cook, stirring, until mixture comes to a boil; reduce heat and simmer for 2 minutes. Remove from heat.

- In a bowl, beat egg yolks or whole egg with a fork; add a small amount (125 mL/$^1/_2$ cup) of the hot mixture to beaten egg, stirring until smooth; return immediately to hot mixture, stirring constantly. (The hot mixture will cook the egg.)

- Stir in sugar substitute and vanilla.

- Pour 125 mL ($^1/_2$ cup) into each of 4 dessert dishes. Cover with plastic wrap to prevent skin from forming on top of pudding. Cool to room temperature or chill in refrigerator.

Makes 500 mL (2 cups), 4 servings

Microwave Directions:
In 1 L (4 cup) microwaveable container, combine 250 mL (1 cup) milk and cornstarch. Microwave at High (100%) for 3 minutes, stirring once. Beat egg into remaining milk. Stir into hot milk mixture. Microwave at High (100%) for 3 minutes. Stir well. Let stand for 1 minute. Stir in sugar substitute and vanilla.

Calculations as above.

Variation:

Chocolate Pudding: In place of the cornstarch in the above recipe, use 50 mL ($^1/_4$ cup) each of cornstarch and dry unsweetened cocoa.

148

Vanilla Creme Custard

Warm or cold, baked custard is one of my comfort foods. It feels nice and tastes good.

Preparation Time: *10 minutes*
Cooking Time: *35 minutes*
Standing Time: *1 hour*

2	eggs	2
375 mL	skim milk	1$^1/_2$ cups
	Sugar substitute equivalent to 30 mL (6 tsp) sugar	
5 mL	vanilla	1 tsp
2	Double Chocolate Oatmeal cookies (recipe, pg 134)	2

- In a bowl, with a whisk or hand beater, gently beat eggs until just mixed. Stir in milk, sugar substitute and vanilla.

- Pour into a 750 mL (3 cup) ovenproof baking dish or casserole. Cover top with foil.

- Place in a larger pan. Pour in hot water to reach 5 cm (2 in) up sides of baking dish.

- Bake in a 180ºC (350ºF) oven for 35 minutes or until tester, inserted between center and outside edge, comes out clean.

- Cool for 10 minutes, then cover and refrigerate until serving time. (Custard can be made 1 day ahead.)

- Crush cookies to make crumbs. Sprinkle over custard.

- Place under broiler for 1 to 2 minutes to toast crumbs. Remove.

- Serve in dessert dishes in the kitchen or at the table.

Makes 4 servings

Variations:

Orange Creme Custard: Add 5 mL (1 tsp) grated orange rind.

Almond Creme Custard: Use 5 mL (1 tsp) almond extract in place of the vanilla extract.

Each Serving: 200 mL($^3/_4$ cup)

1 ◆ Milk Choice (skim)

1 ▲ Fats & Oils Choice

OR

1$^1/_2$ ◆ Milk Choice (2%)

7 g carbohydrate
6 g protein
4 g fat

370 kilojoules
(88 Calories)

Microwave Directions:
In 1 L (4 cup) glass measure, heat milk, uncovered, at High (100%) for 4 minutes. Cool for 1 minute. In 500 mL (2 cup) measure, whisk together egg, sweetener and vanilla until well combined. While whisking, gradually add hot milk in a thin stream. Pour evenly into four 125 mL ($^1/_2$ cup) custard cups placed in a round microwaveable baking dish. Pour hot water around custard cups. Microwave, uncovered, at High (100%) for 5 minutes. Continue as recipe directs.

Calculations as above.

Coconut Rice Pudding

Creamy rice combined with the crunch of coconut makes a delectable and satisfying finishing touch to a meal.

Preparation Time: *10 minutes*

250 mL	cooked short grain rice	1 cup
125 mL	skim milk	$^1/_2$ cup
	Sugar substitute equivalent to 30 mL (6 tsp) sugar	
5 mL	vanilla	1 tsp
25 mL	shredded unsweetened coconut	2 tbsp

Each serving: 125 mL($^1/_2$ cup)

1 ☐ Starchy Choice

1 ◆ Milk Choice (skim)

22 g carbohydrate
4 g protein
1 g fat

470 kilojoules
(113 Calories)

- In a saucepan, combine cooked rice, skim milk, sugar substitute, vanilla and shredded coconut.

- Bring to a boil; reduce heat and simmer, stirring occasionally, for 5 minutes, or until most of moisture evaporates, rice kernels stick together and mixture is creamy.

Makes 250 mL (1 cup), 2 servings

❖ **Timely Tip:**

Cooked rice can be frozen in 250 mL (1 cup) portions in small plastic freezer bags. Push all the air out of the bag of rice, close and secure it with twist-ties. Label it with name, date and instructions for use. It will keep for up to 3 month. To defrost quickly, place the rice in a sieve and pour boiling water over it. When you are in the mood for rice pudding, it sure is handy to have a little rice cooked and ready.

Apple Raisin Rice Pudding

This creamy rice pudding with plump raisins and juicy apple is a good old-fashioned, family favorite. When the rice is pre-cooked it takes only about 10 minutes to make it.

Preparation Time: *10 minutes*

500 mL	cooked short grain rice	2 cups
250 mL	skim milk	1 cup
	Sugar substitute equivalent to 60 mL (12 tsp) sugar	
50 mL	raisins	¹/₄ cup
5 mL	vanilla	1 tsp
1 mL	ground cinnamon	¹/₄ tsp
1 mL	ground nutmeg	¹/₄ tsp
1	apple	1
1 mL	ascorbic acid color keeper	¹/₄ tsp

Each Serving: 125 mL(¹/₂ cup)

1 ☐ Starchy Choice

1 ◆ Milk Choice (skim)

22 g carbohydrate
2 g protein

400 kilojoules
(96 Calories)

- In a saucepan, combine rice, skim milk, sugar substitute, raisins, vanilla, cinnamon and nutmeg. Bring to a boil; reduce heat and simmer, stirring occasionally, for 5 minutes or until most of the moisture evaporates and mixture is creamy.

- Core and shred apple and sprinkle with ascorbic acid color keeper.

- Stir apple into rice mixture. Cook for 2 to 3 minutes longer or until apple is soft.

- Spoon into serving dish or dessert dishes. Serve warm or chilled.

Makes 750 mL (3 cups), 6 servings

Chocolate Layered Pudding

Preparation Time: *10 minutes*
Cooking Time: *30 minutes*

As this rich tasting, chocolaty mixture bakes, three layers form — a smooth bottom layer, a creamy middle one, and a foamy light one on top. It is fun to eat out of the dish in which it is baked.

1	egg, separated	1
10 mL	granulated sugar	2 tsp
10 mL	all-purpose flour	2 tsp
	Sugar substitute equivalent to 30 mL (6 tsp) sugar	
15 mL	dry unsweetened cocoa	1 tbsp
125 mL	skim milk	¹/₂ cup
5 mL	vanilla	1 tsp
Pinch	cream of tartar	Pinch

Each serving: 200 mL(³/₄ cup)

1¹/₂ ◆ Milk Choices (2%)

OR

1 ▨ Fruits & Vegetables

1 ⬕ Protein Choice

11 g carbohydrate
6 g protein
3 g fat

400 kilojoules
(95 Calories)

- In a small bowl, whisk egg yolk, sugar, flour, sugar substitute and cocoa. Stir in milk and vanilla.

- In separate bowl, beat egg white and cream of tartar until stiff peaks form. Fold into egg yolk mixture.

- Pour pudding into small 200 mL (³/₄ cup) custard cups.

- Set custard cups in pan; pour in hot water to reach 2.5 cm (1 in) up sides of cups.

- Bake in a 160ºC (325ºF) oven for 30 minutes.

- Serve warm or cold.

Makes 2 servings

Lemon Layered Pudding

The surprising thing about this lemony, custard-like mixture is that it layers as it bakes. Its tart sweetness pleases both the young at heart and the young in years.

1	egg, separated	1
10 mL	granulated sugar	2 tsp
10 mL	all-purpose flour	2 tsp
	Sugar substitute equivalent to 30 mL (6 tsp) sugar	
10 mL	lemon juice	2 tsp
5 mL	grated lemon rind	1 tsp
125 mL	skim milk	¹/₂ cup
Pinch	cream of tartar	Pinch

- In a small bowl, whisk egg yolk, sugar, flour, sugar substitute and lemon juice. Stir in lemon rind and milk.

- In separate bowl, beat egg white and cream of tartar until stiff peaks form. Fold into egg yolk mixture.

- Pour into 2 small (200 mL/³/₄ cup) custard cups.

- Set custard cups in pan; pour in hot water to reach 2.5 cm (1 in) up sides of cup. Bake in a 160ºC (325ºF) oven for 30 minutes. Serve warm or cold.

Makes 2 servings

Preparation Time: *10 minutes*
Cooking Time: *30 minutes*

Each Serving: 200 mL/³/₄ cup

1 ◢ Fruits & Vegetables

1 ◿ Protein Choice

OR

1¹/₂ ◆ Milk Choice (2%)

9 g carbohydrate
5 g protein
3 g fat

350 kilojoules
(83 Calories)

Date Bread Pudding

Preparation Time: *20 minutes*
Baking Time: *45 minutes*

This good old-fashioned bread pudding is like one my mom made. The sweetness comes mainly from the dates and raisins.

8	pitted dates, finely chopped	8
250 mL	2% milk	1 cup
2 mL	ground cinnamon	¹/₂ tsp
4	slices whole wheat bread	4
1	egg	1
1	egg white	1
1 mL	cream of tartar	¹/₄ tsp
5 mL	granulated sugar*	1 tsp
15 mL	raisins, finely chopped	1 tbsp

Each serving: 175 mL(²/₃ cup)

1 ☐ Starchy Choice
1 ◆ Milk Choice (2%)

22 g carbohydrate
6 g protein
3 g fat

560 kilojoules
(134 Calories)

- In saucepan, combine dates, milk and cinnamon. Heat over medium heat to scalding. Remove from heat and place pan in cool water for 10 minutes or until cool.

- Cut bread into bite-size cubes and place in bowl.

- Beat egg into milk mixture. Pour over bread cubes and stir well.

- With clean beaters, beat egg white and cream of tartar until frothy; add sugar and continue to beat until stiff peaks form.

- Fold into bread mixture along with raisins.

- Spoon into 23 cm (9 in) nonstick or lightly greased baking dish or divide evenly among 5 custard cups.

- Bake in 160°C (325°F) oven for 45 minutes (25 minutes for custard cups) or until tester inserted in center comes out clean.

Makes 5 servings

Microwave Directions:
In 500 mL (2 cup) measuring cup, combine dates, milk and cinnamon. Microwave at High (100%) for 3 minutes, stirring once. Beat together egg, egg white and sugar, then slowly beat milk mixture into eggs. Fold into bread cubes. Spoon into microwaveable baking dish. Microwave, uncovered, at High (100%) for 4 minutes, stirring once. Cover and let stand for 5 minutes.

Fruity Bread Pudding

Here's old-fashioned bread pudding with a tasty difference

6	slices whole wheat bread	6
15 mL	margarine	1 tbsp
15 mL	all-purpose flour	1 tbsp
250 mL	2% milk	1 cup
125 mL	three-fruit dietetic fruit spread	$^1/_2$ cup
50 mL	unsweetened orange juice	$^1/_4$ cup
1	egg, beaten	1
1	egg white, lightly beaten	1
25 mL	granulated sugar*	2 tbsp
5 mL	rum flavoring	1 tsp
1 mL	ground allspice	$^1/_4$ tsp

The added sugar in the recipe has been included in the carbohydrate and Food Choice Values

- Cut bread in 1 cm (1/2 in) cubes. Set aside in 1.5 L (6 cup) casserole or baking dish.

- In heavy-bottomed saucepan, melt margarine. Stir in flour until well blended and cook over low heat for about 1 minute, taking care not to brown mixture. Add milk, stirring and continuing to cook for 5 minutes until mixture thickens.

- Whisk together three-fruit spread, orange juice, beaten egg, egg white, sugar, rum flavoring and allspice.

- Gradually stir into sauce until well mixed. Pour over bread cubes and stir gently just to coat cubes.

- Bake in 180ºC (350ºF) oven for 40 minutes or until top is golden brown and pudding is firm to the touch.

Makes 6 servings

Preparation Time: *20 minutes*
Baking Time: *40 minutes*

Each serving: 200 mL($^3/_4$ cup)

1 ☐ Starchy Choice
1 ◪ Fruits & Vegetables
1 ▲ Fats & Oils Choice

27 g carbohydrate
6 g protein
4 g fat

710 kilojoules
(168 Calories)

Microwave Directions:
Use dry bread cubes. Place in mixing bowl. In 500 mL (2 cup) measuring cup, microwave margarine at high (100%) for 30 seconds until melted. Stir in flour and milk. Microwave at high (100%) for 3 minutes, stirring once, until slightly thickened. Stir orange juice mixture into milk mixture. Stir into bread cubes until evenly mixed. Pour into 1.5 mL (6 cup) microwave proof ring mould. Microwave, uncovered, at High (100%) for 5 minutes or until edges are firm. Cover with plate for 5 minutes.

Blueberry Grunt

Preparation Time: *10 minutes*
Cooking Time: *15 minutes*

I had my first taste of Blueberry Grunt in Newfoundland. And I was surprised when I found out it was all cooked on top of the range in a heavy pot.

750 mL	blueberries	3 cups
	Sugar substitute equivalent to 125 mL (¹/₂ cup) sugar	
125 mL	water	¹/₂ cup
200 mL	all-purpose flour	³/₄ cup
50 mL	natural bran	¹/₄ cup
5 mL	baking powder	1 tsp
5 mL	granulated sugar*	1 tsp
1 mL	salt	¹/₄ tsp
125 mL	2% milk	¹/₂ cup

Each serving: 2 dumplings and 25 mL (2 tbsp) of sauce

1 ☐ Starchy Choice

1 ▨ Fruits & Vegetables

  24 g carbohydrate
  3 g protein
  1 g fat

  520 kilojoules
  (123 Calories)

* The added sugar in the recipe has been included in the carbohydrate and Food Choice Values.

- In large saucepan, combine blueberries, sugar substitute and water. Bring to boil; reduce heat and simmer for 4 minutes or until blueberries are soft.

- Meanwhile, in bowl, combine flour, bran, baking powder, sugar and salt. Stir in milk to make soft dough.

- Drop dough by spoonfuls onto blueberry mixture to make 12 equal-size dumplings.

- Cover saucepan and cook over low heat for 15 minutes or until dumplings puff and are no longer doughy inside. Do not remove cover until cooking is done.

- Serve immediately.

Makes 6 servings.

Apple Clafouti

Inspiration for this country-style dessert came from a classic French Clafouti I have been making for years. It is best described as a light, fruit-filled pancake.

Preparation Time: *10 minutes*
Baking Time: *30 minutes*

2	eggs	2
125 mL	skim milk	1/2 cup
	Sugar substitute equivalent to 30 mL (6 tsp) sugar	
15 mL	all-purpose flour	1 tbsp
5 mL	almond extract	1 tsp
3	medium apples, peeled and sliced	3
1 mL	cinnamon	1/4 tsp
Pinch	ground ginger	Pinch

Each Serving: 1/6 **of dessert**

1 🟥 Fruits & Vegetables

1/2 ⬜ Protein Choice

- In a bowl, combine eggs, milk, sugar substitute, flour and almond extract; mix well.

- Arrange sliced apples in the bottom of a 20 cm (8 in) round or square nonstick baking dish. Sprinkle with cinnamon and ginger.

- Pour egg mixture over apples.

- Bake in a 180ºC (350ºF) oven for 30 to 35 minutes or until set and tester, inserted halfway between centre and edge of dish, comes out clean. Cool.

- To serve, invert on serving plate, if desired, or spoon onto dessert plates from baking dish.

Makes 6 servings

11 g carbohydrate
3 g protein
2 g fat

310 kilojoules
(74 Calories)

Microwave Directions:
In a 2 L (6 cup) microwaveable ring mould, spread apples, sprinkle with cinnamon and ginger and pour batter over top. Sprinkle with a little additional cinnamon, if desired. Cover with waxed paper. Microwave, turning mould halfway through cooking time, at Medium High (70%) for 6 to 7 minutes or until tester inserted in cake comes out clean. Let stand 5 minutes.

Variation:
Peach Clafouti or Pear Clafouti: Substitute 6 peach or pear halves (fresh or canned in their own juice and drained) for the apples.

Calculations as above

Apricot Clafouti

Preparation Time: *15 minutes*
Baking Time: *35 minutes*

Clafouti is like an oven-baked omelette, full of fruit. It originated in the cherry country of France.

16	apricots or 26 apricot halves canned in juice and drained	16
3	eggs	3
75 mL	all-purpose flour	$^1/_3$ cup
75 mL	2% milk	$^1/_3$ cup
75 mL	2% yogurt	$^1/_3$ cup
25 mL	granulated sugar*	2 tbsp
5 mL	almond extract	1 tsp
2 mL	ground nutmeg	$^1/_2$ tsp
	Cottage Cream (p. 225) or whipped dessert topping, optional	

* The added sugar in the recipe has been included in the carbohydrate and Food Choice Values.

Each serving: $^1/_8$ **of clafouti**

1 ▰ Fruits & Vegetables

1 ◆ Milk Choice (2%)

16 g carbohydrate
4 g protein
3 g fat

440 kilojoules
(104 Calories)

- Cut apricots into quarters or eighths and arrange on bottom of 20 cm (8 in) round or square nonstick baking dish or spray dish with nonstick vegetable spray.

- In bowl, combine eggs, flour, milk, yogurt, sugar, almond extract and nutmeg. Mix well.

- Pour over apricots.

- Bake in 180°C (350°F) oven for 30 to 35 minutes or until set and tester inserted halfway between center and edge of dish comes out clean. Let cool.

- To serve, spoon onto dessert plates.

- Top each serving with 15 mL (1 tbsp) Cottage Cream or whipped topping, if desired.

Makes 8 servings.

Variation:
Plum Clafouti: Substitute 10 prune plums for the apricots.

Calculations as above

158

Banana and Peanut Butter Pie

Here's a winner and not just with the kids.

Preparation Time: *30 minutes*
Chilling Time: *4 hours*

Crust

500 mL	cornflakes, crushed	2 cups
125 mL	quick cooking rolled oats, toasted**	$^1/_2$ cup
25 mL	margarine or butter, melted	2 tbsp
	Sugar substitute equivalent to 25 mL (2 tbsp) sugar	
25 mL	water	2 tbsp

Filling

500 mL	2% milk	2 cups
2	small bananas, mashed	2
50 mL	minute tapioca	$^1/_4$ cup
25 mL	granulated sugar*	2 tbsp
25 mL	peanut butter	2 tbsp
5 mL	crushed peanuts	1 tsp

* *The added sugar in the recipe has been included in the carbohydrate and Food Choice Values.*

Each Serving: $^1/_8$ of pie

1 ▢ Starchy Choice
1 ◢ Fruits & Vegetables
1 ▲ Fats & Oils Choice

24 g carbohydrate
5 g protein
7 g fat

730 kilojoules
(173 Calories)

- **Crust:** In small bowl, combine cornflakes, rolled oats, margarine, sugar substitute and water. Reserve 50 mL ($^1/_4$ cup) and set aside. Press remaining mixture on bottom and up sides of 23 cm (9 in) pie plate.
- **Filling:** In heavy-bottomed saucepan, combine milk, mashed bananas, tapioca and sugar.
- Cook, stirring constantly, over low heat for about 5 minutes or until thickened.
- In small saucepan, heat peanut butter over low heat until liquidy. Pour this over tapioca mixture and stir 3 to 4 times to swirl peanut butter into mixture.
- Pour into prepared pie crust.
- Sprinkle with reserved crust mixture and crushed peanuts.
- Cover and chill for at least 4 hours or overnight.

Makes one 23 cm (9 in) pie, 8 servings

♣ **Timely Tip:**

**To toast quick-cooking rolled oats, place them in nonstick skillet. Heat over medium heat, stirring, for about 4 minutes or until golden brown.

Microwave Directions:
Prepare crust in microwaveable pie plate. Microwave at High (100%) for $1^1/_2$ minutes. Set aside. **Filling:** In 1 L (4 cup) microwaveable container, combine milk, mashed bananas, tapioca and sugar. Microwave, stirring halfway through cooking time, at High (100%) for 5 minutes or until thickened. In small microwaveable bowl, microwave peanut butter at High (100%) for 1 minute or until melted. Continue as recipe directs.

Banana Cream Pie

This crumb crust uses a minimum of margarine and is best if it is baked before it is filled.

Preparation Time: *20 minutes*
Baking Time: *10 minutes*

Crust

200 mL	graham wafer crumbs	³/₄ cup
30 mL	margarine or butter	2 tbsp
10 mL	water	2 tsp

Filling

500 mL	2% or skim milk	2 cups
75 mL	cornstarch	¹/₃ cup
2	egg yolks OR 1 whole egg	2
	Sugar substitute equivalent to 75 mL (¹/₃ cup) sugar	
10 mL	vanilla	2 tsp
2	small bananas	2
	Whipped topping, optional	

Each serving: ¹/₆ **of pie**

1 ☐   Starchy Choice

1 ▨   Fruits & Vegetables

1 ▲   Fats & Oils Choice

26 g carbohydrate
4 g protein
7 g fat

770 kilojoules
(183 Calories)

- **Crust:** In a bowl, combine crumbs, margarine and water until crumbly. With fingers, press onto the bottom and sides of a 23 cm (9 in) pie pan.
- Bake in a 190ºC (375ºF) oven for 10 minutes.
- **Filling:** Meanwhile, in a heavy saucepan, combine 125 mL (¹/₂ cup) of the milk and cornstarch; mix well. Add remaining milk. Place over medium heat and cook, stirring, until mixture comes to a boil; reduce heat and simmer, stirring, for 2 minutes. Remove from heat.
- In a bowl, beat egg yolks with a fork; add a small amount (125 mL /¹/₂ cup) of the hot mixture to beaten egg, stirring until smooth. Return immediately to hot mixture, stirring constantly. (The hot mixture will cook the egg.) Stir in sugar substitute and vanilla.
- Slice 1 banana and arrange slices on the bottom of cooled pie crust. Spoon half the pudding mixture over bananas. Slice remaining banana and arrange slices over pudding, then pour remaining pudding over bananas. Refrigerate to chill.
- Garnish with whipped topping, if desired, and serve.

Makes one 23 cm (9 in) pie, 6 servings

Microwave Directions:
Crust: Microwave, uncovered, at High (100%) for 2 minutes. **Filling:** In 1 L (4 cup) microwaveable container, combine all the milk and cornstarch; mix well. Microwave, stirring at half time, at High (100%) for 6 minutes until thick. Beat egg with fork, add small amount of thickened mixture to egg, then mix egg mixture into hot thickened mixture. Continue as recipe directs.

Strawberry Rhubarb Pie

Few Spring desserts are as luscious as this one. However, if it's not Spring and you want a delicious fruit pie, make it using frozen sliced rhubarb and frozen unsweetened strawberries.

Preparation Time: *20 minutes*
Baking Time: *40 minutes*

Crust

200 mL	all-purpose flour	³/₄ cup
125 mL	whole wheat flour	¹/₂ cup
1 mL	salt	¹/₄ tsp
45 mL	margarine or corn oil	3 tbsp
45 mL	ice water	3 tbsp

Filling

500 mL	sliced fresh or frozen unsweetened rhubarb (2.5 cm/1 in pieces)	2 cups
250 mL	fresh or frozen unsweetened strawberries, sliced	1 cup
50 mL	all-purpose flour	¹/₄ cup
	Sugar substitute equivalent to 250 mL (1 cup) sugar	
50 mL	unsweetened dessicated coconut	¹/₄ cup

Each Serving: ¹/₆ **of pie**

1 □ Starchy Choice

1 ◪ Fruits & Vegetables

1 ▲ Fats & Oils Choice

26 g carbohydrate
3 g protein
7 g fat

750 kilojoules
(179 Calories)

- **Crust:** In a bowl, combine flours and salt.

- With a pastry blender or 2 knives, cut in margarine until mixture is crumbly. Add the water gradually, stirring with a fork until mixture is moist but still crumbly.

- Press onto the bottom and sides of a 23 cm (9 in) pie plate with fingers, making sure pastry evenly covers both bottom and sides of the pie pan.

- **Filling:** In the same bowl, combine rhubarb and strawberries. Sprinkle with flour and sugar substitute. Toss gently.

- Spoon into prepared pie crust; spread evenly.

- Bake in a 220ºC (425ºF) oven for 30 minutes.

- Remove from oven. Sprinkle evenly with coconut; return to oven and continue to bake 10 minutes longer or until fruit is tender and top is golden brown.

Makes 1 pie, 6 servings

Homey Puddings and Pies

Recipe	Food Choices per Serving	Energy per Serving kilojoules	Calories	
Vanilla Pudding	1 ☐ Starchy; 1½ ◆ Milk (2%)	520	123	p. 148
Chocolate Pudding	1 ☐ Starchy; 1½ ◆ Milk (2%)	520	123	p. 148
Vanilla Creme Custard	1½ ◆ Milk (2%) OR 1 ◆ Milk (skim); 1 ▲ Fats & Oils	370	88	p. 149
Orange Creme Custard	1½ ◆ Milk (2%) OR 1 ◆ Milk (skim); 1 ▲ Fats & Oils	370	88	p. 149
Almond Creme Custard	1½ ◆ Milk (2%) OR 1 ◆ Milk (skim); 1 ▲ Fats & Oils	370	88	p. 149
Coconut Rice Pudding	1 ☐ Starchy; 1 ◆ Milk (skim)	470	113	p. 150
Apple Raisin Rice Pudding	1 ☐ Starchy; 1 ◆ Milk (skim)	400	96	p. 151
Chocolate Layered Pudding	1½ ◆ Milk (2%) OR 1 ◢ Fruits & Vegetables; 1 ⊘ Protein	400	95	p. 152
Lemon Layered Pudding	1½ ◆ Milk (2%) OR 1 ◢ Fruits & Vegetables; 1 ⊘ Protein	350	83	p. 153
Date Bread Pudding	1 ☐ Starchy; 1 ◆ Milk (2%)	560	134	p. 154
Fruity Bread Pudding	1 ☐ Starchy; 1 ◢ Fruits & Vegetables 1 ▲ Fats & Oils	710	168	p. 155
Blueberry Grunt	1 ☐ Starchy; 1 ◢ Fruits & Vegetables	520	123	p. 156
Apple Clafouti	1 ◢ Fruits & Vegetables; ½ ⊘ Protein	310	74	p. 157
Peach or Pear Clafouti	1 ◢ Fruits & Vegetables; ½ ⊘ Protein	310	74	p. 157
Apricot Clafouti	1 ◢ Fruits & Vegetables; 1 ◆ Milk (2%)	440	104	p. 158
Plum Clafouti	1 ◢ Fruits & Vegetables; 1 ◆ Milk (2%)	440	104	p. 158
Banana and Peanut Butter Pie	1 ☐ Starchy; 1 ◢ Fruits & Vegetables; 1 ▲ Fats & Oils	730	173	p. 159
Banana Cream Pie	1 ☐ Starchy; 1 ◢ Fruits & Vegetables; 1 ▲ Fats & Oils	770	183	p. 160
Strawberry Rhubarb Pie	1 ☐ Starchy; 1 ◢ Fruits & Vegetables; 1 ▲ Fats & Oils	750	179	p. 161

Crêpes and Pancakes

The crêpe seems to have won applause as the classiest pancake. It can be folded, rolled, stacked and stuffed with good things and even buried in sauce for a delectable dessert. Running close behind in my mind and offering all kinds of possibilities are clafoutis, frittatas, omelets and puffy pancakes. You can tuck bits and pieces of fruit and smidgens of spices into their batters and cook up delightful desserts or snacks.

German Pancake

Preparation Time: *30 minutes*
Cooking Time: *15 minutes*

This 'pancake' puffs up quickly in the oven, then drops, forming a hollow to fill with fresh fruit. For best results, serve immediately.

Pancake

125 mL	2% milk	$^1/_2$ cup
1	egg	1
1	egg white	1
Pinch	salt	Pinch
	Sugar substitute equivalent to 25 mL (2 tbsp) sugar	
75 mL	all-purpose flour	$^1/_3$ cup

Filling

250 mL	unsweetened orange juice	1 cup
10 mL	arrowroot flour	2 tsp
	Sugar substitute equivalent to 25 mL (2 tbsp) sugar	
	Summer Mixed Fruit OR Winter Mixed Fruit	

Summer Mixed Fruit

4	medium peaches	4
	Ascorbic acid color keeper	
250 mL	cubed cantaloupe	1 cup
125 mL	seedless green grapes, halved	$^1/_2$ cup
125 mL	blueberries	$^1/_2$ cup

- **Summer Mixed Fruit:** Peel, pit and thinly slice peaches. Sprinkle lightly with ascorbic acid color keeper. In bowl, combine peaches, cantaloupe, grapes and blueberries

OR
Winter Mixed Fruit

4	peach halves canned in juice, drained	4
1	medium apple	1
1	medium orange	1
125 mL	seedless green grapes, halved	$^1/_2$ cup

- **Winter Mixed Fruit**: Cut peach halves into bite-size pieces. Core apple and cut into bite-size pieces (do not peel). Peel and section orange. In bowl, combine peaches, apple, orange and grapes.

- **Pancake:** In mixing bowl, combine milk, egg, egg white, salt and sugar substitute; whisk until light and fluffy.

- Whisk in flour until blended.

- Pour into lightly greased 20 cm (8 in) deep-dish pie plate.

- Bake in 200ºC (400ºF) oven for 12 to 15 minutes or until light brown and puffy.

- Remove and let cool slightly to allow puff to fall before serving.

- **Filling:** In small saucepan, combine orange juice, arrowroot flour and sugar substitute. Cook over low heat, stirring, for about 4 minutes or until mixture thickens and is clear.

- Pour over Summer Mixed Fruit or Winter Mixed Fruit and toss to coat.

- Spoon into pancake.

- Cut into wedges to serve

Makes 8 servings

Each serving: 1/8 of pancake and Summer or Winter Mixed Fruit

2 Fruits & Vegetables

18 g carbohydrate
3 g protein
1 g fat

390 kilojoules
(95 Calories)

Strawberry Omelette

Preparation Time: *5 minutes*
Cooking Time: *5 minutes*

It's fun to share a warm dessert omelette as a finale at a dinner for two.

1	egg	1
1	egg white	1
	Sugar substitute equivalent to 15 mL (1 tbsp) sugar	
25 mL	all-purpose flour	2 tbsp
5 mL	oil	1 tsp
5 mL	vanilla	1 tsp
25 mL	light cream cheese, at room temperature	2 tbsp
8	strawberries	8
	Cinnamon	

- In small bowl, whisk together egg, egg white, sugar substitute, flour, oil and vanilla.

- Pour into nonstick 25 cm (10 in) skillet; swirl to spread evenly.

- Cook over medium-low heat for about 5 minutes or until top of omelette is set.

- Remove from heat; spread light cream cheese evenly over top. Slice strawberries and arrange evenly over cheese.

- Gently fold omelette in half and remove to warm platter.

- Sprinkle lightly with cinnamon and cut in half to serve.

Makes 2 servings

Variation:
Strawberry Roll
Spread 15 mL (1 tbsp) strawberry dietetic fruit spread over cheese instead of berries. Roll omelette for different presentation.

Each serving: ¹/₂ **of omelette**

1 ▨ Fruits & Vegetables
1 ▨ Protein Choice
1 ▲ Fats & Oils Choice

11 g carbohydrate
7 g protein
6 g fat

580 kilojoules
(137 Calories)

Calculations as above

Crêpes

Spread them, fill them, fold them or roll them. They take to fruit fillings and sauces. Remember to count all Food Choices.

Preparation Time: *5 minutes*
Standing Time: *1 hour*
Cooking Time: *20 minutes*

2	eggs	2
375 mL	2% milk	1¹/₂ cup
250 mL	all-purpose flour	1 cup
5 mL	vanilla	1 tsp
	Margarine	

- In bowl, beat together eggs and milk. Whisk in flour until smooth; stir in vanilla. Cover and refrigerate for 1 hour.
- Lightly brush thin coat of margarine on bottom of 15 cm (6 in) omelette or crêpe pan.
- Stir crêpe batter. For each crêpe, spoon 50 mL (¹/₄ cup) batter into hot pan, swirling it around to evenly cover bottom of pan. Cook until top is dry and no longer sticky. Loosen edge with spatula and slip onto plate. Repeat to make 12 crêpes.
- Crêpes may be made ahead, stacked and wrapped in plastic wrap. Store in refrigerator for up to 4 days or in freezer for up to 3 months. (Defrost in refrigerator.)

Makes 12 crêpes.

Each serving: 2 crêpes

1 ◻ Starchy Choice
1 ◆ Milk Choice (2%)

*18 g carbohydrate
6 g protein
3 g fat*

*540 kilojoules
(128 Calories)*

Blueberry Cream Crêpes

Some food lovers might call these blintzes, but these are more delicate and lighter than the blintzes I devoured in New York.

Preparation Time: *15 minutes*

500 mL	2% cottage cheese	2 cups
	Sugar substitute equivalent to 50 mL (¹/₄ cup) sugar	
5 mL	vanilla	1 tsp
250 mL	fresh or frozen blueberries	1 cup
12	Crêpes (recipe above)	12
250 mL	Blueberry Sauce (recipe, p. 224)	1 cup
	Cinnamon	

- In food processor or blender, combine cottage cheese, sugar substitute and vanilla. Process until puréed and smooth. Fold in blueberries.
- Place 60 mL (4 tbsp) on one-half of each crêpe. Roll up. Spoon 20 mL (4 tsp) Blueberry Sauce on each serving plate.
- Place filled crêpe on sauce and lightly sprinkle with cinnamon. Chill before serving, if desired.

Makes 12 servings

Each serving: 1 crêpe

1 ◻ Starchy Choice
1 ▨ Protein Choice
OR
1 ▧ Fruits & Vegetables
1 ◆ Milk Choice (2%)

*16 g carbohydrate
9 g protein
2 g fat*

*510 kilojoules
(121 Calories)*

Crèpes and Pancakes

Recipe	Food Choices per Serving	Energy per Serving kilojoules	Calories	
German Pancake	2 ◪ Fruits & Vegetables	390	95	p. 164
Strawberry Omelette	1 ◪ Fruits & Vegetables; 1 ◪ Protein 1 ◪ Fats & Oils	580	137	p. 166
Blueberry Cream Crèpes	1 ☐ Starchy; 1 ◪ Protein OR 1 ◪ Fruits & Vegetables; 1 ◈ Milk (2%)	510	121	p. 167
Crèpes	1 ☐ Starchy; 1 ◈ Milk (2%)	540	128	p. 167

168

Fruit Fantasies

Whenever I'm caught wondering what to have for dessert, I call on
my standby for all occasions — fruit. It's amazing how many luscious
concoctions you can make with just a few pieces of fruit. My daughter
Susan also has fun creating fruity finalés for her meals and some of
the desserts are her creations.

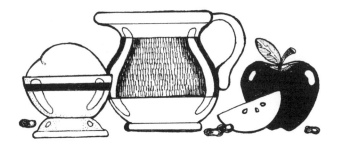

Apricot Fruit Soup

Preparation Time: *10 minutes*
Cooking Time: *10 minutes*

Everything about this fruit soup is exquisite — its brightness, tanginess and smoothness

18	dried apricot halves	18
375 mL	water	1¹/₂ cups
1	stick (7.5 cm/3 in) cinnamon	1
15 mL	granulated sugar*	1 tbsp
200 mL	2% plain yogurt	³/₄ cup
200 mL	2% milk	³/₄ cup
10 mL	finely chopped toasted walnuts	2 tsp

Each serving: 200 mL(³/₄ cup)

1 ◢ Fruits & Vegetable

1 ◆ Milk Choice (2%)

18 g carbohydrate
5 g protein
2 g fat

450 kilojoules
(108 Calories)

*The added sugar in the recipe has been included in the carbohydrate and Food Choice Values

- In saucepan, combine apricots, water, cinnamon stick and sugar. Bring to boil; reduce heat, cover and simmer for 10 minutes.

- Remove cinnamon stick. Pour into food processor or blender. Process for about 1 minute or until smooth. Add yogurt and milk; process for 10 seconds longer.

- Serve immediately in hot bowls or refrigerate in covered container for 2 hours or until chilled. Serve in chilled bowls.

- Garnish with chopped walnuts.

Makes 800 mL (3¹/₄ cups), 4 servings

Microwave Directions:
In 4 cup (1 L) microwaveable container, combine apricots, 1 cup (250 mL) water, cinnamon stick and sugar. Microwave at High (100%) for 5 minutes. Stir in remaining water and continue as recipe directs.

Fruit Soup

One day I served this warm instead of cold. Now it's on my list of comfort foods for chilly days.

Preparation Time: *10 minutes*
Cooking Time: *20 minutes*

2	medium apples	2
1	medium pear	1
750 mL	hot water	3 cups
5 mL	ascorbic acid color keeper	1 tsp
5 mL	grated lemon rind	1 tsp
2 mL	ground cinnamon	$^1/_2$ tsp
Pinch	salt	Pinch
15 mL	cornstarch	1 tbsp
15 mL	cold water	1 tbsp
10 mL	dry sherry or vanilla	2 tsp
10 mL	granulated sugar*	2 tsp
15 mL	2% plain yogurt	1 tbsp

Each serving: 200 mL$^{(3/4}$ cup)

1 ◢ Fruits & Vegetables

11 *g carbohydrate*

230 *kilojoules*
(54 *Calories*)

*The added sugar in the recipe has been included in the carbohydrate and Food Choice Values

- Peel, core and chop 1 of the apples and the pear.

- In saucepan, combine chopped fruits, hot water, ascorbic acid color keeper, lemon rind, cinnamon and salt.

- Bring to boil; reduce heat and simmer for 15 minutes.

- Transfer to food processor or blender. Process for about 30 seconds or until smooth. Return to saucepan.

- Combine cornstarch and cold water until smooth. Stir into fruit purée. Cook, stirring, for about 3 minutes or until thickened.

- Stir in sherry or vanilla and sugar.

- Peel and grate remaining apple. Stir into soup.

- Serve warm or refrigerate for about 2 hours and serve chilled.

- Garnish each serving with drizzle of yogurt.

Makes 1.25 L (4$^1/_2$ cups), 6 servings

Microwave Directions:

In 1 L (4 cup) microwaveable container, combine the chopped apple and pear, 250 mL (1 cup) hot water, color keeper, lemon rind, cinnamon and salt. Microwave at High (100%) for 5 minutes. Stir in cornstarch mixture. Microwave for 1$^1/_2$ minutes, stirring once. Stir in remaining hot water, sherry, grated apple and sugar.

Blueberry Borscht

Preparation Time: *5 minutes*
Cooking Time: *10 minutes*

Here's a delightfully different dessert that can also be served as a starter.

750 mL	fresh or frozen thawed unsweetened blueberries	3 cups
500 mL	water	2 cups
	Sugar substitute equivalent to 25 mL (2 tbsp) sugar	
15 mL	minute tapioca	1 tbsp
90 mL	2% plain yogurt	6 tbsp
2 mL	vanilla	1/2 tsp

Each serving: 175 mL(²/₃ cup)

1  Fruits & Vegetables

10 g carbohydrate
1 g protein
1 g fat

240 kilojoules
(57 Calories)

- In large saucepan, combine berries, water, sugar substitute and tapioca.

- Cook over medium heat, stirring occasionally, for about 10 minutes or until mixture thickens.

- Remove from heat and transfer to blender or food processor. Blend or process until fruit is puréed.

- Combine yogurt and vanilla.

- Pour fruit purée evenly into 6 bowls. Top each with 15 mL (1 tbsp) yogurt-vanilla mixture.

Makes 1 L (4 cups), 6 servings.

Berry Fool

The acidity of the puréed berries blends well with the whipped topping for a fruity whip that's as easy to make as it is to eat. The name is an old one. It comes from the French word fouler, *which means to crush.*

Preparation Time: *5 minutes*
Cooking Time: *5 minutes*
Chilling Time: *30 minutes*

500 mL	blueberries	2 cups
	Sugar substitute equivalent to 125 mL (¹/₂ cup) sugar	
50 mL	water	¹/₄ cup
5 mL	grated orange peel	1 tsp
1	envelope dessert topping mix	1
125 mL	2% milk	¹/₂ cup
5 mL	vanilla	1 tsp

• In saucepan, combine blueberries, sugar substitute, water and orange peel. Bring to boil; reduce heat and simmer for 5 minutes or until berries are tender and saucy. Mash berries; stir well. Set aside to let cool. (If smooth fool is desired, press berry mixture through sieve or purée in processor or blender.)

• In large bowl, beat topping mix with milk and vanilla.

• Fold cool berry mixture into whipped topping until even-colored.

• Spoon into serving bowl, individual stemmed glasses or dessert dishes.

• Chill for at least 30 minutes before serving. Cover and refrigerate for up to 5 days; freeze for up to 4 weeks. Defrost frozen Berry Fool in refrigerator for 1 hour before serving.

Makes 6 servings

Variation:
Raspberry, Blackberry or Gooseberry Fool:
Substitute raspberries, blackberries or gooseberries for the blueberries.

Each serving: 175 mL(²/₃ cup)

1 ▰ Fruits & Vegetables
1 ▲ Fats & Oils Choice

10 g carbohydrate
4 g fat

340 kilojoules
(82 Calories)

Calculations as above

Sesame Baked Bananas

Preparation Time: *5 minutes*
Baking Time: *20 minutes*

Use firm ripe bananas for this comforting warm dessert.

2	small bananas, cut in half lengthwise	2
25 mL	unsweetened orange juice	2 tbsp
10 mL	margarine, melted	2 tsp
	Sugar substitute equivalent to 15 mL (1 tbsp) sugar	
2 mL	vanilla	$^1/_2$ tsp
15 mL	unsweetened dessicated coconut	1 tbsp
15 mL	toasted sesame seeds	1 tbsp
	Whipped dessert topping, optional	

Each serving: $^1/_2$ banana

1 ◢ Fruits & Vegetable

1 ▲ Fats & Oils Choice

12 g carbohydrate
1 g protein
4 g fat

370 kilojoules
(89 Calories)

- In nonstick 20 cm (8 in) square baking dish, arrange bananas cut side down.

- Combine orange juice, margarine, sugar substitute and vanilla.
  Spoon over bananas.

- Sprinkle coconut and sesame seeds evenly over bananas.

- Bake in 180ºC (350ºF) oven for about 20 minutes or until bananas are soft and lightly browned. Serve warm.

- Garnish each serving with 15 mL (1 tbsp) whipped topping, if desired.

Makes 4 servings

Microwave Directions:
Cut banana halves in half. Arrange, like spokes, in round microwaveable baking dish. Spoon orange mixture over bananas; sprinkle with coconut and sesame seeds. Microwave at High (100%) for 2 minutes or until bananas are soft and hot.

Baked Apples

Here's a warm and inviting dessert for nippy autumn days when apples from Canada's orchards are at their prime.

Preparation Time: *15 minutes*
Baking Time: *25 minutes*

4	medium apples	4
125 mL	quick cooking rolled oats	$^1/_2$ cup
15 mL	finely chopped raisins	1 tbsp
15 mL	finely chopped pecans	1 tbsp
10 mL	margarine	2 tsp
1 mL	ground cinnamon	$^1/_4$ tsp
Pinch	ground nutmeg	Pinch
	Sugar substitute equivalent to 25 mL (2 tbsp) sugar	
2 mL	maple extract	$^1/_2$ tsp

- Cut off stem end of apples to 1 cm ($^1/_2$ in) below top. Carefully cut around cores and lift out.

- Scoop out pulp to leave about 2.5 cm (1 in) hollow in centre of apples. Reserve pulp.

- In bowl, combine rolled oats, raisins, pecans, margarine, cinnamon, nutmeg, sugar substitute, maple extract and reserved apple pulp.

- Evenly divide mixture and pack into apples.

- Arrange apples in baking dish.

- Bake in 180ºC (350ºF) oven for 30 minutes or until pulp is soft but skin is still tight.

Makes 4 servings

Each serving: 1 apple

1 ☐ Starchy Choice
1 ◢ Fruits & Vegetable
1 ▲ Fats & Oils Choice

26 g carbohydrate
2 g protein
4 g fat

680 kilojoules
(161 Calories)

Microwave Directions:
Arrange stuffed apples in a circle in microwaveable pie plate so they don't touch each other or edge of dish. Cover with microwave plastic wrap, leaving no vent so apples are airtight. Microwave at High (100%) for 5 minutes, rotating quarter turn halfway through, until apples are tender but not collapsed. Pierce plastic wrap to let out steam. Let stand for 2 minutes to steam. Spoon juice over apples.

Brandied Oranges

Preparation Time: *15 minutes*
Cooking Time: *10 minutes*

Here's a simple dessert for two. It's luscious and elegant.

2	small oranges	2
125 mL	unsweetened orange juice	$^1/_2$ cup
50 mL	water	$^1/_4$ cup
2 mL	ground cinnamon	$^1/_2$ tsp
Pinch	ground cloves	Pinch
Pinch	ground nutmeg	Pinch
15 mL	brandy OR 2 mL ($^1/_2$ tsp) brandy extract	1 tbsp
	Sugar substitute equivalent to 15 mL (1 tbsp) sugar	
10 mL	arrowroot	2 tsp

Each serving: 1 orange with 50 mL ($^1/_4$ cup) sauce with peel

2 ▟ Fruits & Vegetables

21 g carbohydrate
1 g protein

340 kilojoules
(82 Calories)

- With paring knife, peel oranges, removing all white membrane. Set fruit aside.

- Scrape white pith from peel of half an orange. Cut peel into very thin strips. Pour boiling water over peel and let stand.

- In medium, heavy-bottomed saucepan, combine orange juice, water, cinnamon, cloves, nutmeg, brandy or brandy extract and sugar substitute. Drain and add peel to saucepan.

- Bring to boil; reduce heat and add peeled oranges. Simmer for about 10 minutes, turning oranges once or twice, or until heated through. (Most of the alcohol in this recipe evaporates.)

Microwave Directions:
Omit water. In glass measuring cup, combine orange juice, cinnamon, cloves, nutmeg, brandy and sweetener. Add drained peel. Microwave at High (100%) for 2 minutes or until hot. Place oranges in small microwaveable dish. Pour juice mixture over top. Microwave at High (100%) for 2 minutes. Remove oranges to serving dishes. Stir arrowroot mixture into liquid in dish. Microwave at High (100%) for 2 minutes or until sauce is thickened. Pour over oranges.

- With slotted spoon, remove oranges to serving dish.

- Stir arrowroot flour into 15 mL (1 tbsp) cold water, then into liquid in saucepan. Cook, stirring, for 2 minutes or until sauce is thickened and clear. Pour over oranges.

- Serve warm.

Makes 2 servings

Baked Grapefruit Meringue

All fruits seem sweeter when they are warm or at room temperature, especially citrus fruits. That's why I like broiled grapefruit.

Preparation Time: *10 minutes*
Baking Time: *10 minutes*

2	pink or white grapefruit	2
1	egg white	1
Pinch	cream of tartar	Pinch
10 mL	brown sugar*	2 tsp
10 mL	unsweetened desiccated coconut	2 tsp

*The added sugar in the recipe has been included in the carbohydrate and Food Choice Values

- With sharp knife, cut grapefruit in half. Cut around and inside membranes to loosen segments. Place cut side up in shallow baking dish.

- In small mixing bowl, beat egg white and cream of tartar until foamy; add sugar and continue beating until stiff peaks form. Spoon evenly over top of each grapefruit half, spreading meringue to edges. With back of spoon, swirl and peak meringue.

- Sprinkle each with coconut.

- Bake in 190ºC (375ºF) oven for 10 minutes or until lightly browned.

Makes 4 servings

Each serving: half grapefruit with meringue

1 ◪ Fruits & Vegetables

> *11 g carbohydrate*
> *2 g protein*
> *1 g fat*

> *230 kilojoules*
> *(55 Calories)*

Microwave Directions:
Microwave meringue topped grapefruit at High (100%) for $1^{1}/_{2}$ minutes.

Blushing Poached Pears

Preparation Time: *15 minutes*
Cooking Time: *15 minutes*

These blushing rose pears have a tantalizing , tangy flavor.

200 mL	unsweetened orange juice	³/₄ cup
50 mL	dry red wine	¹/₄ cup
50 mL	water	¹/₄ cup
15 mL	grated lemon rind	1 tbsp
	Sugar substitute equivalent to 15 mL (1 tbsp) sugar	
Pinch	ground cinnamon	Pinch
Pinch	ground cloves	Pinch
2	medium pears	2
10 mL	arrowroot flour	2 tsp

Each serving: **¹/₂ pear with 50 mL (¹/₄ cup) sauce**

2 ◣ Fruits & Vegetables

19 g carbohydrate
1 g protein

350 kilojoules
(84 Calories)

- In medium, heavy-bottomed saucepan, combine orange juice, wine, water, lemon rind, sugar substitute, cinnamon and cloves.

- Bring to boil; reduce heat and simmer. (Most of the alcohol in this recipe evaporates.)

- Meanwhile, peel pears. Cut in half lengthwise and remove cores.

- Add pear halves to saucepan. Continue to simmer for about 10 minutes, turning once or twice, until pears are soft rose color and heated through.

- With slotted spoon, remove pear halves to serving dish.

- Stir arrowroot flour into 15 mL (1 tbsp) water and then into liquid in saucepan. Cook, stirring, for about 2 minutes or until sauce is thickened and opaque.

- Spoon sauce evenly over pears. Serve warm.

Makes 4 servings.

Fresh Applesauce

It only takes a few minutes to turn fresh apples into a refreshingly different dessert. But please don't peel them. The peel provides additional fiber and makes the sauce colorful.

Preparation Time: *7 minutes*

2	small red apples	2
2 mL	ascorbic acid color keeper	$^1/_2$ tsp
1	slice white bread, crust removed	1
5 mL	lime or lemon juice	1 tsp
2 mL	rum extract, optional	$^1/_2$ tsp
2 mL	ground cinnamon	$^1/_2$ tsp
	Sugar substitute equivalent to 15 mL (1 tbsp) sugar	

- Quarter and core apples. Cut into pieces. Sprinkle with ascorbic acid color keeper.

- Tear bread into pieces.

- In food processor, combine apples, bread, lime juice, rum extract, if desired, and cinnamon. Process for about 2 minutes or until smooth and mushy. Add sugar substitute and process for 10 seconds longer. (If food processor is unavailable, shred apples with vegetable shredder and combine with crumbled bread and other ingredients.)

- Serve at room temperature or chilled.

Makes 2 servings

Each Serving:
$^1/_2$ **of applesauce,**
125 mL ($^1/_2$ cup)

2 ▰ Fruits & Vegetables

19 g carbohydrate
1 g protein
1 g fat

400 kilojoules
(95 Calories)

Glazed Fruit Bowl

Preparation Time: *15 minutes*
Cooking Time: *4 minutes*
Chilling Time: *30-45 minutes*

A pretty combination of colorful, glistening fruit is scrumptious served at lunch or supper.

1	small orange	1
1	small grapefruit	1
500 mL	strawberries	2 cups
200 mL	seedless green grapes	3/4 cup
200 mL	unsweetened orange juice	3/4 cup
125 mL	water	1/2 cup
	Sugar substitute equivalent to 50 mL (1/4 cup) sugar	
15 mL	arrowroot flour	1 tbsp

- With paring knife, peel orange and grapefruit, removing all white membrane. Remove sections to bowl.

- Slice strawberries and grapes. Add to bowl and set aside.

- Scrape white pith from half of the orange peel. Cut peel into very thin strips. Pour boiling water over peel and let stand.

- In saucepan, combine orange juice, water, sugar substitute and arrowroot flour. Drain and add peel to saucepan.

- Cook over medium heat, stirring, for about 4 minutes or until mixture is thickened and clear.

- Pour over fruit and mix until fruit is covered and glazed.

- Refrigerate, covered, for 30 to 45 minutes or until chilled.

Makes 8 servings

Each serving: 175 mL(²/₃ cup)

1 ◣ Fruits & Vegetables

12 g carbohydrate
1 g protein

220 kilojoules
(52 Calories)

Microwave Directions:
Prepare fruit as recipe directs. In 1 L (4 cup) microwaveable container, combine orange juice, water and arrowroot flour. Microwave, stirring halfway through cooking time, at High (100%) for 3¹/₂ minutes or until thickened and clear. Cool for 2 minutes. Stir in sweetener. Continue as recipe directs.

Grape and Peach Ambrosia

The dictionary says ambrosia is an exquisite dish. And this one is —
cool, juicy fruit and crunchy nuts bathed in wine-scented yogurt.

Preparation Time: *10 minutes*
Chilling Time: *1 hour*

250 mL	seedless green grapes	1 cup
2	medium peaches, peeled OR 3 peach halves canned in juice, drained	2
1	medium apple, unpeeled	1
25 mL	chopped walnuts	2 tbsp
125 mL	2% plain yogurt	¹/₂ cup
	Sugar substitute equivalent to 15 mL (1 tbsp) sugar	
15 mL	dry sherry or Marsala wine	1 tbsp

- Place grapes in bowl.

- Cut peaches and apple into bite-size pieces. Add to bowl along with walnuts.

- Combine yogurt, sugar substitute and sherry.

- Pour over fruit and toss gently to thoroughly coat fruit.

- Chill for at least 1 hour. Stir gently and serve.

Makes 750 mL (3 cups), 4 servings

Each Serving: 200 mL (³/₄ cup)

2 ▰ Fruits & Vegetables
1 ▲ Fats & Oils Choice

OR

1 ▰ Fruits & Vegetables
1 ◆ Milk Choice (2%)

18 g carbohydrate
3 g protein
3 g fat
1 g alcohol

480 kilojoules
(115 Calories)

Fruit Fantasies

Recipe	Food Choices per Serving	Energy per Serving kilojoules	Calories	
Apricot Fruit Soup	1 ▨ Fruits & Vegetables; 1 ◆ Milk (2%)	450	108	p. 170
Fruit Soup	1 ▨ Fruits & Vegetables	230	54	p. 171
Blueberry Borscht	1 ▨ Fruits & Vegetables	240	57	p. 172
Berry Fool	1 ▨ Fruits & Vegetables; 1 ▲ Fats & Oils	340	82	p. 173
Sesame Baked Bananas	1 ▨ Fruits & Vegetables; 1 ▲ Fats & Oils	370	89	p. 174
Baked Apples	1 ▢ Starchy: 1 ▨ Fruits & Vegetables 1 ▲ Fats & Oils	680	161	p. 175
Brandied Oranges	2 ▨ Fruits & Vegetables	340	82	p. 176
Baked Grapefruit Meringue	1 ▨ Fruits & Vegetables	230	55	p. 177
Blushing Poached Pears	2 ▨ Fruits & Vegetables	350	84	p. 178
Fresh Applesauce	2 ▨ Fruits & Vegetables	400	95	p. 179
Glazed Fruit Bowl	1 ▨ Fruits & Vegetables	220	52	p. 180
Grape and Peach Ambrosia	2 ▨ Fruits & Vegetables; 1 ▲ Fats & Oils **OR** 1 ▨ Fruits & Vegetables; 1 ◆ Milk (2%)	480	115	p. 181

Cool Jellies and Mousses

Since these shimmering jellies and fluffy mousses are refreshingly light, I've classified them as cool, mouth-watering winners for warm summer days. They're also winners with busy cooks because they can be made ahead and wait in the refrigerator until serving time.

Ambrosia

Preparation Time: *10 minutes*
Chilling Time: *2 ¹/₂ hours*

Jelly desserts are a joy because they can be made in advance yet always seem fresh.

1	envelope unflavored gelatin	1
125 mL	water	¹/₂ cup
250 mL	unsweetened orange juice	1 cup
250 mL	unsweetened crushed pineapple drained	1 cup
50 mL	unsweetened dessicated coconut	¹/₄ cup

- In small custard cup or dish, sprinkle gelatin over water and let stand for 4 to 5 minutes to soften.

- In small saucepan, heat 125 mL (¹/₂ cup) of the orange juice. Add softened gelatin to hot liquid and stir until gelatin dissolves completely.

- In medium bowl, combine gelatin mixture with remaining 125 mL (¹/₂ cup) orange juice.

- Chill in refrigerator for 20 minutes or until consistency of egg whites and partially set.

- Fold in pineapple and coconut.

- Return to refrigerator to chill for at least 2 hours or until set.

Makes 6 servings

Each serving: 125 mL(¹/₂ cup)

1 Fruits & Vegetables

1 Fats & Oils Choice

12 g carbohydrate
2 g protein
3 g fat

310 kilojoules
(74 Calories)

Microwave Directions:
In small microwaveable dish, sprinkle gelatin over cold water; let stand until gelatin softens. Microwave at High (100%) for 2 minutes or until gelatin dissolves. Gradually stir into orange juice. Continue as recipe directs.

Melon Mousse

If the beaters, bowl and evaporated milk are ice cold, the whipped milk will be fluffier with more volume. This adds more lightness to the mousse.

Preparation Time: *15 minutes*
Chilling Time: *4 to 6 $1/4$ hours*

1	cantaloupe	1
Pinch	salt	Pinch
2	envelopes unflavored gelatin	2
125 mL	water	$1/2$ cup
50 mL	orange juice	$1/4$ cup
75 mL	ice cold evaporated skim milk	$1/3$ cup
	Sugar substitute equivalent to 15 mL (1 tbsp) sugar	
5 mL	vanilla	1 tsp
12	seedless green grapes OR	12
1	kiwifruit, peeled and sliced	1
	Cottage Cream (recipe, p. 225) or whipped dessert topping, optional	

Each Serving: $1/6$ **of Mousse**

1 ▰ Fruits & Vegetables

12 g carbohydrate
3 g protein

260 kilojoules
(61 Calories)

- Quarter cantaloupe; remove seeds and peel. Cut into chunks.

- In food processor or blender, combine cantaloupe and salt. Process until puréed and transfer to bowl.

- In small saucepan, sprinkle gelatin over water and orange juice. Let stand for 3 minutes to soften. Heat over low heat, stirring, until gelatin dissolves.

- Stir into puréed cantaloupe. Chill in refrigerator for about 15 minutes or until partially set.

- Beat evaporated milk until stiff; beat in sugar substitute and vanilla. Fold into melon mixture until evenly distributed.

- Spoon into 2 L (8 cup) mold or individual dessert dishes. Cover and chill for 4 to 6 hours or until firm.

- Unmold and garnish with grapes or kiwifruit. Garnish each serving with 15 mL (1 tbsp) Cottage Cream or whipped topping, if desired

Makes 6 servings

Nectarine Lemonade Mousse

Preparation Time: *15 minutes*
Chilling Time: *4 ½ hours*

The nectarine slices appear to float in this creamy lemonade gel.

2	envelopes unflavored gelatin	2
500 mL	diet lemonade	2 cups
250 mL	boiling water	1 cup
2	egg whites	2
2 mL	cream of tartar	½ tsp
25 mL	granulated sugar*	2 tbsp
250 mL	plain low-fat yogurt	1 cup
2	nectarines	2

* *The added sugar in the recipe has been included in the carbohydrate and Food Choice Values.*

Each serving: 250 mL (1 cup)

1 ◪ Fruits & Vegetables

1 ◆ Milk Choice (2%)

15 g carbohydrate
7 g protein
1 g fat

400 kilojoules
(96 Calories)

- In bowl, sprinkle gelatin over 125 mL (½ cup) lemonade and let stand for about 5 minutes to soften. Add boiling water and stir until gelatin is completely dissolved.

- Stir in remaining lemonade. Chill in refrigerator for about 20 minutes or until mixture just mounds on spoon. Whisk for about 2 minutes or until light.

- Beat egg whites with cream of tartar until fluffy. Beat in sugar and continue until stiff peaks form.

- Fold ⅓ of egg whites into gelatin mixture until texture is smooth. Fold in remaining egg whites until texture is smooth.

- Gently fold in yogurt.

- Peel and thinly slice nectarines. Fold half into lemonade mixture. Reserve remaining half.

- Spoon into glass bowl. Garnish with reserved nectarine slices.

- Cover and chill for about 4 hours or until firm, or overnight.

Makes 5 servings.

Rosé Fruit Parfait

Every time the word parfait is mentioned, I imagine a dessert dressed up for a party. This combination of fruit layered with both a creamy and a sparkling gel portrays that image.

Preparation Time: *10 minutes*
Chilling Time: *1 ½ hours*

1	envelope unflavored gelatin	1
250 mL	water	1 cup
200 mL	dry rosé wine	³/₄ cup
	Sugar substitute equivalent to 15 mL (1 tbsp) sugar	
1	egg white	1
1	small banana, coarsely chopped	1
1	kiwifruit, peeled & coarsely chopped	1
200 mL	strawberries, sliced & quartered	³/₄ cup

Each Serving: 1 parfait

1 ▧ Fruits & Vegetables
1 ▲ Fats & Oils Choice

11 g protein
3 g fat
4 g alcohol

280 kilojoules
(70 Calories)

- In small saucepan, sprinkle gelatin over 125 mL (¹/₂ cup) of the water and let stand for 5 minutes to soften. Heat over low heat, stirring, until gelatin dissolves.

- Stir in remaining water, rosé wine and sugar substitute.

- Chill in refrigerator for about 30 minutes or until partially set and mixture just mounds on spoon.

- Beat egg white until stiff peaks form. Beat in half of the gelatin mixture.

- Toss fruit together and divide into 4 equal portions.

- In 4 parfait or stemmed glasses, alternately layer equal amounts of fruit, gelatin mixture and egg white mixture.

- Return to refrigerator and chill for 1 hour or until set.

Makes 4 servings

Note: The alcohol in the rosé wine gives Calories. A Fats & Oils Choice is given to cover the Calories

Variation:
Peach, Blueberry and Kiwi Parfait:
Use the following fruit combination in place of banana, strawberries and kiwifruit: 2 medium peaches, peeled & chopped, 125 mL (¹/₂ cup) fresh blueberries and 1 kiwifruit, peeled & chopped.

Calculations as above

Apricot Bavarian Cream

Preparation Time: *40 minutes*
Chilling Time: *4 ½ hours*

This is creamy and luscious like a Bavarian cream should be, but it's lighter and not as rich.

12	dried apricot halves	12
1	stick cinnamon, 8 cm (3 in) long	1
125 mL	water	¹/₂ cup
	Sugar substitute equivalent to 15 mL (1 tbsp) sugar	
75 mL	2% plain yogurt	¹/₃ cup
75 mL	2% milk	¹/₃ cup
1	envelope unflavored gelatin	1
50 mL	cold water	¹/₄ cup
1	envelope dessert topping, whipped	1

Each serving: 175 mL(²/₃ cup)

1 Fruits & Vegetables

1 ◣ Fats & Oils Choice

11 g carbohydrate
3 g protein
4 g fat

370 kilojoules
(88 Calories)

Microwave Directions:
In a 1 L (4 cup) microwaveable dish, combine apricots, cinnamon stick and water. Microwave at High (100%) for 5 minutes or until apricots are tender. Remove cinnamon stick. Process with yogurt and milk as directed. In small microwaveable bowl or cup, sprinkle gelatin over water. Let stand 2 minutes to soften. Microwave at High (100%) for 1 minute or until gelatin melts. Stir into apricot mixture. Add sweetener. Continue as recipe directs.

- In saucepan, combine apricots, cinnamon stick, water and sugar substitute. Bring to boil; reduce heat, cover and simmer for 10 minutes or until apricots are tender. Remove cinnamon stick.

- Pour into food processor or blender. Process for about 1 minute or until smooth. Add yogurt and milk; process for 10 seconds longer. Remove to bowl and set aside to let cool.

- In small saucepan, sprinkle gelatin over cold water and let stand for about 5 minutes to soften. Heat over low heat, stirring, until gelatin is completely dissolved. Stir into apricot mixture; mix well.

- Chill in refrigerator for about 30 minutes or until partially set and mixture just mounds on spoon.

- Fold in whipped topping until blended.

- Pour into 1 L (4 cup) mold. Cover and chill in refrigerator for about 4 hours or until set.

- At serving time, unmold on serving plate.

Makes 6 servings

Snow Gelatin

This light dessert is adapted from the cuisine of Japan. The Japanese always decorate it with a pretty garnish of colorful fruit.

Preparation Time: *10 minutes*
Standing Time: *30 minutes*
Chilling Time: *2 to 4 hours*

1	envelope unflavored gelatin	1
250 mL	water	1 cup
	Sugar substitute equivalent to 125 mL (¹/₂ cup) sugar	
25 mL	fresh lime or lemon juice	2 tbsp
5 mL	vanilla	1 tsp
2	egg whites	2
6	strawberries or orange slices	6

Each Serving: 125 mL(¹/₂ cup)

1 ┣┫ Extra

- In a small saucepan, sprinkle gelatin over water and let stand for 5 minutes to soften. Place over low heat and stir until gelatin dissolves. Stir in sugar substitute, lime juice and vanilla.

2 g carbohydrate
2 g protein

- Chill in the refrigerator about 25 to 30 minutes or until partially set and the consistency of raw egg white.

70 kilojoules
(16 Calories)

- Beat egg whites until stiff peaks form. Fold into gelatin mixture. Pour into a 20 cm (8 in) square pan or a 1 L (4 cup) mold.

- Chill in refrigerator for 3 to 4 hours or until set.

Microwave Directions:
In small microwaveable bowl, sprinkle gelatin over water and let stand for 2 minutes until softened. Microwave at High (100%) for 2 minutes or until gelatin dissolves. Continue as recipe directs.

- Cut gelatin in pan into 6 squares. Remove with spatula to dessert plates. Garnish each with a strawberry cut in slices or an orange slice cut in half. (If gelatin is in a mold, unmold it onto a plate and garnish attractively with strawberry or orange slices.)

Makes 750 mL (3 cups), 6 servings

Variation:

Cranberry Chiffon: In place of water and lemon juice, use 375 mL (1¹/₂ cups) cranberry juice cocktail. Omit the strawberry or orange slice garnish.

Each Serving: 125 mL(¹/₂ cup)

1 ◢ Fruits & Vegetables

10 g carbohydrate
2 g protein

210 kilojoules
(51 Calories)

Chocolate Mousse Soufflé

Preparation Time: *20 minutes*
Standing Time: *4 hours*

Gelatin gives the mousse a little more body. Dusting with shaved chocolate gives it an elegant touch.

1	envelope unflavored gelatin	1
75 mL	unsweetened orange juice	$^1/_3$ cup
250 mL	skim milk	1 cup
50 mL	dry unsweetened cocoa	$^1/_4$ cup
2	eggs, separated	2
5 mL	vanilla	1 tsp
	Sugar substitute equivalent to 50 mL ($^1/_4$ cup) sugar	
Pinch	cinnamon	Pinch
Pinch	cream of tartar	Pinch
10 mL	grated semi-sweet chocolate ($^1/_2$ square)	2 tsp
	Whipped topping, optional	

Each serving: 200 mL(³/₄ cup)

1 ◆ Milk Choice (homo)

OR

1 ◆ Milk Choice (skim)

¹/₂ ▲ Fats & Oils Choice

7 g carbohydrate
5 g protein
3 g fat

320 kilojoules
(75 Calories)

- In a small bowl or cup, sprinkle gelatin over orange juice and let stand for 5 minutes to soften.

- In saucepan, whisk together milk and cocoa until there are no dry lumps of cocoa. Place over medium heat. Bring to a boil; reduce heat and cook over low heat, stirring frequently, about 7 minutes or until slightly thickened. Remove from heat.

- Beat egg yolks with a fork; stir about 125 mL ($^1/_2$ cup) of the hot mixture into beaten yolks, stirring until smooth. Immediately return this egg yolk mixture to the chocolate mixture, stirring well.

- Stir in gelatin until it dissolves, then add vanilla, sugar substitute and cinnamon; mix well.

- Pour into medium bowl. Cover and chill in refrigerator about 30 minutes or until partially set.

- Beat egg whites with cream of tartar until stiff peaks form.

- Stir one-quarter of the beaten egg whites into partially set chocolate mixture, then fold in remaining stiffly beaten egg whites until there are no white streaks.

- Spoon into straight-sided soufflé dish or mold. Chill about 4 hours or until set.

- Unmold onto serving plate. Garnish with shredded chocolate and whipped topping, if desired.

Makes 6 servings

Chocolate Mousse

Rich and creamy, this smooth mousse is a perfect make-ahead dessert for a special dinner.

Preparation Time: *15 minutes*
Standing Time: *2 hours*

250 mL	evaporated skim milk	1 cup
50 mL	dry unsweetened cocoa	$^1/_4$ cup
2	eggs, separated	2
5 mL	almond extract or vanilla	1 tsp
	Sugar substitute equivalent to 50 mL ($^1/_4$ cup) sugar	
Pinch	cream of tartar	Pinch
5 mL	granulated sugar	1 tsp
	Strawberries, raspberries or whipped topping	

- In a medium saucepan, whisk together milk and cocoa until there are no dry lumps of cocoa.

- Place over medium heat. Bring to a boil; reduce heat and cook over low heat, stirring frequently, about 7 minutes or until smooth and slightly thickened. Remove from heat.

- Beat egg yolks with a fork. Stir 125 mL ($^1/_2$ cup) of the hot mixture into beaten yolks, stirring until smooth; immediately return to chocolate mixture, stirring well. Stir in almond extract and sugar substitute.

- Pour into medium bowl; cover and chill for 1 hour.

- Beat egg whites and cream of tartar until soft peaks form. Add sugar and beat until stiff.

- Stir one-quarter of beaten egg whites into cooled chocolate mixture to lighten it, then fold in remaining stiffly beaten egg whites until there are no white streaks.

- Spoon into small parfait glasses or cups. Cover and chill for at least 2 hours. (Will keep refrigerated up to 3 days.)

- Garnish each with a strawberry, a few raspberries or dollop of whipped topping.

Makes 750 mL (3 cups), 6 servings

Each Serving: 125 mL($^1/_2$ cup)

1 ◆ Milk Choice (homo)

OR

1 ◆ Milk Choice (skim)
1 ▲ Fats & Oils Choice

5 g carbohydrate
4 g protein
4 g fat

300 kilojoules
(72 Calories)

Cool Jellies and Mousses

Recipe	Food Choices per Serving		Energy per Serving		
			kilojoules	Calories	
Ambrosia	1 ◪ Fruits & Vegetables; 1 ▲ Fats & Oils		310	74	p. 184
Melon Mousse	1 ◪ Fruits & Vegetables		260	61	p. 185
Nectarine Lemonade Mousse	1 ◪ Fruits & Vegetables; 1 ◆ Milk (2%)		400	96	p. 186
Rosé Fruit Parfait	1 ◪ Fruits & Vegetables; 1 ▲ Fats & Oils		280	70	p. 187
Apricot Bavarian Cream	1 ◪ Fruits & Vegetables; 1 ▲ Fats & Oils		370	88	p. 188
Snow Gelatin	1 ✚✚ Extra		70	16	p. 189
Cranberry Chiffon	1 ◪ Fruits & Vegetables		210	51	p. 189
Chocolate Mousse Soufflé	1 ◆ Milk (homo) **OR** 1 ◆ Milk (skim); ½ ▲ Fats & Oils		320	75	p. 190
Chocolate Mousse	1 ◆ Milk (homo) **OR** 1 ◆ Milk (skim); 1 ▲ Fats & Oils		300	72	p. 191

Notes

over: *Melon Mousse*

Notes

over: *Citrus Banana Cheesecake*

Icy Sherbets and Freezes

My dictionary says freeze means to become congealed into ice by cold. In this cookbook, a freeze is an icy cold, frozen banana puréed with fruit or chocolate resulting in a creamy, smooth concoction with the texture of soft ice cream.

Sorbets are fruit juices frozen into a refreshing icy slush. The sherbets are the same but have a little milk or yogurt added.

A blender is essential for making a banana freeze and an ice cream maker produces the best-textured sherbet or sorbet. However, both desserts can be made by freezing, mixing by hand, then refreezing. It's the mixing of the frozen icy slush that breaks up the ice crystals and smooths out the texture.

Frozen Vanilla Yogurt

Preparation Time: *10 minutes*
Freezing Time: *4 hrs to 4 wks*

Cool and light! This frozen treat is refreshing on top of a piece of Angel Cake or fruit, or floating on top of a colorful fruit sauce.

500 mL	2% plain yogurt	2 cups
15 mL	vanilla	1 tbsp
	Sugar substitute equivalent to 25 mL (2 tbsp) sugar	

Each serving: 75 mL(⅓ cup)

1 ◆ Milk Choice (2%)

7 g carbohydrate
4 g protein
1 g fat

250 kilojoules
(60 Calories)

- In mixing bowl, combine yogurt, vanilla and sugar substitute until well blended. Pour into ice cube or freezer tray. (Or transfer to ice cream maker and follow manufacturer's directions, then transfer to container and freeze.)

- Freeze for about 1 hour or until ice crystals form around edges.

- With fork or whisk, mix crystals back into mixture and return to freezer.

- Freeze for 30 minutes longer and repeat stirring. Repeat once more.

- Transfer to cold plastic container. Cover and freeze for at least 2 hours longer or until firm. (Mixture will keep for up to 4 weeks.)

- To serve, let stand for 20 minutes in refrigerator before scraping into serving dishes.

Makes 500 mL (2 cups), 6 servings

Apricot Sherbet

This fruity, icy sherbet is light and lively. It helps to 'cleanse the palate'.

Preparation Time: *5 minutes*
Freezing Time: *8 hours*

1	can (398 mL/14 oz) calorie-reduced apricots (no sugar added)	1

Sugar substitute equivalent
to 10 mL (2 tsp) sugar

- Place unopened can of fruit in freezer of refrigerator for about 8 hours or overnight.

- Take can from freezer; open it. With a knife, cut into frozen fruit to help loosen it; then spoon frozen fruit with juice into container of food processor fitted with a steel blade; add sugar substitute.

- Process with an on/off action about 2 minutes or until puréed and slushy.

- Spoon immediately into chilled dessert dishes to serve immediately or transfer to a chilled plastic container, cover and store in freezer.

Makes 500 mL (2 cups) sherbet, 6 servings

Each Serving: 75 mL (¹⁄₃ cup)

1 ◪ Fruits & Vegetables

11 g carbohydrate
1 g protein

200 kilojoules
(48 Calories)

Variation:

Frozen Apricot Yogurt: Add 125 mL (¹⁄₂ cup) yogurt to the fruit and sugar substitute. Process until puréed. Serve immediately or transfer to plastic container, cover and freeze.

Makes 625 mL (2¹⁄₂ cups), 6 servings

Each Serving: 100 mL(¹⁄₃ cup plus 2 tbsp)

1 ◪ Fruits & Vegetables
¹⁄₂ ◆ Milk Choice (2%)

13 g carbohydrate
2 g protein
1 g fat

290 kilojoules
(69 Calories)

Cranberry Sherbet

Preparation Time: *10 minutes*
Freezing Time: *4 hrs to 4 wks*

If you're ever looking for a light, refreshing finale for a special meal, this is perfect. I like it with Macaroons (recipe, p. 137)

| 450 mL | cranberry juice cocktail | 1³/₄ cup |
| 50 mL | 2% plain yogurt | ¹/₄ cup |

Each serving: 75 mL(¹/₃ cup)

1 ▨ Fruits & Vegetables

12 g carbohydrate
1 g protein

210 kilojoules
(49 Calories)

- In bowl, combine cranberry juice and yogurt. Pour into ice cube or freezer tray (OR transfer to ice cream maker and follow manufacturer's directions for making sherbet.)
- Freeze for about 1 hour or until crystals form around edges. With fork or whisk, vigorously mix crystals back into mixture and return to freezer.
- Freeze for 30 minutes longer and repeat stirring. Repeat once more. (The more the sherbet is stirred, the finer the texture will be.)
- Transfer to cold plastic container. Cover and freeze for at least 2 hours longer or until firm. (Mixture will keep for up to 4 weeks.)
- To serve, let stand for 20 minutes in refrigerator before scraping into serving dishes.

Makes 500 mL (2 cups), 6 servings.

Pineapple Sherbet

Preparation Time: *5 minutes*
Freezing Time: *4 hrs to 4 wks*

When a heat wave makes everyone feel wilted, the sure cure is a refreshing, cooling dessert.

375 mL	unsweetened pineapple juice	1¹/₂ cups
125 mL	water	¹/₂ cup
50 mL	2% plain yogurt	¹/₄ cup

Each Serving: 125 mL(¹/₂ cup)

1 ▨ Fruits & Vegetables

11 g carbohydrate
1 g protein

210 kilojoules
(49 Calories)

- Combine pineapple juice, water and yogurt. Pour into ice cube or freezer tray. (OR transfer to ice cream maker and follow manufacturer's directions for making sherbet. Then transfer to container and freeze.)
- Proceed with second step in Cranberry Sherbet.

Makes 625 mL (2¹/₂ cups), 5 servings

Instant Strawberry Freeze

This dessert has no cream at all, but is so smooth it tastes as if it does.

Preparation Time: *10 minutes*

250 mL	fresh or frozen unsweetened strawberries	1 cup
1	frozen small banana*, sliced	1
50 mL	buttermilk or 2% milk	1/4 cup
5 mL	lemon juice	1 tsp
	Sugar substitute equivalent to 25 mL (2 tbsp) sugar	
2	ice cubes	2

- In blender or food processor, combine strawberries, banana, buttermilk, lemon juice, sugar substitute and ice cubes.

- Process for 2 minutes or until smooth and creamy and ice cubes are crushed.

- Serve immediately.

Makes 2 servings.

* To freeze banana: Peel; wrap in plastic wrap and place in freezer overnight.

Each serving: 200 mL(³/₄ cup)

2 ◪ Fruits & Vegetables

19 g carbohydrate
1 g protein
2 g fat

370 kilojoules
(89 Calories)

Chocolate Banana Freeze

Preparation Time: *10 minutes*
Freezing Time: *Up to 4 weeks*

Chocolate lovers, this is for you. It's rich and sweet-tasting.

2	small frozen bananas*, sliced	2
	Sugar substitute equivalent to 10 mL (2 tsp) sugar	
1	square unsweetened chocolate, melted	1

- Combine banana and sugar substitute in food processor and process using on/off motion for 2 to 3 minutes or until banana is puréed and fluffy.

- With processor running, slowly drizzle melted chocolate through feed tube. Continue to process until little flecks of chocolate are evenly distributed throughout mixture.

- Serve immediately in chilled dessert dishes or transfer to chilled container, cover and freeze for up to 4 weeks. (Let container of frozen dessert stand in refrigerator for about 20 minutes before serving.)

Makes 500 mL (2 cups), 4 servings

* *To freeze bananas: Peel, wrap in plastic wrap and place in freezer overnight.*

Each serving: 125 mL(½ cup)

1 ◢ Fruits & Vegetables

1 ▲ Fats & Oils Choice

12 g carbohydrate
4 g fat

340 kilojoules
(80 Calories)

Just Banana Freeze

It is amazing how similar this creamy smooth, ice-cold concoction is to soft ice cream. It is light and refreshing but it is difficult to create the fluffy light texture without the aid of a food processor.

Preparation Time: *10 minutes*
Freezing Time: *two 4-hour sessions*

2	small bananas	2
Pinch	ascorbic acid color keeper	Pinch
50 mL	instant skim milk powder	$^1/_4$ cup
5 mL	vanilla	1 tsp
Pinch	ground cinnamon	Pinch

- Peel bananas; cut into thick slices and sprinkle with a pinch of ascorbic acid color keeper, wrap in plastic wrap and place in the freezer at least 4 hours or overnight until frozen solid.

- Unwrap bananas and place in the container of food processor fitted with metal blade. Add skim milk powder, vanilla and cinnamon. Process with an on/off motion, scraping down bowl occasionally, for about 2 minutes or until very smooth and creamy.

- Serve immediately or spoon into container, cover and store in freezer.

Makes 4 servings

Variations:

Strawberry Banana Freeze: Add 8 fresh or unsweetened frozen strawberries to banana mixture in processor.

Each Serving: 200 mL($^3/_4$ cup)

1   ▰   Fruits & Vegetables

$^1/_2$ ◆   Milk Choice (skim)

14 g carbohydrate
2 g protein

270 kilojoules
(64 Calories)

Calculations as above

Peach Ice Cream

Preparation Time: *10 minutes*
Freezing Time: *4 hrs to 4 wks*

It's creamy and fruity. And everything will seem peachy and cool after the first spoonful.

2	medium peaches or 3 peach halves, canned in juice, drained	2
15 mL	granulated sugar*	1 tbsp
10 mL	brandy or vanilla	2 tsp
Pinch	ground coriander	Pinch
1	envelope dessert topping mix	1
125 mL	2% milk	1/2 cup

Each serving: 125 mL(1/2 cup)

1 🔲 Fruits & Vegetables

1 🔺 Fats & Oils Choice

10 g carbohydrate
1 g protein
3 g fat

310 kilojoules
(74 Calories)

* The added sugar in the recipe has been included in the carbohydrate and Food Choice Values.

- Peel, pit and cut peaches into quarters.

- In food processor or blender, combine peaches, sugar, brandy or vanilla and coriander. Process until puréed.

- Meanwhile, in mixing bowl, combine topping mix and milk. Beat until stiff.

- Beat peach purée into whipped topping until evenly colored.

- Spoon into chilled plastic container. Cover and freeze. (OR transfer to ice cream maker and follow manufacturer's directions, then transfer to container and store in freezer.)

- If put directly in freezer, freeze for 3 to 4 hours or until firm. Spoon into mixing bowl; beat for 1 minute or until ice crystals are broken up. Return to container and freeze. (Mixture will keep for up to 4 weeks.)

- To serve, let stand for 20 minutes in refrigerator before scraping or scooping into serving dishes.

Makes 750 mL (3 cups), 6 servings.

Rosé Rhubarb Granita

Every spring I'm out in the garden coaxing the rhubarb along because I'm looking forward to a spoonful of this ice.

Preparation Time: *5 minutes*
Chilling Time: *4 hrs to 4 wks*

750 mL	chopped rhubarb	3 cups
500 mL	water	2 cups
	Sugar substitute equivalent to 125 mL ($^1/_2$ cup) sugar	
125 mL	dry rosé wine	$^1/_2$ cup
10 mL	lemon juice	2 tsp

Each Serving: 250 mL(1 cup)

1   Fruits & Vegetables

    9 g carbohydrate
    1 g protein

    180 kilojoules
    (42 Calories)

- In saucepan, combine rhubarb and water. Bring to boil and cook for 5 minutes or until rhubarb is tender. Strain into clean saucepan.

- Stir in sugar substitute, rosé wine and lemon juice. Bring to boil and boil for about 2 minutes. Set aside to let cool. (Most of the alcohol in this recipe evaporates.)

- When cool, pour mixture into chilled plastic container. Cover and freeze. (Or transfer to ice cream maker and follow manufacturer's directions, then transfer to container and freeze.)

- If put directly in freezer, freeze for 3 to 4 hours or until firm. Spoon into mixing bowl; beat for 1 minute or until ice crystals are broken up. Return to container and freeze. (Mixture will keep for up to 4 weeks.)

- To serve, let stand for 20 minutes in refrigerator before scraping or scooping into dessert dishes.

Makes 750 mL (3 cups), 3 servings

Icy Sherbets and Freezes

Recipe	Food Choices per Serving	Energy per Serving		
		kilojoules	Calories	
Frozen Vanilla Yogurt	1 ◆ Milk (2%)	250	60	p. 194
Apricot Sherbet	1 ▨ Fruits & Vegetables	200	48	p. 195
Frozen Apricot Yogurt	1 ▨ Fruits & Vegetables; ½ ◆ Milk (2%)	290	69	p. 195
Cranberry Sherbet	1 ▨ Fruits & Vegetables	210	49	p. 196
Pineapple Sherbet	1 ▨ Fruits & Vegetables	210	49	p. 196
Instant Strawberry Freeze	2 ▨ Fruits & Vegetables	370	89	p. 197
Chocolate Banana Freeze	1 ▨ Fruits & Vegetables; 1 ▲ Fats & Oils	340	80	p. 198
Just Banana Freeze	1 ▨ Fruits & Vegetables; ½ ◆ Milk (skim)	270	64	p. 199
Strawberry Banana Freeze	1 ▨ Fruits & Vegetables; ½ ◆ Milk (skim)	270	64	p. 199
Peach Ice Cream	1 ▨ Fruits & Vegetables; 1 ▲ Fats & Oils	310	74	p. 200
Rosé Rhubarb Granita	1 ▨ Fruits & Vegetables	180	42	p. 201

Celebration Concoctions

These are the show-off desserts for special gatherings — birthday parties, anniversaries, reunions. They're more complicated to make than the others in this cookbook, but most have an easy two-step procedure with the parts coming together when the dessert is assembled.

One of my friends is surprised that recipes for tortes, cheesecakes, cream rolls and trifle are in *Light & Easy Choices and Desserts*. But these versions use the bare minimum of sugar and fat and meet all my criteria for lightness.

Chocolate Fondue

Preparation Time: *20 minutes*
Cooking Time: *10 minutes*

When you want a fun dessert or special snack to enjoy with friends, make this fondue.

175 mL	dry unsweetened cocoa	²/₃ cup
1 mL	cinnamon	¹/₄ tsp
250 mL	skim milk	1 cup
2 mL	vanilla or almond extract	¹/₂ tsp
	Sugar substitute equivalent to 125 mL (¹/₂ cup) sugar	
1	apple, cored and cut in bite-size chunks	1
1	banana	1
250 mL	seedless green grapes	1 cup
150 mL	unsweetened pineapple chunks	²/₃ cup
125 mL	bran flakes, crushed	¹/₂ cup
50 mL	chopped walnuts	¹/₄ cup
50 mL	dessicated unsweetened coconut	¹/₄ cup

Each serving: ¹/₈ of fruit, 50 mL (¹/₄ cup) sauce

2 ▰ Fruits & Vegetables
1 ▲ Fats & Oils Choice

19 g carbohydrate
3 g protein
4 g fat

520 kilojoules
(124 Calories)

- In a heavy saucepan, combine cocoa, cinnamon and milk; stir or whisk until there are no dry lumps of cocoa. Stir and cook over medium heat until mixture comes to a boil. Reduce heat; boil gently, stirring often, for 5 minutes or until mixture is thick and smooth. Cool slightly.

- Stir in vanilla and sugar substitute.

- Pour into a small enamelled fondue pot or heatproof ceramic bowl. Set on holder over candle or source of heat to keep warm.

- In small dishes, place fruits, crushed cereal, walnuts and coconut around fondue pot.

- Provide each diner with long bamboo or wooden picks or fondue forks. Each person pierces a chunk of fruit and dips it into the fondue, then into one of the accompaniments, if desired, and then enjoys.

Makes 8 servings

Microwave Directions: Chocolate Sauce: In 1 L (4 cup) microwaveable container, combine cocoa, cinnamon and milk. Microwave, stirring several times throughout cooking, for 5 minutes or until smooth and thickened. Continue as recipe directs.

Orange Cheesecake

Because the Citrus Banana Cheesecake in the original Light & Easy Choices was so popular, I created this one.

Preparation Time: *30 minutes*
Chilling Time: *2 to 4 hours*

Crust

250 mL	soft whole wheat bread crumbs	1 cup
50 mL	natural bran	1/4 cup
	Sugar substitute equivalent to 50 mL (1/4 cup) sugar	
2 mL	ground cinnamon	1/2 tsp
25 mL	butter or margarine	2 tbsp

Filling

1	envelope unflavored gelatin	1
75 mL	water	1/3 cup
500 mL	2% cottage cheese	2 cups
75 mL	orange juice	1/3 cup
5 mL	orange rind	1 tsp
1	small banana	1
	Sugar substitute equivalent to 25 mL (2 tbsp) sugar	
5 mL	lemon juice	1 tsp
1	small orange	1
8	strawberries or seedless green grapes	8

Each serving: 1/8 of cheesecake

1 ▨ Fruits & Vegetables
1 ▨ Protein Choice

12 g carbohydrate
10 g protein
4 g fat

520 kilojoules
(124 Calories)

- **Crust:** In bowl, combine bread crumbs, bran, sugar substitute and cinnamon. With fingers, rub in butter until mixture is crumbly. Press onto bottom of 16 cm (7") springform pan.
- **Filling:** In small saucepan, sprinkle gelatin over water and let stand for about 5 minutes to soften. Place over low heat, stirring, until gelatin dissolves. Cool to room temperature.
- In food processor or blender, combine cottage cheese, orange juice, orange rind, banana, sugar substitute, lemon juice and dissolved gelatin. Purée until smooth (or mash cottage cheese and banana along with sugar substitute, juices and gelatin or press through sieve). Pour over prepared crust.
- Cover and chill in refrigerator for 2 to 4 hours or until set.
- At serving time, remove side from pan. With wide metal lifter, slip cheesecake off bottom of pan onto serving plate or leave on base of springform pan.
- Peel orange, removing pith and thin membrane. Remove sections.
- Slice strawberries or grapes. Arrange on top of cheesecake along with orange sections.

Makes 8 servings

Citrus Banana Cheesecake

Preparation Time: *15 minutes*
Standing Time: *2 to 4 hours*

A blender is not absolutely necessary to make this creamy cheesecake as long as you can mash the banana and cottage cheese together until they are as smooth as possible.

Crust

250 mL	soft whole wheat breadcrumbs	1 cup
	Sugar substitute equivalent to 50 mL (¹/₄ cup) sugar	
Pinch	cardamom	Pinch
25 mL	margarine	2 tbsp

Each serving: ¹/₈ **of cheesecake**

1¹/₂ 🔲 Fruits & Vegetables

1 🔲 Protein Choice

OR

1 🔲 Starchy Choice

1 🔲 Protein Choice

14 g carbohydrate
9 g protein
4 g fat

540 kilojoules
(128 Calories)

Filling

1	envelope unflavored gelatin	1
175 mL	unsweetened grapefruit juice	²/₃ cup
500 mL	2% cottage cheese	2 cups
1	small banana	1
	Sugar substitute equivalent to 25 mL (2 tbsp) sugar	
5 mL	vanilla	1 tsp
1	small pink grapefruit	1
4	fresh strawberries, optional	4

- **Crust:** In a bowl, combine bread crumbs, sugar substitute and cardamom. With fingers, rub in margarine. Press onto bottom of a 20 cm (8 in) springform pan.
- **Filling:** In a small dish or measure, sprinkle gelatin over 50 mL(¹/₄ cup) of the grapefruit juice and let stand for 5 minutes to soften. Place dish of gelatin in pan of hot water and stir until gelatin dissolves completely. Cool to room temperature.
- In food processor or blender, combine cottage cheese, banana, sugar substitute and remaining juice. Purée until smooth. (Or, mash cottage cheese and banana with sugar substitute and juice or press through sieve.)
- Stir in dissolved gelatin and vanilla. Pour into crust.
- Cover and chill in refrigerator for 2 to 4 hours or until set.
- Remove sides from pan and with wide metal lifter, slip cheesecake off bottom of pan onto serving plate, or leave on base of springform pan.
- Peel grapefruit, removing all white pith. Separate into segments and arrange on top of cheesecake. Slice strawberries and add to garnish if desired.

Makes 8 servings

English Summer Pudding

This has always been in my collection of recipes for summer specialties. Now I make it all through the year with frozen berries.

Preparation Time: *35 minutes*
Chilling Time: *8 hours*

500 mL	frozen unsweetened strawberries (300 g package), thawed	2 cups
500 mL	frozen unsweetened blueberries (300 g package), thawed	2 cups
500 mL	frozen unsweetened raspberries (300 g package), thawed	2 cups
125 mL	water	$^1/_2$ cup
	Sugar substitute equivalent to 125 mL ($^1/_2$ cup) sugar	
10	slices firm white bread, crusts removed	10
	Whipped dessert topping, optional	

Each serving: $^1/_8$ of pudding

1 ☐   Starchy Choice

1 ▨   Fruits & Vegetables

23 g carbohydrate
3 g protein
1 g fat

530 kilojoules
(125 Calories)

- In large saucepan, combine thawed strawberries, blueberries, raspberries and water. Bring to boil; reduce heat, cover and simmer for 2 minutes. Stir in sugar substitute.

- Line 1L (4 cup) bowl with bread slices (about 8), fitting to cover bottom and up sides of bowl, trimming as necessary.

- Remove 25 mL (2 tbsp) juice from berry mixture and reserve.

- Spoon berry mixture into bread-lined bowl. Cover with remaining bread slices and trim, fitting bread together to cover mixture.

- Select plate a little smaller than circumference of bowl where top layer of bread is. Place on bread layer and weight with heavy object, such as juice can.

- Refrigerate for 8 hours or overnight.

- Remove weight and plate. Invert onto serving plate. Spoon reserved juice over any bread not colored by fruit mixture.

- Garnish with whipped dessert topping, allowing only 15 mL (1 tbsp) per serving.

Makes 8 servings

Light Coeur à la Crème

Preparation Time: *10 minutes*
Chilling Time: *2 days*

In France, cheese and fruit are served at dinner. Often it is a cheese heart with fresh fruit. It's a perfect finale for a Valentine dinner or special romantic celebrations.

250 mL	2% cottage cheese	1 cup
250 mL	2% plain yogurt	1 cup
	Sugar substitute equivalent to 75 mL (¹/₃ cup) sugar	
10 mL	dry sherry or vanilla	2 tsp
1.2 L	strawberries	5 cups

- In food processor or blender, combine cottage cheese, yogurt, sugar substitute and sherry or vanilla. Purée for about 3 minutes or until very smooth, scraping down sides of container occasionally.

- Line heart-shaped mold with perforated bottom or small sieve with cheesecloth.

- Spoon cottage cheese mixture into lined mold. Cover with plastic wrap.

- Place mold on plate or dish to collect liquid as it drains from mold.

- Refrigerate for 48 hours or until about 125 mL (¹/₂ cup) has drained from mold. Center of mold should feel fairly firm.

- At serving time, invert onto serving plate. Peel away cheesecloth. Discard liquid.

- Slice or halve strawberries.

- Surround Light Coeur à la Crème with strawberries.

Makes 6 servings

Variation:
Coeur à la Crème with Peaches:
In place of strawberries, use 5 medium peaches. Peel, pit and slice peaches. Sprinkle lightly with ascorbic acid color keeper.

Each serving: ¹/₆ **of mold and fruit**

1 Fruits & Vegetables

1 Protein Choice

10 g carbohydrate
8 g protein
2 g fat

370 kilojoules
(89 Calories)

Calculations as above

Light and Easy Trifle

All the elements of a good English trifle are here except the rich custard and real cream.

Preparation Time: *25 minutes*
Chilling Time: *2 hours*

1	envelope dessert topping mix	1
125 mL	raspberry dietetic fruit spread	1/2 cup
15 mL	brandy or 5 mL (1 tsp) brandy extract	1 tbsp
15 mL	water	1 tbsp
250 mL	2% plain yogurt	1 cup
	Sugar substitute equivalent to 15 mL (1 tbsp) sugar	
1 mL	ground cinnamon	1/4 tsp
4	medium peaches or 6 peach halves canned in juice, drained	4
	Ascorbic acid color keeper	
1/2	Chiffon Cake (recipe, p.139)	1/2

Each serving: 200 mL (³/₄ cup)

1 ☐ Starchy Choice

1 � Fruits & Vegetables

1 ▲ Fats & Oils Choice

25 g carbohydrate
4 g protein
6 g fat

700 kilojoules
(167 Calories)

- Prepare dessert topping, following package directions.
- In small dish, combine raspberry fruit spread, brandy or brandy extract and water; mix well. Set aside.
- In bowl, combine yogurt, sugar substitute and cinnamon.
- Peel and pit peaches. Cut 3 into thin slices; finely chop 4th. Lightly sprinkle with ascorbic acid color keeper. Set aside 8 slices for garnish.
- Fold 200 mL (3/4 cup) whipped topping into yogurt mixture. Stir in chopped peach. Set aside remaining whipped topping.
- Break Chiffon Cake into bite-size pieces. scatter a layer on bottom of 1 L (4 cup) glass bowl.
- Spread half of the raspberry mixture over cake. Cover with half of the peach slices.
- Pour half of the yogurt mixture over peaches.
- Repeat layering once more.
- Spread reserved whipped topping over final yogurt layer.
- Garnish with reserved peach slices. Cover and chill in refrigerator for 2 hours.
- Divide into 10 equal portions.

Makes 10 servings

Strawberry Cream Torte

Preparation Time: *25 minutes*
Chilling Time: *2 hours*

Deluxe desserts often take hours to prepare, not this one.

1	Chiffon Cake (recipe, p. 139)	1
1	envelope dessert topping mix	1
125 mL	2% milk	$^{1}/_{2}$ cup
5 mL	vanilla	1 tsp
250 mL	strawberry dietetic fruit spread	1 cup
250 mL	strawberries, cut in half	1 cup

- Prepare and bake cake. Invert pan and let cool for at least 4 hours, preferably overnight. Cake can be made 2 to 3 days ahead, if desired. If made ahead, remove from pan, wrap well in plastic wrap and store in refrigerator.

- In mixing bowl, whip topping mix with milk and vanilla until stiff.

- Beat in fruit spread until well combined.

- Cut cake horizontally into 3 even layers.

- Place widest layer (top layer) top side down on flat cake plate.

- Spread with 250 mL (1 cup) whipped topping mixture.

- Top with second cake layer and another 250 mL (1 cup) whipped topping mixture. Place remaining cake layer on top.

- Spread top and sides with remaining whipped topping mixture.

- Garnish with strawberry halves, cut side down.

- Chill for about 2 hours before serving. Store any remaining torte in refrigerator.

Makes 15 servings

Each serving: $^{1}/_{15}$ **of torte**

1 ☐ Starchy Choice
1 ◪ Fruits & Vegetables
1 ▲ Fats & Oils Choice

23 g carbohydrate
2 g protein
6 g fat

640 kilojoules
(153 Calories)

Fruited Cream and Chocolate Torte

Easy-to-make Chocolate Chiffon Cake is all dressed up for a party when it's filled and frosted with fruity whipped topping.

Preparation Time: *20 minutes*
Chilling Time: *2 hours*

1	Chocolate Chiffon Cake (recipe, p. 140)	1
1	envelope dessert topping mix	1
125 mL	2% milk	1/2 cup
5 mL	vanilla	1 tsp
5 mL	brandy or lemon juice	1 tsp
250 mL	three-fruit dietetic fruit spread	1 cup

- Prepare and bake cake. Invert pan and let cool for at least 4 hours, preferably overnight. Cake can be made 2 to 3 days ahead, if desired. If made ahead, remove from pan, wrap well in plastic wrap and store in refrigerator.

- In mixing bowl, whip topping mix with milk, vanilla and brandy or lemon juice until stiff.

- Beat in fruit spread until well combined.

- Cut cake horizontally into 3 even layers.

- Place widest layer (top layer) top side down on flat cake plate.

- Spread with 250 mL (1 cup) whipped topping mixture.

- Top with second cake layer and another 250 mL (1 cup) whipped topping mixture. Place remaining cake layer on top.

- Spread top, and sides with remaining whipped topping mixture.

- Chill for about 2 hours before serving. Store any remaining torte in refrigerator.

Makes 14 servings

Each serving: 1/14 **of torte**

1 ☐ Starchy Choice

1 ◪ Fruits & Vegetables

1 ▲ Fats & Oils Choice

24 g carbohydrate
3 g protein
7 g fat

670 kilojoules
(160 Calories)

Jelly Cream Roll

Preparation Time: *35 minutes*
Baking Time: *12 minutes*
Chilling Time: *1 hr to 3 days*

This jelly roll is surprisingly easy to make.

1	batter for Chiffon Cake (recipe, p. 139)	1
250 mL	raspberry dietetic fruit spread	1 cup
1	envelope dessert topping mix	1
5 mL	brandy or vanilla	1 tsp
	Cinnamon, optional	

- Line 2 L (15x11 in) jelly roll pan with waxed paper. Prepare Chiffon Cake batter; pour into prepared jelly roll pan. Bake in 200°C (400°F) oven for 12 minutes or until top springs back when lightly touched.

- Lay clean tea towel on work surface; with knife, loosen around sides of jelly roll. Invert onto towel and remove pan.

- Lift off waxed paper. Immediately, while jelly roll is still warm, fold end of towel over one narrow end of jelly roll. Roll up with towel. Place seam side down in refrigerator for 20 minutes or until cool.

- Unroll jelly roll and remove cloth.

- Spread fruit spread on inside of roll right to edges.

- Whip dessert topping mix following package directions, using brandy or vanilla. Spread evenly over fruit spread.

- Roll up jelly roll snugly so there are no air pockets. Place seam side down on serving platter. Cover and chill in refrigerator for at least 1 hour or up to 3 days.

- Sprinkle lightly with cinnamon, if desired.

- Cut into slices to serve. Cover and store any remaining jelly roll in refrigerator.

Makes14 servings

Each serving: ¹⁄₁₄ **of roll**

1 ☐ Starchy Choice

1 ▨ Fruits & Vegetables

1 ▲ Fats & Oils Choice

24 g carbohydrate
3 g protein
7 g fat

670 kilojoules
(160 Calories)

Variation:

Cherry Chocolate Roll: In place of Chiffon Cake batter, use Chocolate Chiffon Cake batter and use cherry fruit spread instead of raspberry fruit spread.

Calculations as above

212

Chocolate Log

If you aim for lightness but still yearn for the taste of a classic specialty, create this log. It's an adaptation of bûche de Nöel.

Preparation Time: *35 minutes*
Baking Time: *12 minutes*
Chilling Time: *1 hr to 3 days*

1	batter for Chocolate Chiffon Cake (recipe, p. 140)	
250 mL	water	1 cup
125 mL	unsweetened cocoa powder	$^1/_2$ cup
	Sugar substitute equivalent to 50 mL ($^1/_4$ cup) sugar	
1	envelope unflavored gelatin	1
1	envelope dessert topping mix	1

- Prepare Chocolate Chiffon Cake batter; pour into wax paper-lined jelly roll pan. Bake in 200°C (400°F) oven for 12 minutes or until top springs back when lightly touched.
- Lay clean tea towel on work surface; with knife, loosen around sides of jelly roll. Invert onto towel and remove pan.
- Lift off waxed paper. Immediately, while jelly roll is still warm, fold end of towel over one narrow end of jelly roll. Roll up with towel. Place seam side down in refrigerator for 20 minutes or until cool.
- In small saucepan, combine 200 mL ($^3/_4$ cup) of the water and cocoa. Whisk until there are no lumps of cocoa.
- Stir sugar substitute into remaining water. Sprinkle with gelatin and let stand for 5 minutes to soften.
- Cook cocoa mixture over medium heat, stirring, for about 5 minutes or until smooth and thickened. Stir in gelatin mixture until dissolved.
- Transfer to bowl. Cover and chill in refrigerator for 20 minutes or until mixture mounds on spoon.
- Prepare dessert topping mix, following package directions. Fold half of the cocoa mixture into whipped topping until evenly colored. Fold in remaining cocoa mixture until well blended.
- Unroll chocolate roll and remove cloth. Spread half of the whipped topping mixture on inside of roll right to edges.
- Roll up chocolate roll snugly so there are no air pockets. Place seam side down on serving platter. Spread remaining whipped topping mixture evenly on outside of roll. Refrigerate for at least 1 hour or up to 3 days.
- Cut into slices to serve. Cover and store any remaining Chocolate Log in refrigerator.

Makes 18 servings

Each serving: $^1/_{18}$ **of log**

1 ▢ Starchy Choice

1 ▲ Fats & Oils Choice

15 g carbohydrate
3 g protein
5 g fat

470 kilojoules
(113 Calories)

Strawberry Shortcake

Preparation Time: *15 minutes*
Baking Time: *12 minutes*

Ruby red strawberries are stunning sandwiched with creamy topping in fresh-from-the-oven flaky biscuits.

Biscuit

250 mL	all-purpose flour	1 cup
125 mL	whole wheat flour	¹/₂ cup
15 mL	baking powder	1 tbsp
15 mL	granulated sugar*	1 tbsp
2 mL	salt	¹/₂ tsp
50 mL	margarine	¹/₄ cup
175 mL	2% milk	³/₄ cup

Filling

1 L	strawberries, hulled	4 cups
15 mL	granulated sugar*	1 tbsp
5 mL	vanilla	1 tsp

Whipped dessert topping, optional

Each serving: 1 individual shortcake

1 ▢ Starchy Choice
1 ◩ Fruits & Vegetables
1 ▲ Fats & Oils Choice

24 g carbohydrate
3 g protein
6 g fat

680 kilojoules
(163 Calories)

*The added sugar in the recipe has been included in the carbohydrate and Food Choice Values

- **Biscuit:** In bowl, combine flours, baking powder, sugar and salt. With pastry blender or two knives, cut in margarine until mixture resembles fine crumbs. Add milk and stir quickly until moist ball forms.
- Turn out onto lightly floured board. Knead 6 to 7 strokes. Roll out or pat down to 8 mm (¹/₃ in) thick. Cut into nine 7.5 cm (3 in) rounds, squares or wedges. Place on nonstick baking sheet
- Bake in 220ºC (450ºF) oven for 12 minutes or until brown.
- **Filling:** Slice strawberries, reserving 9 whole ones for garnish.
- In bowl, combine sliced strawberries, sugar and vanilla.
- Split warm biscuits in half horizontally. Top each bottom with 1/9 of the berry slices. Replace top of biscuits
- Garnish each with 15 mL (1 tbsp) whipped topping, if desired. Cut reserved berries in half. Garnish each shortcake with two halves.

Makes 9 servings

Calculations as above

Variation:
Peach Shortcake: In place of strawberries use 4 medium peaches. Peel, pit and thinly slice peaches. Sprinkle lightly with ascorbic acid color keeper and combine with sugar and vanilla, reserving 18 slices for garnish. Divide remaining peach slices among the 9 biscuits.

214

Rice Crispy Party Cake

This popular combination makes an unusual birthday cake when made in a tube pan. It cuts easily with a serrated knife.

1 L	miniature marshmallows	4 cups
15 mL	water	1 tbsp
5 mL	vanilla	1 tsp
2 L	rice crispy cereal	8 cups

- In large saucepan, combine marshmallows and water. Warm over low heat, stirring constantly, until melted. Remove from heat.

- Stir in vanilla.

- Gradually stir in rice crispy cereal until well combined. Mixture will be sticky.

- Lightly press into 3 L (10 in) tube pan lightly sprayed with nonstick vegetable coating or lightly buttered.

- Let stand for about 1 hour or until cool before unmolding.

Makes 36 servings

Preparation Time: *10 minutes*
Cooking Time: *5 minutes*

Each serving: ¹⁄₃₆ **of cake**

1 ◢ Fruits & Vegetables

10 g carbohydrate
1 g protein

180 kilojoules
(42 Calories)

Microwave Directions:
In a microwaveable 1.5 L (6 cup) bowl, combine marshmallows and water. Microwave at Medium (50%) for 3 minutes, stirring at halftime. Continue as above.

Celebration Concoctions

Recipe	Food Choices per Serving			Energy per Serving kilojoules Calories		
Chocolate Fondue	2 ◩ Fruits & Vegetables; 1 ▲ Fats & Oils			520	124	p. 204
Orange Cheesecake	1 ◩ Fruits & Vegetables; 1 ◪ Protein			520	124	p. 205
Citrus Banana Cheesecake	1½ ◩ Fruits & Vegetables; 1 ◪ Protein OR 1 ☐ Starchy; 1 ◪ Protein			540	128	p. 206
English Summer Pudding	1 ☐ Starchy; 1 ◩ Fruits & Vegetables			530	125	p. 207
Light Coeur à la Crème	1 ◩ Fruits & Vegetables; 1 ◪ Protein			370	89	p. 208
Light and Easy Trifle	1 ☐ Starchy; 1 ◩ Fruits & Vegetables; 1 ▲ Fats & Oils			700	167	p. 209
Strawberry Cream Torte	1 ☐ Starchy: 1 ◩ Fruits & Vegetables; 1 ▲ Fats & Oils			640	153	p. 210
Fruited Cream & Chocolate Torte	1 ☐ Starchy: 1 ◩ Fruits & Vegetables; 1 ▲ Fats & Oils			670	160	p. 211
Jelly Cream Roll	1 ☐ Starchy; 1 ◩ Fruits & Vegetables; 1 ▲ Fats & Oils			670	160	p. 212
Cherry Chocolate Roll	1 ☐ Starchy; 1 ◩ Fruits & Vegetables; 1 ▲ Fats & Oils			670	160	p. 212
Chocolate Log	1 ☐ Starchy; 1 ▲ Fats & Oils			470	113	p. 213
Strawberry Shortcake	1 ☐ Starchy: 1 ◩ Fruits & Vegetables; 1 ▲ Fats & Oils			680	163	p. 214
Rice Crispie Party Cake	1 ◩ Fruits & Vegetables			180	42	p. 215

Little Treats

A few morsels of these candy-like goodies make a welcome treat. The calculations are there to help you make wise choices.

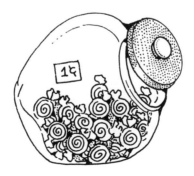

Fruit Jelly Jubes

Preparation Time: *10 minutes*
Standing Time: *4 hours*

For fruit jellies with a tasty, zingier flavor, use grapefruit juice in place of the orange juice; just be sure it is unsweetened.

5	envelopes unsweetened gelatin	5
375 mL	unsweetened orange juice	1$^1/_2$ cups
10 mL	lemon juice	2 tsp
	Sugar substitute equivalent to 125 mL ($^1/_2$ cup) sugar	
4	drops yellow food coloring	4
4	drops red food coloring	4

Each serving: 4 squares

1 **++** Extra

2 g carbohydrate
1 g protein

50 kilojoules
(12 Calories)

- In a small saucepan, sprinkle gelatin over orange juice; let stand for 5 minutes to soften.

- Heat over low heat just to simmering, stirring until gelatin dissolves. Remove from heat. Stir in lemon juice and sugar substitute.

- Pour into a 20 cm (8 in) square baking dish. Let stand for 4 hours at room temperature until firm.

- To remove from pan, cut around outside edges with sharp knife; place pan in shallow pan of hot water for about 30 seconds, just to soften bottom; loosen one corner, then quickly flip gel out onto a clean cutting surface.

- With a sharp knife, cut gel into 2 cm (3/4 in) squares.

- Line a small box with waxed paper. Store gels in single layers with waxed paper between layers. Cover box and store in refrigerator.

Makes 100 squares, 25 servings

Calculations as in
basic recipe

Variations:

Mint Jelly Jubes: Add 5 to 10 mL (1 to 2 tsp) peppermint flavoring and about 20 drops of green food coloring in place of yellow and red coloring.

Grape Jelly Jubes: Use unsweetened grape juice in place of orange juice. No food coloring is required.

Icy Fruity Creamsicles

Kids love these summer treats and so do adults.

Preparation Time: *20 minutes*
Chilling Time: *12 hours or overnight*

250 mL	chopped rhubarb	1 cup
375 mL	fresh or frozen unsweetened strawberries	1¹/₂ cups
250 mL	fresh or frozen unsweetened raspberries	1 cup
50 mL	2% plain yogurt	¹/₄ cup
50 mL	2% cottage cheese	¹/₄ cup
	Sugar substitute equivalent to 75 mL (¹/₃ cup) sugar	
5 mL	vanilla	1 tsp

Each Serving: 2 creamsicles

1 ◢ Fruits & Vegetables

8 g carbohydrate
3 g protein
1 g fat

240 kilojoules
(56 Calories)

- In saucepan, combine rhubarb and 15 mL (1 tbsp) water; cover and cook, stirring occasionally, for 7 minutes or until soft. Let cool.

- In food processor or blender, combine rhubarb, strawberries, raspberries, yogurt, cottage cheese, sugar substitute and vanilla. Process until mixture is smooth.

- Pour 50 mL (¹/₄ cup) of mixture into each of 10 Popsicle forms. Place Popsicle stick in center of each.

- Freeze for 12 hours or overnight. (Check after about 30 minutes and make sure sticks are centered in holders.)

- Dip holders in hot water for a few seconds to remove creamsicles.

Makes 10 creamsicles

Fruit Chews

Preparation Time: *15 minutes*
Baking Time: *15 minutes*
Drying Time: *overnight*

This fruity, chewy treat is perfect when a snack is in order.

6	dried apricot halves	6
1	medium apple	1
250 mL	dry skim milk powder	1 cup
50 mL	dried currants	$^1/_4$ cup
25 mL	unsweetened dessicated coconut	2 tbsp
	Sugar substitute equivalent to 25 mL (2 tbsp) sugar	
15 mL	finely chopped almonds	1 tbsp
2 mL	ground cinnamon	$^1/_2$ tsp
2 mL	baking powder	$^1/_2$ tsp
1 mL	salt	$^1/_4$ tsp

Each serving: 2 chews

1 ◪ Fruits & Vegetables

  8 g carbohydrate
  2 g protein
  1 g fat

  210 kilojoules
  (50 Calories)

Each serving: 4 chews

1 ◪ Fruits & Vegetables

1 ◆ Milk Choice (2%)

  16 g carbohydrate
  5 g protein
  2 g fat

  420 kilojoules
  (100 Calories)

- Finely chop apricots and place in mixing bowl.

- Peel, core and grate apple. Add to apricots.

- Stir in skim milk powder, currants, coconut, sugar substitute, almonds, cinnamon, baking powder and salt. Mix well. Stir in 15 to 25 mL (1 to 2 tbsp) water to moisten slightly. Continue to mix thoroughly, using hands if necessary. This is a stiff mixture.

- Drop by rounded 5 mL (1 tsp), about 5 cm (2 in) apart, onto nonstick baking sheet.

- With tines of fork dipped in cold water, flatten to make 2 cm ($^3/_4$ in) rounds.

- Bake in 190ºC (375ºF) oven for 15 minutes or until dry on top.

- Transfer to wire rack to let cool. Let sit out overnight to dry.

Makes 24 chews.

Strawberry Creams

These are a takeoff of Jelly Jubes.

500 mL	fresh or frozen unsweetened strawberries	2 cups
5	envelopes unflavored gelatin	5
	Sugar substitute equivalent to 125 mL (¹/₂ cup) sugar	
125 mL	2% plain yogurt	¹/₂ cup

Preparation Time: *10 minutes*
Chilling Time: *4 hours*

- In food processor or blender, purée strawberries with 125 mL (¹/₂ cup) water.

- To strain out seeds, press through fine sieve into large measuring cup. Add water if necessary to make 500 mL (2 cups).

- In small saucepan, sprinkle gelatin over 250 (1 cup) of the strained strawberry juice; let stand for 5 minutes to soften.

- Heat over low heat, stirring, until gelatin dissolves.

- Pour remaining strawberry juice into bowl; stir in gelatin mixture. Stir in sugar substitute and yogurt until well mixed.

- Pour into 20 cm (8 in) square baking dish. Let stand for 4 hours at room temperature or until firm.

- To remove from pan, cut around edges with sharp knife. Place dish in shallow pan of hot water for about 30 seconds just to slightly soften bottom. Loosen one corner, then quickly flip gel out onto clean cutting surface.

- With sharp knife, cut evenly in 10 one way and in 10 the other way.

- Place in container, cover and refrigerate.

- Strawberry Creams stay firm at room temperature but melt if left in hot sunlight. Always refrigerate any leftovers. Will keep for up to 1 week in refrigerator.

Makes 100 squares

Each Serving: 4 squares

1 ➕➕ Extra

1 g carbohydrate
2 g protein

60 kilojoules
(13 Calories)

Each Serving: 18 squares

1 ◆ Milk Choice (2%)

6 g carbohydrate
7 g protein
1 g fat

240 kilojoules
(57 Calories)

Little Treats

Recipe	Food Choices per Serving		Energy per Serving		
			kilojoules	Calories	
Fruit Jelly Jubes	1 **++**	Extra	50	12	p. 218
Mint Jelly Jubes	1 **++**	Extra	50	12	p. 218
Grape Jelly Jubes	1 **++**	Extra	50	12	p. 218
Icy Fruity Creamsicles	1	Fruits & Vegetables	240	56	p. 219
Fruit Chews (2)	1	Fruits & Vegetables **OR**	210	50	p. 220
(4)	1	Fruits & Vegetables; 1 ◆ Milk (2%)	420	100	p. 220
Strawberry Creams (4)	1 **++**	Extra **OR**	60	13	p. 221
(18)	1 ◆	Milk (2%)	240	57	p. 221

222

Finishing Touches

A dollop of topping or a drizzle of sauce can turn plain-looking desserts into glamorous presentations. Use them to complement cakes, puddings or ice cream. Small amounts can count as an Extra, as the calculations indicate.

Blueberry Spread or Sauce

Preparation Time: *5 minutes*
Cooking Time: *25 minutes*

Raspberries, gooseberries and blackberries can be used instead of blueberries. I like to make several small batches of spread when the berries are in season.

500 mL	fresh or frozen unsweetened blueberries	2 cups
15 mL	frozen unsweetened orange juice concentrate	1 tbsp
	Sugar substitute equivalent to 125 mL ($^1/_2$ cup) sugar	

Each serving: 15 mL(1 tbsp) as spread

1 ➕ Extra

   2 g carbohydrate

   60 kilojoules
   (13 Calories)

- In saucepan, combine blueberries and orange juice concentrate.

- Bring to boil; reduce heat slightly and cook, stirring, for 20 minutes or until juice has nearly evaporated.

- Stir in sugar substitute. Cook for 5 minutes longer.

- Spoon into sterilized container. Seal with sterilized lid.

- Store in cool, dry, dark place.

- Or spoon into clean dish or jar, cover and store in refrigerator for up to 4 weeks.

Makes 250 mL (1 cup)

Each serving: 50 mL($^1/_4$ cup) as sauce

1 ◢ Fruits & Vegetables

   10 g carbohydrate
   1 g protein

   210 kilojoules
   (50 Calories)

Calculations as above

Variation:
Raspberry, Goosebery or Blackberry Spread:
Substitute raspberries, gooseberries or blackberries for the blueberries.

Cottage Cream

Here's a creamy alternative to whipped topping. Use a little as garnish for a serving of fruit or as a spread for muffins.

500 mL	2% cottage cheese	2 cups
	Sugar substitute equivalent to 25 mL (2 tbsp) sugar	
5 mL	vanilla or dry sherry	1 tsp

- In food processor, combine cottage cheese, sugar substitute and vanilla or sherry. Process for about 1 to 2 minutes or until very smooth and creamy, scraping down sides of container occasionally.

- Store in covered container in refrigerator for up to 5 days.

Makes 500 mL (2 cups)

Preparation Time: *5 minutes*

For topping:
Each serving: 15 mL (1 tbsp)

1 ▉ Extra

1 g carbohydrate
2 g protein

60 kilojoules
(13 Calories)

For filling:
Each serving: 50 mL ($^1/_4$ cup)

1 ▉ Protein Choice

2 g carbohydrate
8 g protein
1 g fat

230 kilojoules
(54 Calories)

Yogurt Dipping Sauce

Dip chunks of fruit or cubes of Chiffon or Angel Cake into this tangy, creamy sauce. Or pour over sliced fruit for a finishing touch.

500 mL	2% plain yogurt	2 cups
	Sugar substitute equivalent to 25 mL (2 tbsp) sugar	
5 mL	vanilla	1 tsp

- In bowl, combine yogurt, sugar substitute and vanilla.

- Store in covered container in refrigerator for up to 1 week.

Makes 500 mL (2 cups)

Preparation Time: *5 minutes*

Each serving: 15 mL (1 tbsp)

1 ▉ Extra

1 g carbohydrate
1 g protein

40 kilojoules
(10 Calories)

Each serving: 75 mL ($^1/_3$ cup)

1 ◆ Milk Choice (2%)

6 g carbohydrate
4 g protein
1 g fat

230 kilojoules
(55 Calories)

Apple Butter

Preparation Time: *5 minutes*
Cooking Time: *15 minutes*

This sauce is so thick and tasty, it makes a scrumptious spread for toast or even French toast.

4	small unpleeled apples, cored	4
	Juice and pulp of half an orange	
2 mL	ground cinnamon	1/2 tsp
1 mL	ground cardamom	1/4 tsp
	Sugar substitute equivalent to 10 mL (2 tsp) sugar	

Each serving: 50 mL (¹/₄ cup)

1 ▨ Fruits & Vegetables

12 g carbohydrate

200 kilojoules
(48 Calories)

OR

Each serving: 15 mL (1 tbsp)

1 ✛ Extra

3 g carbohydrate

50 kilojoules
(12 Calories)

- Finely chop apple pieces.

- In a cold saucepan, combine apples, orange pulp and juice, cinnamon and cardamom. Bring to a boil over medium heat; stir well, reduce heat, and simmer, covered, for 5 minutes.

- Remove cover and continue to simmer, stirring, until no juice shows on the bottom of the pan. Remove from heat before any browning takes place.

- Stir in sugar substitute.

Makes 250 (1 cup), 4 servings

Microwave Directions:
In 1 L (4 cup) microwaveable container, combine apple pieces, orange pulp and juice, cinnamon and cardamom. Microwave at High (100%), stirring 2 to 3 times, for 10 minutes or until apples are very soft and smooth. Stir in sweetener.

Brandied Peach Sauce

It's fresh, fruity and spicy. Good with crepes, ices and Angel Cake recipe, p. 138)

Angel Cake recipe, p. 138)

Preparation Time: *5 minutes*

1	large peach or 2 peach halves, canned in juice, drained	1
50 mL	water	$^1/_4$ cup
	Sugar substitute equivalent to 15 mL (1 tbsp) sugar	
Pinch	allspice	Pinch
Pinch	curry powder	Pinch
15 mL	brandy or 5 mL (1 tsp) artificial brandy extract	1 tbsp

- Peel peach; cut into pieces and place in blender or food processor.

- Add water, sugar substitute, allspice, curry and brandy or brandy extract. Process for about 1 minute or until puréed.

- Serve chilled, at room temperature or place in small saucepan and heat over medium heat until warm.

Makes 250 mL (1 cup)

Each serving: 25 mL (2 tbsp)

1 ➕ Extra

2 g carbohydrate
1 g alcohol

50 kilojoules
(11 Calories)

227

Finishing Touches

Recipe	Food Choices per Serving			Energy per Serving		
				kilojoules	Calories	
Blueberry Spread	1	➕ Extra	(15 mL/1 tbsp)	60	13	p. 224
or Sauce	1	◢ Fruits & Vegetables (50 mL/¼ cup)		210	50	p. 224
Cottage Cream	1	➕ Extra	(15 mL/1 tbsp)	60	13	p. 225
	1	⊘ Protein	(50 mL/¼ cup)	230	54	p. 225
Yogurt Dipping Sauce	1	➕ Extra	(15 mL/1 tbsp)	40	10	p. 225
	1	◆ Milk (2%)	(75 mL/⅓ cup)	230	55	p. 225
Apple Butter	1	◢ Fruits & Vegetables (50 mL/¼ cup)		200	48	p. 226
	1	➕ Extra	(15 mL/1 tbsp)	50	12	p. 226
Brandied Peach Sauce	1	➕ Extra		50	11	p. 227

Foods on the Go

All of us at times are so busy we end up eating on the run or grabbing a bite from a restaurant or fast food outlet. For a person with diabetes, that food on the run has to be right even if it is rushed.

Having each meal or snack properly balanced helps to regulate blood sugar levels during the day and keeps your energy level up. It means choosing one or more foods from each of the food groups (see chart) to make a meal with the right combination of carbohydrate, protein and fat. By choosing a variety each day, you will have a diet that contains vitamins and minerals essential for good health as well as enough food energy (kilojoules/Calories) to supply the energy you need every day to keep you healthy and active.

Eating on the go also means cafeteria food. Wherever the food is found, there are a few rules for people with diabetes and, indeed, for all people concerned with good health, to follow:

- Talk to the person taking the order and ask for your food with little or no fat — baked, broiled, poached or roasted — and salads with oily dressings 'on the side' so you can control the amount you add. Most people will be helpful when they know your diet is controlled because of diabetes.

- Make up small cards with lists of food choices to keep in your pocket of pocket book. Use your list as a guide for selecting foods when you are eating away from home.

- A small carry-along form of the Good Health Eating Guide is available from the Canadian Diabetes Association and it has a place for you to write in your meal plan.

- Eat only the amount of food your food plan allows. There is no need to clean off the plate. Restaurant servings are often much too large. Share the extra, take it home in a doggy bag for another meal, or leave it on your plate.

- Just admire the gorgeous, gooey goodies. Imagine they are plastic and not good to eat.

229

Here are a few tips to help you make the right choice in restaurants and cafeterias.

- Nibble on a few celery sticks and radishes from the relish tray. They are considered **++** Extra Vegetables.

- Clear fat-free broths are also fine for an **++** Extra appetizer.

- Have tomato juice as a starter or a small fresh fruit cup. Remember to count either one as a **◢** Fruits & Vegetables Choice.

- Count bread, rolls, melba toast and crackers as **☐** Starchy Choices. It's a source of food energy that's easily forgotten but may show up later as unwanted weight gain. Too much may interfere with the action of your insulin.

- Rely on plain greens with lemon juice as dressing for another **++** Extra Vegetables.

- The best fillings for sandwiches are lean meats, poultry and slices of cheese. You can never be sure how much mayonnaise or other rich ingredients might be in filling mixtures.

- Ask for mayonnaise or relishes on the side so you can control the amount you use.

- Avoid gravies, cream cheese fillings, cream sauces, fried foods and sweet desserts at all times. Pies, pastries and puddings are usually full of sugar and fat.

- Fresh fruit is the best choice for dessert. Plain ice cream can be substituted for fruit and fat in your food plan on a special occasion.

Foods To Go

For a person with diabetes, it may be much easier to carry a lunch than to puzzle over what to buy from a restaurant or cafeteria. At home the pieces go together more easily because you know what your Choices are. And it does not mean having peanut butter sandwiches every day.

Choose a combination of foods to equal your allowed number of Food Choices for a properly balanced meal, then look at the foods you can prepare from these recipes. Select ones that are easy to carry. Some of the foods from this book are easy to take along to the school or office.

Lemonade or Limeade
Frothy Rich Hot Chocolate
Creamy Vegetable Soup
Clamato Chowder
Broccoli Soup
Keeps-A-Week Coleslaw
Chick Pea and Tomato Salad
Pasta E Fagioli (Pasta and Beans)
Meatball Ragout
Lime-Broiled or Poached Chicken
Mexican Beans and Rice
Lentil Curry

If the carting back and forth can be handled, a wide-mouthed Thermos container is perfect for hot or cold dishes. A small 250 mL (1 cup) one for drinks will solve the beverage problems.

It is also smart to include any mid-morning or mid-afternoon snacks, from your food plan, in your packed lunch. Or non-perishable snacks for a whole week can be packed at the beginning of the week and kept at school.

If you are at school, let your teacher or coach know about your need for a snack. If you prefer not to eat your snack in the classroom or on the playing field, you can be excused for the short time necessary to eat it.

231

Brown Bag Totable Lunches that Work

1. Hard-cooked egg, salad in Thermos, muffin and fruit.

2. Hearty soup in a Thermos, scones, fruit, Butterscotch Peanut Cookies.

3. Cottage cheese with crunchy greens like celery and green pepper, small whole wheat roll, milk and fruit.

4. Pita sandwiches filled with sliced meat, poultry or cheese; raw cauliflower and broccoli florets, fresh fruit and milk in a Thermos.

5. Leftover dinner in a Thermos, zucchini sticks, Apricot Loaf and yogurt.

6. Eggnog, muffin and fruit.

7. Fresh fruit, muffin, cheese, celery sticks, milk.

INDEX